war
d

Dogs are inducted into the Army at Front Royal, Virginia in August 1942. World War II was the first war in which the United States officially brought dogs into its military. Over 10,000 US dogs served during World War II and most were donated to the cause by patriotic civilians who offered their pets for service.

Courtesy of the US National Archives and Records Administration

war
dogs

TALES OF CANINE HEROISM,
HISTORY, AND LOVE

REBECCA FRANKEL

FOREWORD BY THOMAS E. RICKS

St. Martin's Griffin

New York

For the handlers who let me get close to their dogs, and
for the dogs who let me get close to their handlers.

For Tippy and Rippy—the dogs who came first.

www.stmartins.com

All photographs are courtesy of the author except where indicated.

Library of Congress Cataloging-in-Publication Data

Frankel, Rebecca.
    War dogs : tales of canine heroism, history, and love / Rebecca Frankel ; foreword by Thomas E. Ricks.
        pages   cm
    ISBN 978-1-137-27968-2 (hardback)
    1. Dogs—War use—United States. 2. Dogs—Training. 3. Dogs—War use—History. I. Title.
UH100.F83 2014
355.4'24—dc23

                                                                    2014004874

ISBN 978-1-250-07507-9 (trade paperback)
ISBN 978-1-137-45661-8 (e-book)

Our books may be purchased for educational, business, or promotional use. For information on bulk purchases, please contact the Macmillan Corporate and Premium Sales Department at 1-800-221-7945, extension 5442, or write to specialmarkets@macmillan.com.

Design by Letra Libre, Inc.

First published in 2014 by Palgrave Macmillan Trade

First St. Martin's Griffin Edition: October 2015

10 9 8 7 6 5 4 3 2 1

contents

foreword

This is a lovely book. The image of a small but enthusiastic dog pulling the author up a hill at dusk in the Arizona desert in a military training exercise will stay with me.

But it is also a surprising book. I opened it looking forward to reading a few good stories about the use of dogs in war. But midway through, the realization hit me that this is something larger than that, and far deeper: it is a meditation on war and humans. It illuminates conflict from the unexpected angle of the allure of war, and the damage it does to both species.

This book is the account of a journey. We accompany the author, Rebecca Frankel, into the small but lively world of military dogs and their handlers. She brings a gimlet eye for its idiosyncrasies, such as the jockeying to be the handler with the toughest dog. We learn about what makes a "good" dog as opposed to a weak one. We become aware of the danger of the trainer "melting the dog." We see that the essential ingredient in partnering with a dog, as with a human, is trust. "The dog will often rather lay down life itself than betray its trust," we are told. Frankel posits that dogs, unlike other animals, have been "hardwired" by evolution to develop trust in certain humans. I believe it.

But this volume about dogs is also a very human story. Some of its best passages are about the dogs' handlers. They take deserved pride in their line of work. But like many soldiers, they also feel misjudged by the larger military world, yet for an unusual reason: "Leadership doesn't understand us . . . Don't quite grasp us because they don't understand dogs."

Frankel adeptly shows us how bonds form and expand between handler and animal. I did not know that dogs and handlers often work together for years. We meet one team that was joined for a decade, until canine death did them part. Nor did I know that the drive of the handler is the single most important ingredient in a team, or that handlers are taught to "see" spots in the flow of air where dogs might best detect odors.

But, in keeping with the deeper themes of the book, we also learn that dogs require proportionally larger doses of morphine to ease pain than do people. And when one handler wrestling with severe PTSD dies, a comrade comments, "Well, officially it's written up as an accident. But I know it wasn't."

Frankel is a good and observant writer. She brings a fresh eye to military affairs. Our recent wars have made us familiar with the grainy, green images produced by night vision goggles. But I had never seen the image captured quite as well as her phrase herein, "shades of neon lemon and lime."

There is also some interesting history here. I didn't know that dogs were introduced to the Iraq war relatively late and were not part of the invasion force. It is significant also that they were not initially brought to help detect roadside bombs but turned to that task once there. This makes them a central part of the Iraq story, because the roadside bomb, or IED, is the characteristic feature of the war there, just as trenches and machine guns were during World War I.

As shown here, the tale of the US military war dog is the history of the US military buildups and drawdowns in miniature. Old lessons are relearned in new wars, and then forgotten as units demobilize in the postwar era.

Indeed, the world of the canine military is an obscure part of our huge armed forces establishment, somewhat akin to, say, meteorology or airborne medicine. But as Frankel drills deep into it, it becomes clear that this is the most military of worlds, hard-core in its own way. One true lesson: "If you aren't humble and honest with yourself and what you're really capable of . . . then you need to get the hell out of the way and let somebody else do it." Another one that rings true: "Shortcuts get people killed."

The bonus is that anyone who reads this book and has a pet dog will come away with a greater appreciation for, and understanding of, their companion. As I write this, one of my terriers, a rescue dog with fear issues, is sleeping by my feet. Frankel's observation that the leash is the wire through which emotions and feelings are transmitted, both ways, will change the way I think about my walks with him and my other, calmer dog. Most of all, I will think of the daily requirement to earn and retain their trust. Or, as that bumper sticker says, to be the person my dogs think I am.

Thomas E. Ricks

author's note

Here are a few things that I feel might be worth explaining before readers begin.

To head off the understandable questions (and readers with a copy-editing eye) about the spelling of some of the military dogs' names that appear in these pages, those that begin with two of the same letter are not spelling errors. The US Military Working Dog program breeds dogs, and the resulting puppies are identified by names that begin with the same double letter. For example, in June 2010 a litter of Belgian Malinois puppies were born into the "R" litter and were given names like Rrespect, Rromano, Rruck, and Rrisky.

You'll notice too that when I write of "the handler" or "the working dog" at large, I employ "he" or "his." I did this for consistency's sake—it should not be viewed as gender bias or emblematic of a working dog culture that is still dominated by males, but rather because it was simpler.

I also made a conscious decision at the beginning of writing this book not to assign the pronoun "it" when talking about these dogs. Therefore, they are always "he," "she," or "who." In my mind "it" refers to a thing, and dogs are not things; they are our feeling and emotionally engaged companions. And, especially in this book, they are oftentimes more than that, certainly nothing less.

dogs in the time of war

People have been trying to understand dogs ever since the beginning of time. One never knows what they'll do. You can read every day where a dog saved the life of a drowning child, or lay down his life for his master. Some people call this loyalty. I don't. I may be wrong, but I call it love—the deepest kind of love. . . .

It's a shame that people all over the world can't have that kind of love in their hearts. . . . There would be no wars, slaughter, or murder; no greed or selfishness. It would be the kind of world that God wants us to have—a wonderful world.

—Wilson Rawls, *Where the Red Fern Grows*

Despite the many distant stars, there was no moon, and the night sky was all the blacker for it. The desert air had chilled but the tension in the village was palpable and rising. Gunfire crackled down the market lane, rapid and loud. A high-pitched hiss sizzled in the distance, followed by the deep shudder of an explosion. *Boom!* Then came another, and another.

Shouts chorused through the cramped alleyway. Someone in the unit had been hit. There was the scuffle of boots, the cries for "Medic!" and the sound of gravel scratching across the ground in a rush to get to the wounded.

Inside a hut, a group of soldiers huddled around the injured party while the damage was assessed—it was a broken leg and a bad one at that. Only the casualty wasn't one of the men kneeling, but the dog lying next to them.

When Staff Sergeant Fred Roberts, the dog's handler, went to treat his partner's wounds, the panicked dog resisted, thrashing and twisting, his hind legs kicking. It took two able-bodied men to hold Turbo down and Roberts was rattled, his hands fumbling over the gauze as he struggled to set the bone and wrap the bandage. Finally, after what felt like many breath-held minutes, the dressing was secure.

Roberts leaned back, sweat slick across his brow. Turbo lay panting, the fight in him subsiding as if he knew the worst was over. And it was, at least for that night. After all, this had only been a careful simulation, part of a predeployment training session taking place not in the throes of a warzone but on a remote military base in Yuma, Arizona. There were no insurgents' bullets flying; the injuries were feigned, only pretend.

I stood watching a few steps away, my heart pounding inside my chest. Though the scene unfolding before me was practice, the anxiety and the adrenaline rush had been real. It was March 2012, and I was observing not only Roberts and Turbo, but a slew of 17 dog teams from all military branches—Marine Corps, Air Force, Army, and Navy—as they readied themselves for war.

The Inter-Service Advance Skills K-9 (ISAK) course hosted at the Yuma Proving Ground in the Arizona desert is designed to prepare handlers and their dogs for what awaits them in a combat theater. Perhaps Roberts slept better that night, knowing that if his dog were ever hit—if it happened for real—he and Turbo would be better prepared to face it. Either way, they would be deploying soon enough.

As events would unfold in the months that followed, the end of spring and into the summer, most of these handlers and their dogs would deploy; many of them would go to war. Not all of them would return.

It's not known, not really, when the first dog took the battle-field to wage war alongside his human companions. Historians believe that millennia ago, the ancient Egyptians used canines to carry messages. The Corinthians surrounded their seashore citadel with guard dogs in 400 BC, and the Romans employed them to raise alarms for their garrisons. The feared invasion forces of Attila the Hun brought ferocious hounds with them to protect their camps during battle.[1]

The United States, historically, has been woefully behind in adopting dogs into its military ranks, not doing so officially until 1942 with the Army's Dogs for Defense program. So crucial were these animals during World War II that the US canine ranks swelled to over 10,000 dogs strong. In Vietnam, scout dogs were so successful at thwarting the ambush tactics of the Vietcong that bounties exceeding $20,000 were placed on their heads while only half as much was promised for their human handlers. In recent years, working outside the wire in Iraq and Afghanistan, military dogs have become the single greatest advantage allied forces have against the signature weapon of the post-9/11 era—the improvised explosive device, or IED. Try though the military has to outdo them with technology and electronic machinery, nothing has been more effective at uncovering these unpredictably lethal roadside bombs than a handler and his detection dog.

But what is a war dog exactly? A furry but devoted weapon? A faithful fighter? A fierce soldier? A guardian who keeps watch in the night? A war dog is at once all of these things and still somehow more than the mere sum of those collected roles and qualities. Never so dire or profound is that exchange of dependence and trust between a man and his dog than on the battlefield. In combat lives are at stake, and so the capacity to expand that bond between handler and dog—to have it deepen in intensity and feeling—is exceptionally great.

It is a relationship built first on a mutual trust, one that can flourish into something more intimate—trust with a greater sense of loyalty and even love. It's this bond that, in a combat zone, encourages the dog's desire to work his keen senses to the advantage of his human companions and inspires heroic feats of bravery when the instinct to flee or sense of fear might dictate otherwise. Together this team endures what seems unendurable—trauma, injury, and even death. And if all this proves too much to bear, the handler and dog who suffer the same afflictions can even heal together. It is a symbiotic relationship that challenges and changes the way a person experiences war.

The journey that took me to Yuma that March night in 2012 really began with a photograph I found during the winter of 2010—an image of a Marine battalion kicking back at Camp Huskers, located along the outskirts of Marjah, Afghanistan. In the photo, the sunlight slanted warmly over these Marines and the bomb-sniffing dogs who were sprawled across their laps and curled close against their sides.

In my tenure as an editor of *Foreign Policy* magazine, I spent many hours curating and editing large photo collections. During much of this time the United States was still fully engaged in wars in Afghanistan and Iraq. As a side effect of this work, I'd grown more or less accustomed to graphic warzone scenery—the searing reds and whites of RPG blasts, sand clouds kicked up by Chinook helicopters, the bloodied limbs of soldiers and civilians, frozen moments of anguish and death. But this photo surprised me for another reason; I was struck by the unfamiliar sense of contentment radiating from these Marines and their dogs. There were no furrowed brows, no Kevlar vests or helmets, no Ray-Ban sunglasses obscuring their eyes. These young men looked tranquil, happy; the dogs were all but grinning. It evoked a sweet pang of home, if a makeshift barracks in the middle of a warzone could be called home.

I shared the image with Tom Ricks (former senior Pentagon correspondent for the *Washington Post* and, perhaps more importantly, a great lover of dogs), thinking he might like to post the photograph on *The Best Defense*, his *Foreign Policy* blog. On his suggestion, we partnered in a new Friday feature, "Rebecca's War Dog of the Week," and he anointed me Chief Canine Correspondent. And so opened my eyes to the wide world of war dogs.

My biggest fear in stepping into this world was that I had no business in it. I have never held rank in the military. Even as a journalist writing about the policies and events surrounding these wars, or as an editor working with reporters and photo journalists assigned to cover these regions, or dissecting and promoting expert analysis, I was at best a distant observer—perhaps well informed and well intentioned, but an outsider all the same.

I suppose in this way, I was more like most of my fellow Americans than not. The United States has been engaged on two war fronts for over a decade, and less than 1 percent of the American population has served on the front lines. The rest of the country is fatigued by the news of drone strikes and suicide bombings. We are now a country long tired of war.

And yet every time I talked with someone in the Military Working Dog (MWD) community—whether it was a handler on deployment in Iraq, a veterinary technician stationed in Afghanistan, a veteran scout-dog handler from Vietnam, or a volunteer for a therapy dog nonprofit—the barriers I feared might separate us melted away. You don't have to walk a mile down a bomb-laden road in Kandahar to know the pull of devotion of a dog, or the sadness you feel when it becomes clear that the four-legged member of your family is fading and it is time to say good-bye. It's a feeling that transcends the individualized experiences that otherwise would put us on distant life plains. To love an animal is to share a kinship.

When we cannot make that human connection over war, when we cannot empathize or imagine the far-off world of a combat zone, we can still understand what it means to love a dog. These military working dogs are a bridge over the divide, the gap that separates civilians and military, participants and onlookers. The stories of their heroism and sacrifice connect those of us who have no other tie to the battlefield, to the roads in Afghanistan where our service men and women have been laying down their lives. There is something less complicated (and ironically more human) about relating to war through the story of a dog.

In May 2011, the world was riveted by the news that Cairo, a dog reportedly attached to a Navy SEAL team, had helped take down Osama bin Laden. There was an explosion of interest in the topic of war dogs. The idea that a canine was part of this historic event was exhilarating. When it came time to pull together the world's most capable and specialized military team to hunt down and take out the world's most wanted man, they made sure a military working dog was at this team's disposal.

I have spent more than a year exploring the world of war dogs for this book. A vast domain, it extends further and wider than I could've imagined, containing communities within communities. It is a place infused with tremendous spirit and solidarity. I thought I would be writing a book about dogs who live their lives in the service of the military, whether they come to this life by way of breeding, training, or happenstance. But as much as it is about dogs, this is a book about the indelible mark they have left and will leave on their handlers, their community inside the military, as well as all of us who depend on their bravery. In some ways, I was surprised when I realized I was actually writing a book about people, the people who bear this mark the most deeply. And in the end that included me as well. When I was offered a leash during an explosives-finding exercise, I picked it up. When I was offered a bite suit to catch a dog (teeth first), I put it on; a rucksack, I carried it as long and far as I was able.

This is also a book about cycles, wartime and otherwise. After years of reporting on this topic, I couldn't find a way around writing about our militaristic future, which inevitably led me to review our military's past. And war dog history tends to repeat itself, for though dogs have been used to great success in conflict after conflict, when a war dies down, the dogs are scaled back, their programs depleted of their resources and the advances in skill and design made at the height of conflict are shelved or otherwise lost. And when the call for the dogs comes again—as it inevitably will—years and energy are spent rebuilding and reinventing.

I avoid the question of whether or not it is ethical to involve animals in fighting our wars. There are legitimate cases to be made on both sides, but we do employ animals in war and we rely on them heavily. This book starts with the reality that their role is significant on a level that has evolved far beyond function, servitude, and base usefulness. The one question worth asking and answering at more than one turn is this: Does taking dogs into war—wherever the battleground—really make a difference? The answer is, over and over, a resounding *Yes*. Dogs are integral to our efforts abroad as well as to our safety at home and in this role have proven their mettle again and again. A dog belongs by our side—whether as a fighter, detector, protector, companion, empathizer, or healer. As long as we have a military made of men and women, we should have military dogs.

part i

ONE

when dogs
become soldiers

*I actually got jealous when I saw some of the soldiers over there with dogs
deeply attached to them. It was the nearest thing to civilization in this weird
foreign life of ours.*

—Ernie Pyle, *Brave Men*

As the plane dropped it felt like falling, but the turns were too tight, too controlled. The C-17 twisted in a swift plummet—down, down, down—without slowing. The dogs in their crates registered the strange sensation, a few hovering on the floor of their kennels, legs splayed, eyes darting and nervous. Neither they nor their 12 handlers who had left San Diego some 20 hours earlier were enjoying this motion. Some gripped their seats, others had their eyes closed, no doubt fighting a thick wave of nausea. The corkscrew landing pattern of the plane's descent was a combat zone necessity, as was the short approach to the flight line. They came down so hard and so fast that as the plane met the ground, the g-force slapped against their bodies.

When the men stepped off the plane and into the Iraq air, there was nothing but darkness, no way to discern where they were. The three Special Forces guys who had also been on their flight had already melted away into the night.

Only a couple of days before, Staff Sergeant Sean Lulofs and the 11 other Air Force handlers had been at Camp Pendleton in California for their in-processing: filling out the necessary paper work at the Marine Corps base before they could begin their deployment. A lieutenant colonel gave them their first briefing for the mission they would undertake, Operation Phantom Fury. She did not mince words. "The Marine Corps," she told them, "anticipates that at least two to three of you will be killed in action."

The response in the room had been utter silence. At first the handlers thought this woman had to be bullshitting them, that she was just saying this because the Marine Corps thought they were weak-ass Air Force guys. But it soon sunk in that this was not the lieutenant colonel's motivation. She was letting them know how deadly serious their deployment was going to be: they would be embedding deep within the Marines' infantry units, and it was crucial that they understand the risk implicit in this assignment. It would be so dangerous, in fact, that when the Marine Corps had conducted its objective assessment of their upcoming mission, it fully expected this group of handlers to come back at a loss.

Holy shit, Lulofs had thought. *I'm not going home.*

Truth be told, he hadn't wanted to deploy in the first place. The news of four American contractors who'd been killed that March had dominated the headlines; the images of a mob pulling charred corpses through the streets to then dangle them from a bridge over the Euphrates were fresh in his mind.[1] From the outside, the Iraqis appeared to be full of rage and they were directing their ire at Americans.

When Lulofs's commander had told him he and his dog Aaslan would be deploying, they'd given him less than eight hours' notice. Almost his whole life he'd dreamed of joining the Air Force to be a narcotics detection dog handler, and then, all of a sudden, he was frenzied, packing his bags to go to war. The thought of what it really meant scared the living crap out of him. Iraq was the last place in the world he wanted to be.

But there he was. The 12 handlers stood on the tarmac, in the dark with no idea where the hell they were. There was a mandatory military blackout so they couldn't use lights. They hadn't packed night vision goggles; they didn't know they were going to need them. Lulofs wondered what else they might need that they would have to do without. After a few minutes the men began to load their weapons. Then a deep voice sounded nearby. "Are you the Air Force guys?"

Lulofs felt a twinge of relief; this voice was familiar. It was Gunnery Sergeant William Kartune, a rugged, no-bullshit Marine in charge of all the dog teams in Iraq from Baghdad to Al Anbar. He had come to collect the handlers.

It was March 2004. With their arrival, the call for approximately 30 Air Force and Marine Corps dog teams was complete. For the first time in nearly three decades the United States had dispatched a force of military dogs and their handlers to fight a war.

After that night, the dozen air force handlers sectioned off into smaller groups. Lulofs ended up with another handler, a staff sergeant with a big chip on his compact shoulder named Joshua Farnsworth. Together they took their dogs to Camp Baharia, the post for which none of the others had volunteered. An assignment to Camp Baharia meant lots of time in Fallujah. At that time, Fallujah had become the epicenter of violence since US forces invaded in 2003. Nobody wanted Fallujah.

Located just two miles southeast, Camp Baharia was the closest base to Fallujah, known as the city of mosques, which had a population of 285,000.[2] It was so close that Lulofs could see the cars on the main highway heading in and out of the city. Once upon a time, the area that became Camp Baharia in 2003 had been known as Dreamland, formerly a Ba'ath Party retreat. Palm trees surrounded a man-made lake, where Saddam Hussein's sons had watched boats race back and forth across the water. In the last few months the area had been torn up by fighting. Many of the buildings on base had been gutted, including the handlers' living quarters, the glass in the windows blown out. Lulofs and another handler found plywood and sandbags and rebuilt walls where needed. They even managed to construct a couple of bunk beds. It was palatial compared to the floor of a Humvee, where some of the other handlers were sleeping.

That first morning on base, Lulofs woke early, just as the sun was rising, and took Aaslan outside. He unclipped his dog's leash to give him free range of the dirt and rock that made up the bank of the lake's shoreline. Lulofs's somber eyes lifted behind his wire-rimmed glasses as he smiled and watched Aaslan, with his shadowy dark coloring around his narrow face, sniff around the lake. Aaslan, a trim Belgian Malinois, had a civil temperament: he never growled at people, never barked at other dogs, and he would bite only when asked to, only when he knew it was okay. He was a tough dog, and when he ran at decoys during their bite work in training, Aaslan hit hard, once even breaking his own legs during a drill. That kind of fight was in his blood; his mother, Boyca, had been legendary for her hardiness. During one training session, she'd pounced with such force on a human decoy that even though the man had been wearing a full-padded bite suit, she'd cracked three of his ribs.

US Air Force Staff Sergeant Sean Lulofs on patrol with MWD Aaslan in Iraq in 2004. Courtesy of Sean Lulofs

Lulofs watched Aaslan skirt the bank looking for the right spot to do his business. No sooner had he raised his leg when Lulofs saw the wrinkling of the dog's nose and watched Aaslan cock his head to the side. The dog paused, leg in the air, and stopped pissing midstream. Lulofs's blood went cold. Aaslan was on bomb. *But how can that be possible?* he wondered. They were *inside* the base.

As he watched Aaslan begin to search, nose to the ground, twisting and sniffing, Lulofs told himself the dog had to be picking up on some kind of residual odor, something left over from an unexploded ordnance. He stared in disbelief as Aaslan nuzzled around a coffee can and planted his hindquarters on the ground. "Oh shit," he said to himself. "That's not good." Lulofs called Aaslan back to him and away from whatever was in that coffee can.

The EOD team—the tactical specialists whose job it is to safely detonate any live explosives—came to investigate. The can, the harmless piece of trash filled with rocks and disarranged wires, also contained rocket propellant. According to the EOD guys, it had gotten waterlogged sitting idle for so long and thus had become even more volatile.

The night before, while Lulofs and Farnsworth were making introductions with the Marines on base, they'd hung out in this yard by the water, talking, smoking, shooting the shit. One of the Marines had been sent a fishing rod because of the lake, and the guys were casting it out onto the bank, seeing if they could hook up stray bits of garbage. The fucked-up thing was, they'd been messing around with that very same coffee can. Lulofs had even taken a picture of one Marine holding it up, a lit cigarette dangling from his lip. They'd been playing with an IED.

The next day the base was hit with roughly 18 rounds of indirect fire. They got their asses handed to them. Lulofs and Aaslan had been in Iraq a grand total of two days and they were in the thick of the war, as close to it as they could possibly be.

Just 12 months earlier, bombs had rained down on Baghdad. In March 2003, President George W. Bush had stood before the nation and announced that, on his orders, coalition forces were going into Iraq to disarm Saddam Hussein and save the world from grave danger. "Our nation enters this conflict reluctantly—yet, our purpose is sure. The people of the United States and our friends and allies will not live at the mercy of an outlaw regime that threatens the peace with weapons of mass murder. We will meet that threat now, with our Army, Air Force, Navy, Coast Guard and Marines, so that we do not have to meet it later with armies of fire fighters and police and doctors on the streets of our cities."[3]

By late 2003, the use of IEDs by insurgents to inflict terror increased tremendously—40 to 60 percent of all attacks started with an IED, attacks to which US and coalition forces were extremely vulnerable.[4] How to deal with the IED problem quickly became an utmost priority. A number of solutions were investigated, and different ideas were teased out and tested. In early 2004, General James Mattis issued an order down the chain of command inside the Marine Corps to investigate whether or not dogs might be brought in to help with the growing threat.[5] Was it possible for dogs to become a permanent part of a Marine battalion? Could dogs attach to a unit? Could they be paired easily with infantrymen? The idea evolved and morphed and eventually the task—and its funding—came under the jurisdiction of the Marine Corps MWD program. The Marine Corps determined that roughly 30 dogs were needed, and they combed their own units, as well as the ranks of dog handlers in other branches of the military, for the best dog teams available.

It would take almost a full year after the 2003 invasion before the Marines fulfilled that order to send dogs into Operation Iraqi Freedom, deploying six dog teams from their own service along with others from the Air Force. These were the first dog teams flown into a combat area since Vietnam. No US dogs had been used in a war as an on-the-ground force in over three decades.

However, these teams of Marine Corps and Air Force handlers were law enforcement teams, trained for patrol work—searching cars, detaining suspects, finding drugs and maybe bomb materials. They had not been trained for war. And they were categorically unprepared for what awaited them in Iraq. They hadn't been trained in conducting a roadway search, or how to hunt for an IED. The dogs hadn't been conditioned to search for buried explosives for the simple reason that this specific hazard did not exist stateside or during wartime (not in recent decades) and therefore hadn't been anticipated, at least not until these first patrols started and units were going out onto roads and getting blown up by roadside IEDs. Since the US military's working dogs hadn't been trained to fight an asymmetric force of insurgents armed to the teeth with guerrilla tactics since the days of Vietnam, the dog handlers in Iraq were basically starting from scratch. They had to make it up as they went along.

When Marine handler Corporal Mark Vierig arrived in Iraq in 2004 with his dog Duc, he knew next to nothing about what was waiting for them. Born and raised in Utah, Vierig had, at the age of 17, made off for Texas with a friend to ride bulls professionally. At 25 years old, after breaking his leg twice as well as an arm, and shattering an ankle, he promised himself he wasn't going to end up a beat-up, broken-down cowboy. Instead he enlisted in the Marines. In some ways it wasn't much of a leap—the daredevil drive that pulsed behind the thrill he got from working the rodeo was perhaps the thing that drove him to volunteer for a combat tour. A combat mindset came to him naturally, and even though no one in-country seemed to know what to do with Vierig or his dog, he put himself to work.

In between missions, Vierig trained Duc on whatever they could find, hiding old mortars and RPGs so the dog could learn the scent. At first Vierig had to ask for missions in order to prove that he and Duc could be useful. He would approach company commanders and battalion commanders and say, "My dog finds bombs. Put us out in front."

After a short time, the Special Forces teams started to request Vierig and Duc—they all wanted Duc out with them on their missions. Sometime in the spring, after he and Duc had been in-country for a few months, Vierig overheard one of the other Marines say that it'd be more demoralizing for them if Duc were to be killed than if they lost another Marine. He didn't really know until he heard that remark just how much the other guys were depending on the skill of his dog.

Their reputation spread further, beyond their fellow Marines and beyond their base. Whenever he worked with the Iraqi border police, Vierig
showed them just how well his dog could find explosives. "Go ahead," he'd
say to them, "hide it. Anywhere you want. My dog will find it." The Iraqi
police officers would take a nonexplosive piece of material and tuck it away
somewhere. Minutes later Duc would find it. Soon enough, while they were
on patrol in the streets, the Iraqi civilians would point at the dog and say to
Vierig, "Duc?" They knew his dog's name.

Vierig and Duc were stationed in Husaybah, an Iraqi border town
known for its unwieldy lawlessness. A city of about 30,000 people, it was
so treacherous even Saddam Hussein hadn't been able to keep control
over it. It was a dangerous, violent, and volatile place located right on the
Syrian border and along the western side of the Euphrates. The Marines
there were constantly engaged in firefights with the insurgents. They practically had the routine down pat: after an exchange of gunfire, the Marines would give chase, down the streets running past shops and houses.
Then the insurgents would rush into a mosque, knowing the Marines
would not follow. It was a religious place, a sacred space and off limits. So
the Marines had no choice but to wait. Sometimes the insurgents would
emerge and the fight would begin again; other times they'd stay shut in
and the Marines would disengage, knowing the firefight would just pick
up again another day.

The insurgents would leave notes for them on the doors of the
mosque. These were hateful messages, threats of violence and revenge.
One day Vierig was in front of the mosque and a note caught his eye—
some of it was in Arabic, some of it was in English. It had the standard
threats promising the decapitation of American heads and cooking their
brains, when he saw a word he recognized: "Duck." It was spelled like the
waterfowl, but the bounty it promised was for a hit on his dog. Next to it
was a number: 10,000. Whether it was the guarantee of dollars or some
other currency, Vierig wasn't sure, but he knew the enemy was gunning
for his dog. And that was when the impact he and Duc were making
became real.

When he first arrived in Iraq in 2004, Sean Lulofs was a fairly religious man. Being someone who put a lot of stock in quiet humility, he just couldn't contend with Farnsworth's behavior—his foul mouth, his lewd jokes, or his cocky strut. They were the only two canine handlers stationed at Camp Baharia, and while the men didn't butt heads exactly, they spent those first weeks living together in an uncomfortable quiet. But eventually a grudging respect grew between them. Farnsworth, in his late 20s, had small, dark eyes below a substantial brow and a high rising forehead. Lulofs could see that behind the bullshit bravado, he was a competent handler. Lulofs liked the way the guy worked his dog, Eesau. And sharing such close living quarters, he would sometimes overhear Farnsworth making calls home to his wife, catching bits of their conversation. Somewhere along the way the distance between the men closed, and soon the handlers and their dogs became a tight-knit unit of four.

From day to day, their job was mostly running traffic control points, or TCPs, in different locations along the main routes in and out of Fallujah. Lulofs and Farnsworth eventually got their own Humvee from two other Marine handlers so they could travel with their dogs. It was a Frankenstein hybrid, a blend of ill-fitting pieces—part pickup truck, part jeep, part tractor. After a couple of months, it took on the look of a hardened scab—dinged, dented, scorched, and bruised.

When Lulofs and Farnsworth started taking the vehicle on missions, making the trip between Camp Baharia and Fallujah, the Humvee didn't have any armor—nothing, not even a bulletproof windshield. They were given a couple of Kevlar blankets, which couldn't have stopped a bullet or warded off shrapnel. Still, it was all they had, so they draped them along the carriage in the back where they kept the dog kennels. It was a paltry safeguard, especially as Lulofs and Farnsworth knew that without Aaslan and Eesau they had no real place in this war. Bit by bit they clamped on additions to their Humvee, stitching together mismatched patches of metal and canvas, adding the L-shaped armored doors for the driver and passenger side, and the homemade AC unit they jerry-rigged to a generator and lobbed onto the roof. It was an eyesore of a combat vehicle, one that stood out in any convoy, and it became a prime and sought-after target.

It didn't take long before there was a bounty on their heads—Lulofs's and Aaslan's, Farnsworth's and Eesau's—handlers and dogs together. Shortly after those first teams arrived in 2004, the going rate for taking them out was $10,000. Lulofs was hell-bent on pissing off the enemy so much that by the time they left Iraq the bounty would be worth at least $25,000.[6]

Early one day in August they were riding in a convoy on their way to set up a TCP. There were very few cars on MSR (Main Supply Route) Mobile that morning. Lulofs could feel that something was off as soon as they rolled out onto the paved thoroughfare; it was too quiet. The main six-lane highway that traverses the outside edge of the city of Fallujah usually saw more traffic at this time of day.[7] They guessed that word of some impending threat had spread among the people living in the city, and so the civilians were avoiding their normal route, using instead the makeshift dirt road that ran alongside MSR Mobile.

After some back and forth on their radios, Lulofs, Farnsworth, and the other Marines in their convoy determined that what they were looking at was likely a single IED attack. So they slowed down their normal speed of 45 miles per hour to about 25, taking the road nice and easy. Lulofs drove, keeping his eyes locked on the road, looking for disturbances—a suspicious bump, a rock pile—anything that could be a bomb.

They'd been creeping along for some time when the convoy pushed past a certain point and there was an explosion. But it wasn't just a single IED—that was just the trigger signal. The enemy, lying in wait, now had the target in its sights and started unloading its arsenal. The onslaught hit the convoy from the left side, so while Lulofs was driving, focused on steering around any IEDs, he was also aiming his weapon out the window, shooting as they pushed ahead. Farnsworth, who didn't have a clear shot from the passenger's seat, kept his eyes glued in front: watching for danger, calling out directions, and reloading Lulofs's weapon. The incoming fire pelted them as they pressed forward on the road, like ants in a line unable to scatter.

One of the rounds hit their Humvee—a bullet piercing its armor, passing right between Lulofs's knees, striking the steering wheel column and then ricocheting up, exploding the dashboard and spraying little blackened bits of shrapnel everywhere, breaking the skin along his hands, legs, chest, and arms.

Lulofs barely had time to react when Farnsworth shouted, "RPG!" Lulofs flinched and slammed the break, keeping the rocket-propelled grenade from hitting the driver's side door. The barrage continued; Farnsworth was so pissed that he climbed out his side of the vehicle while it was still moving to position himself so he could return fire over the back end of the truck. He wasn't there for very long—within a few minutes' time they'd almost made it out of the danger zone. The guys in the vehicle behind theirs watched as Lulofs's and Farnsworth's Humvee got slammed and counted at least six RPGs that sailed past or hit the vehicle. Each time, they missed or hit without detonating, clanking against the armor at an angle and flying back up into the air. It had been a relentless, nonstop hail of bullets and mortars that lasted the full stretch of a mile.

When they finally were able to pull over, the first thing they did was check on their dogs, who were still in their kennels in the back. While Aaslan had weathered the barrage, Eesau had not; he refused to get out of his kennel. Even after Farnsworth managed to coax him out, Eesau still wouldn't work. The stress was so great, the dog just shut down. The dogs had protection against bullets, yes, but it had been modest at best. And as each round hit the side of their vehicle close to where the dogs were riding, Lulofs couldn't help but think that they'd been killed or at least wounded. Amazingly, they weren't even scratched. But they had come close. On the outside of the vehicle, right by the dogs' kennels, was a compartment where they kept their MREs, Meals Ready to Eat, the prepackaged field rations. Later, when they opened up an MRE, they found a bullet lodged inside.

It was after that August ambush that Lulofs began to change. He'd been deployed for nearly six months, and the devout man he'd been when he arrived in Iraq was seeing things differently. Where before he'd have shaken his head in offense at the sound of swearing, profanity now spouted freely from his mouth. Farnsworth noticed the difference in his friend and tried to talk to Lulofs about it; he reasoned that if a guy who wouldn't even utter a curse word put his Bible in a bag and never touched it again, it meant something wasn't right.

But it was more than that. Lulofs had grown complacent. It wasn't laziness but a kind of mania that gripped him. When they went out on missions, Lulofs stopped carrying his rifle, taking only his sidearm. He started to think himself invincible, believing that bullets and bombs couldn't touch him. He'd already faced them all and survived. God wasn't going to let him die, not here. Not in Fallujah.

The nearer he came to the end of his deployment, the more the thought of going home began to consume Lulofs. He began to approach each mission with a ravenous sense of purpose, working his handlers and their dogs to the breaking point. On one mission during those last weeks, he worked his team with such belligerent intent that he didn't even realize they had pushed their way past the front line—putting his dog teams between the Marines and the enemy. When he finally noticed they were in the kill zone, Lulofs simply told his handlers to keep moving even as they were getting shot at, telling them to ignore it. They were less than 100 yards from artillery shells. He knew how dangerous it was but he didn't care.

Lulofs rationalized away the risks he was taking. The sooner they were done with this mission, the sooner they could begin the next and then, only then, could they leave this godforsaken place and go home.

A single moment of clarity managed to prick its way through the fog of Lulofs's complacency. While he and Farnsworth were out together on a mission, Lulofs saw a master gunnery sergeant, with Special Ops standing a few feet away, watching the pair of them. The sergeant walked over and looked Lulofs straight in the eye. "You two have been here too long," he told him.

The sense of fearlessness and invincibility he felt on missions was, he would realize later, purely selfish, and it put him recklessly close to the edge of death. Looking back now, Lulofs believes he survived the war because of two things. One of those things was luck; the other was Aaslan. The dog had been his lone emotional crutch and the real reason why he'd been able to retain as much of himself as he could hold onto in Fallujah.

The other men relied on Aaslan too. During their deployment in Iraq, Lulofs had one rule about his dog. No one could pet Aaslan while they were working. The Marines on their patrols knew this rule and respected it. They would wait for each mission to be over because that's when Aaslan was free—free to be loved on, free to play.

There would be a lot of bad days in Iraq, "bad" meaning that they had severe casualties. After one very bad day, Lulofs and Aaslan were waiting with the Marines to remount so they could get back to their base. Lulofs watched while one Marine broke down, put his head on Aaslan's shoulder, and wept.

Any handler who has brought a dog with him or her to war will say it made all the difference in the world. They will say that the dog by their side provided them with something more than just a living, breathing piece of home—the dog acted as a talisman, insulating them from whatever horrors unfolded, bringing them peace in turbulence, offering companionship in times of loneliness. The dog's presence made the path through war bearable, the unendurable somehow endurable, and many will say they came through the other side more stable.

During wartime or otherwise, no matter how far one strays from working dogs, whether to venture into different military jobs or once back in civilian life, K-9 is a lifelong state of mind. It's like a bloodline, deep and tangled, the mark of which lives on long past the dogs, long after the wars are over.

Sean Lulofs knew he wanted to be a handler when he was five years old. His mother brought him to a police demonstration. He watched as an officer placed a bag of cocaine in a woman's purse. Then a dog was brought in and, within minutes, found the cocaine. Awestruck, he turned to his mother and declared his life's goal—to become a K-9 police officer.

Dog handlers are their own breed. In Lulofs's estimation handlers have their own place in the military world; they are like drops of oil floating in water—distinct, separate. It's all part of the personality, he says. They see themselves as outsiders within the larger world of the military. Shunned, misunderstood. "Leadership doesn't understand us," he says, "because they don't understand our mindset. They don't quite grasp us because they don't understand dogs."

Even though he didn't fully leave the MWD program, Lulofs stopped handling dogs in 2009 to take a managerial role. Advancing as a dog handler in the military often means giving up the work he loves—the higher the rank, the further into the world of administration one goes, and the further he is from working with the dogs. Still, the familiar ring of K-9 pride colors Lulofs's voice. It's the same sound that carries in Ron Aiello's voice, just as it does with most handlers whether they're retired or active, young or old.

A scout dog handler who served in Vietnam, Ron Aiello still beams with pride for Stormy, the dog who accompanied him to war. From the way Aiello talks about her—immediate, vivid, and joyful—it's as if Stormy is somehow still at his feet or dozing in the next room, instead of a memory from a lifetime nearly half a century old. She did more, Aiello believes, than merely save the lives of the men on the patrols he led through the jungles of Vietnam, alerting them to snipers, ambushes, and explosives. Had it not been for Stormy, he says, "I would've come back a different person."

When Ron Aiello was a little boy, he would spend Friday nights riding in the front seat of his grandfather's taxicab. When they dropped off a fare, his grandfather, a heavy man who'd immigrated to the United States from Italy as a teenager, would tell their passenger, "Give the tip to my grandson," and Aiello would collect a dime or, if he was really lucky, a quarter. It was a lot of money for an eight-year-old kid in 1953.

Even then Aiello knew he would become a Marine. He grew up in his grandparents' home in the Italian section of Trenton, New Jersey, in a house filled with love, food, dogs, and family. One of Aiello's favorite uncles was a Marine. So in the summer of 1964, when he was 18, Aiello threw some clothes into the back of his '57 Cadillac and drove down to Virginia Beach and enlisted. A few weeks later he was an infantry grunt stationed at Camp

Lejeune in North Carolina. One day coming back from maneuvers Aiello spotted a guy posting a three-by-five index card on a bulletin board. It was asking for volunteers for dog school. Aiello thought if he had to go to Vietnam, what better way to do it than to go with a dog?

By December 1965, he was assigned and training with the Army's dog program at Fort Benning in Georgia. It was there Aiello met the dog he would take to war with him, an 18-month-old German shepherd mix named Stormy. The first time he approached her kennel he did so cautiously, leash in hand. She was smaller than the male dogs and she stood in the back of the run, staring at him. She didn't bark or move. And so Aiello held still too, looking back at her. They both just stood there, staring. Ten minutes must've gone by before he got up the courage to open the kennel and walk in. Day after day they trained together—day patrols, then night patrols, learning how to follow airborne scent and alert on booby-traps, the scent of gun oil, and the sound of snipers high in the trees. The training drew them close, and pretty soon it felt to Aiello that Stormy could read his mind. In 1966, the 21-year-old Marine corporal and his scout dog were on their way to Vietnam.

As a scout dog team, their role was to lead night patrols through the jungle undetected and in one piece. Aiello always kept her leash wrapped tight around his left wrist. Stormy, confident in her job, would lead out in front. When the leash was taut and pulling, the tension held between them, she was moving and it was safe to follow. But as a soon as the leash went slack, it meant Stormy had stopped; it was her way of alerting him. Aiello would then halt the troops behind them. Whatever held her attention, whichever direction her head was turned, that was where the threat could be found.

Before each mission Aiello would sit with Stormy and talk through his orders with her. "Stormy," he'd say, bending his dark head of Italian hair down to the dog, "We're going out on a patrol tonight. We're gonna go to an old cemetery." As he would talk his way through the mission, mapping it out klick by klick, she would sit, listening intently, studying his face. And when Aiello heard his name called up, he'd look down at her and say,

"C'mon, Stormy. Let's go." All the worry had gone out of him because she'd been there to listen.

Stormy was a loveable, friendly dog. In fact, she was so friendly that when a senior officer instructed Aiello to use Stormy to intimidate a Vietcong they were holding captive for questioning, Aiello panicked. Stormy was too gentle a dog to be violent without provocation, without some kind of imminent threat. As Aiello approached the man—who was on his knees, blindfolded, with hands tied behind his back—he tightened his grip on Stormy's leash, not because he was afraid she would bite the prisoner, but because he was afraid if she got too close, she would lick his face.

But that sweet disposition would change if warranted. One afternoon on base, Aiello was crossing a field with Stormy. Tired and deep in thought, he didn't notice a South Vietnamese Army soldier who was also crossing the field and heading right toward him. The soldier was similarly unaware of Aiello and his dog. Stormy however, had seen this man coming at them and, perhaps because she didn't know him or because she smelled his gun, had marked him as a threat. She stopped in front of Aiello, crouched to the ground and growled. The soldier, reacting, pointed his gun at the dog. Aiello reached for his .45-caliber pistol and pointed it at the man's head. He had no idea if the Vietnamese soldier would understand him but he told him anyway, "If you try to shoot my dog, I will blow your head off." The soldier lowered his weapon and very slowly backed away. Aiello lowered his weapon and then, sensing that someone was close by, turned around. Behind him were three other Marines who'd watched this soldier point his gun at Stormy and had their M-14s raised, ready to shoot the man who would harm her.

After one handler was shot and wounded, Aiello and Stormy took over his assignment for a day patrol; their orders were to search a village suspected of harboring Vietcong. Before they began their search, an airstrike came through to clear the village. Artillery hailed down in front of them, and the sound of roaring jets filled the air above them. The ground shook as the 500-pound bombs hit the village, rattling the earth.

They stood on a hillside and watched as the village started to burn, blazing into a fiery inferno. While they waited for it to cool, a sick feeling filled Aiello; he knew they weren't prepared for what lay ahead. Aiello was drenched with sweat from the intense heat, from all that burning, from sweating at the sight of it. The trees were still scorching, the lush green leaves smoldering and smoking, like coals in a fire, their ash lifting into the mess of black clouds above them even as they made their way to the bottom of the hill.

When they entered the village, Stormy made a sound Aiello had never heard before—a deep, strangled moan. As they pushed deeper into the wreckage, she kept moaning. The dog had been trained not just to alert on ammunition and gun oil but also on human scent, and she was overwhelmed by the smell of charred flesh—it was all around them. Aiello realized there was no way she could work like this. But in the end it didn't matter. As they walked from village to village, Aiello couldn't understand what the hell they were doing there, there was nothing but bodies left to find—in pieces and parts strewn everywhere. The village was like a hotbox, the temperature upward of 120 degrees. It was as if they'd entered the underside of hell.

The memory of that day would be one he would repress, hiding in the recesses of his mind until it reemerged on a steamy summer night nearly 40 years later.

On July 4, 2000, Aiello was sitting on the porch of his New Jersey home, a lit cigar between his fingertips. It was late in the evening; the day was fizzling to an end. Earlier, his teenaged sons had set off roman candles and firecrackers in the yard. Maybe it was the sound of the fireworks, or the starbursts pluming in the distant sky, or even the hazy heat of the night, but the vision hit him suddenly and clearly, as did the sensation of being completely soaked. He flashed back to his younger self, standing at the top of that hill in 1966, surveying the burning wreckage of that Vietnamese village.

Perhaps more traumatizing than the memory of that day is that Aiello never knew what became of Stormy. When his tour in Vietnam was over in 1967, Stormy stayed behind in Vietnam, as each dog did when his handler finished a tour. Back then, the dogs stayed where they were and partnered up with new handlers. Aiello remembers the April afternoon when his captain announced that the replacement handlers were already en route and would be arriving the next day. It was, he told them, the last night they would have with their dogs. Almost all of the handlers, including Aiello, brought blankets out to the kennels to sleep on the ground next to their dogs, wanting to be with them until the very last moment.

For years Aiello wrote to the Marine Corps trying to find Stormy, putting in his bid to take her, mailing letters, making phone calls, but to no avail. He never received a response and was left only to wonder what had become of her. Like the majority of the some 10,000 handlers who served in Vietnam, Aiello never saw his dog again.

Of the nearly 5,000 dogs who served their tours in Vietnam from 1964 to 1975, only 204 dogs left the country, and none were out-processed to a

Marine handler Ron Aiello and his scout dog Stormy deployed to Vietnam together in 1966. Aiello, whose tour ended in 1967, never knew what became of his canine partner.
Courtesy of Ron Aiello

life beyond the military.[8] The dogs still in-country at the time the US forces evacuated were either euthanized or turned over the South Vietnamese Army, which likely meant death. Their handlers, who left Vietnam believing they would see their partners again, were in the dark about the fates of their dogs. Many wouldn't discover the truth until years later. And many, to this day, have not recovered from the pain of knowing their dogs were left behind.

In the early 1990s Aiello and some of his Vietnam handler buddies saw a notice circulating for a war dog reunion out in Ocean City, Maryland. They decided to go. They didn't realize their mistake until they got to the hotel—it was actually a reunion for World War II handlers, not for the guys who served in Vietnam. In the end, Aiello said it didn't matter—not the difference in wars or the generations between them. They were all handlers.

Aiello and the other Vietnam veterans spent those three days laughing, talking, and sharing memories of their dogs with the old timers. "They would close their eyes and listen," he says. "Their stories were our stories."

TWO

the house of
misfit dogs

Now the most important point . . . is this question of the keepers. It is more important than that of the dog.

—Lieutenant Colonel E. H. Richardson

In the late 1990s, at the Lackland Air Force Base kennels in Texas, there was one dog so aggressive, so vicious and unapproachable that Dr. Stewart Hilliard, chief of the Department of Defense's Military Working Dog Training Course and resident animal behaviorist, started to document the efforts to train him. Taint was an ornery, raging beast of a dog; a notorious biter who had grown to deserve his disparaging name.

Curious to see if even a problem dog like Taint could be used in the program, Hilliard asked handler Staff Sergeant Chris Jakubin to work alongside him in testing Taint's boundaries. Jakubin was eager to help. He had a great respect for Hilliard, whom he called "Doc," and often trailed around after him, peppering Hilliard with questions about training techniques or a dog he was having trouble with. After they mounted a video camera on the top of the kennel so they could film these attempts, Jakubin donned the necessary protective layers and pulled on a pair of gloves to shield his hands. They were expecting the worst.

But when Jakubin opened the door and went in, nothing happened. Taint accepted the hot dog Jakubin offered and let him walk right into his kennel. Jakubin didn't have any issues with Taint that day or in the days that would follow. He would just walk up to the kennel, feed Taint a hot dog, and go on in. On the way out, the dog followed him willingly. And this was how Taint the problem dog became Jakubin's dog.

When Jakubin's assignment at Lackland came to an end, a Marine stepped up to take over handling Taint. Jakubin was very clear about how to work with the dog to keep his temperament in check, carefully outlining a long list of do's and don'ts. The Marine assured him he could manage Taint. But one day, not long after Jakubin departed, the Marine handler tried to get too close and Taint mauled him so badly that Lackland's behavioral veterinarians were ready to destroy the dog. When word got back to Jakubin that they were planning on putting Taint down, he pleaded with them not to do it. "I will take him," he told them. "I will deal with him."

His request was approved, and soon Taint was on a plane to Colorado, where Jakubin had taken a position at the United States Air Force Academy as kennel master. When he went to pick Taint up, Jakubin was nervous. It'd been months since he'd last seen his old partner, so he put on gloves before opening Taint's crate, just in case the dog had changed his attitude. But Taint came out of his crate happy. Together, Jakubin and Taint would go on to prove the naysayers wrong, winning multiple competitions and meeting the regular requirements for detection work without difficulty.

By 2009, time caught up with Taint. The ten-year-old dog's health had deteriorated: his bladder was shot and his cataracts were so bad he was nearly blind. But the tenacious Belgian Malinois continued running drills, his accuracy at detection spot-on perfect. Even as his body was riddled with illness and infirmity, he was outperforming dogs half his age with twice his strength. Those who knew and watched them together as a team—like Sergeant Timothy Bailey, Jakubin's head trainer—believe the dog's iron will to survive derived solely from his attachment to Jakubin.

One day Bailey was supposed to take Taint in for a routine veterinary visit, but when Jakubin saw them getting ready to leave, he decided he wanted to be the one to go. After they got there, it only took the vet a little while to determine that the dog was dying. Taint's lungs were filling with fluid. It was unlikely, the vet told Jakubin, that he would survive the night. So Jakubin brought Taint back outside and they walked for nearly two miles before going back to the vet and saying good-bye.

When Jakubin returned to the kennels, he came back alone. He didn't hide his grief. It was the first time any of his handlers saw Jakubin so emotionally bare; the first time they ever saw Jakubin cry.

When Bailey spoke to the sizeable crowd at Taint's memorial service, he tried to impart to those gathered how rare Jakubin's relationship with Taint really was. Their relationship spanned the dog's life. "Jak and Taint could probably almost go in for records of being the longest team together," he said. "Your average K-9 military dog team is together for maybe three to four years and that's the max."

Jakubin and Taint were together for ten.

The muzzle on this dog is already speckled with gray and white, even though he is barely five years old. This coloring is the reason why the other handlers at the United States Air Force Academy call Mack, a moderately sized Belgian Malinois, the "ghost-faced killer."

It's a cold December morning in Colorado Springs, Colorado. Mack is riding in the back of one of the kennel's vehicles outfitted especially for their dogs. Kennel Master Chris Jakubin, or Jak, as most of his handlers call him, is driving. His six-foot-four frame fills the cab of the car so that he has to hunch over the steering wheel. Dog hair dusts his black fleece. Jakubin and Mack are on their way to meet the handlers stationed at Buckley, another Colorado Air Force base located nearby, for a day of intrabase kennel training.

Mack doesn't sit quietly, nor does he use the hour of downtime in the moving car to rest; he is constantly twisting and shifting or frenetically scratching at the metal interior of the made-for-canine backseat. He barks randomly at the cars he sees flying by his window on the highway, the sound throaty, hoarse, and loud. A smoker's bark, Jakubin calls it. He grins.

He has a special shine for Mack, the dog he fondly calls the reincarnation of Taint.

In the backseat, Mack seems more stir-crazy than like the vicious impressions conjured by stories of Taint. But Mack hasn't been an easy dog to work with, so in a way, Mack is continuing Taint's legacy because in Taint's legacy there is inherently a challenge. And Jakubin loves a good challenge—especially when it comes to training dogs. He calls it "polishing the turds."

Chris Jakubin, kennel master of the US Air Force Academy, works with MWD Oli at a training facility in Colorado Springs, Colorado in December 2011.

There's been a long line of turds, or problem dogs, who have graced the kennels under Jakubin's command. In fact, he's actively sought out difficult dogs from other kennels; it's become something of a tradition. The very first dog to officially join the US Air Force Academy kennels after they opened in 2002 was Agbhar, a German shepherd. Agbhar was an asshole. Jakubin says this sheepishly but without hesitation because it's the truth. Agbhar did not like people. Agbhar was not friendly. Agbhar was a problem dog.

"Agbhar was in a way a misfit dog. Taint was a misfit dog," Jakubin says. "Like the home for misfit toys, we're the home for misfit dogs."

A kennel master is pretty much exactly what it sounds like—the officer responsible for maintaining the kennels and overseeing the handlers and dogs who work there. It's a high-ranking position in the dog-handling field. It's also a role that comes with a lot of managerial responsibilities—from ordering the dogs' food to assigning handlers to base patrol duty. Much of the work can have little to do with hands-on training. So how much a kennel master works with the dogs is entirely up to the kennel master. Will he be a desk man or a dog man?

Jakubin is decidedly a dog man. He operates under the philosophy that there is no single, cookie-cutter way to train a dog. Each dog is unique, and it's the handler's job to study that dog and learn *that* dog's behavior. As Jakubin sees it, dogs tell their handlers how they need to be trained, not the other way around. All the handlers have to do is listen. His technique—which he honed while working with dogs like Taint, Agbhar, and Mack—begins with simple observation: first, uncover each dog's weak points until they're fully explored and understood; next, work through those weak points; and finally, build the dog's confidence until that dog is performing at his highest potential. It is a long investigative process but one that comes with great reward—a dog who can contribute, a dog who can save lives.

Jakubin has been training dogs for nearly 30 years, almost his whole adult life. Getting on with dogs comes naturally to him. It all goes back to his first dog bite. One day in winter when he was just a kid, the family dog, a springer spaniel called Silly, went missing. They found the dog a couple of days later at a neighbor's house. When young Jakubin went to retrieve Silly, the neighbor's boxer bit him hard, the dog's incisors puncturing his leg. Rather than scaring him off dogs for good, the experience fortified his desire to work with them—he calls it his Peter Parker moment. That was a long time ago and now, in his mid-forties, Jakubin's arms and legs are pocked and colored with dog-bite scars.

Jakubin retired from the Air Force in 2005, so he's free to wear civilian clothes while he works. On his head is either a Cubs baseball hat or a black wool skullcap that reveals the poke of a smooth ponytail just above his shirt collar. The long hair is a personal grooming choice that he takes shit for, constantly. An avid hiker, much of his spare time is spent tackling trails and peaks, knocking out the list of 14ers that he scales with three longtime hiking buddies. He walks with a slow, sometimes uneven gait. It's not hard to see how, on a military base with some 4,000 cadets, someone might mistake him for a wayward backpacker.

One afternoon, as we drive back into the Springs from a day of training, the mountains rise up ahead of us, cutting across the sky, impossibly large. He looks over at me, his face brightening as if he's just spotted old friends. "See that?" he says, nodding to the range as if there was any way I could miss it. "When I first saw those mountains I knew I was home."

The Academy kennels are set back away from the road on the widespread campus, nestled against the outline of more Colorado mountains. Two mesh wire sculptures contoured in the shape of dogs guard the front door, flanking the walkway. A worn, black leather couch takes up room in the hallway, the walls of which are lined with framed photographs of each dog who has called this kennel home. Underneath each photo are rectangular pieces of wood, plaques listing the dog's individual achievements: Taint's drug find in May 2003 (five grams of marijuana); Ginger's 115 individual bomb searches in August 2003 alone; and Agbhar's second-place finish in bomb detection at the Tucson K-9 trials in 2003. This wall of colorful photos and the kennel's modest, fenced-in training yard out back, with its seesaw plank of wood and cement tunnel, are reminiscent of a nursery school playground.

Just to the left is the door leading to the kennels themselves, and before that a clean and organized kitchen area. On the counter is a hand-written reminder not to feed Benga because he has a vet appointment the following day. Plastic specimen containers are lined up above the kitchen cabinets; inside, ghostly white, cocoon-shaped orbs float in a yellowish liquid, some kind of preservative. They are dog testicles. An homage of sorts, however bizarre, to the kennel's dogs.

At the other end of the hall, Jakubin's office is comfortable but cluttered. His desk is a mess of papers; equipment and gear are lumped in piles on the floor. Shelves and file cabinets are crowded with awards etched with achievements Jakubin has never mentioned. Across the hall, in what appears to be a little-used conference room, an old-fashioned mantelpiece hangs on the wall. The antique polished wood looks out of place, a relic in a room outfitted with more modern amenities—a large-screen television and plastic office chairs. It is the only thing Jakubin took from the original kennel, and on it sits a row of decorative tin boxes. Their sweetly curled pastel ribbons belie their contents: the ashes of the dogs the kennel has lost to illness and old age.

Jakubin is always affable, quick to make jokes and easy with his self-deprecating humor. "If there were no dogs," he likes to say, "I don't know what I'd be doing. I'd be working in a video store." Still, he somehow manages to remain at arm's length even when he's talking about his wife and their two sons or describing the day that Taint died. If you ask him how he won Taint over, he'll just kind of shrug and tell you he did it with a pocketful of hot dogs.

One afternoon as we walk through the campus, Jakubin runs into one of his handlers who has Benga, a German shepherd, in tow. The dog had banged his head, which caused a hematoma, the third on this ear. Now his left ear drooped, maybe from the weight of the stitches but more likely, said the vet, a lasting result of the repeated injury. That ear would probably never stand up straight again.

When the pair walks in, Benga lights up, immediately excited to see Jakubin, who is standing about three feet away, just out of his reach. The dog wants to get to him—his ears are snapped as high and tall as they will go, his eyes are wide and seeking, a high-pitched whine catches in his throat as he tap-dances his paws up and down, desperate to be closer.

In 1914, at the beginning of WWI, there was one man, Lieutenant Colonel E. H. Richardson, who stood as the lone advocate for integrating canines into Her Majesty's battalions, arguing that their potential to assist on the battlefield would be unparalleled. Other countries, he argued, were already using dogs to great advantage: the Germans employed dogs, as did the Russians. The Bulgarians and Albanians positioned them as sentry guards. France was trying to integrate dogs into its army. Italy and Sweden were also experimenting with canines as a military force. But Richardson's petition fell on deaf ears.

Firm in his belief that dogs could be trained to great advantage for England's cause, Richardson carried on his campaign until finally, in 1916, an officer from the Royal Artillery sent a request for trained dogs to "keep up communications between his outpost and the battery during heavy bombardment."[1]

Lieutenant Colonel E. H. Richardson, "the father of war dogs" (at least as we know them today), pulls bandages from the kit of a British Red Cross dog, circa 1914.
Courtesy of the Library of Congress, Prints and Photographs Division

In the years that followed, Richardson's success with dogs was unsurpassed. He would write of his progress with his dogs in two highly regarded tomes: *British War Dogs: Their Training and Psychology* and *Watch Dogs: Their Training and Management.* When the US Marine Corps began its official program, the Dogs for Defense, in 1942, his techniques served as a guidebook of sorts, the holy bible of war dogs.

Through his writings the colonel revealed himself to be a man of incredible open-mindedness and gentility, especially when it came to the treatment of his dogs. He was kind to the animals, intolerant of cruelty, and expected dog handlers, or "keepers" as they were called, to act as he did. Of the "first importance," he writes, is the character of the keeper:

> This must be accompanied by a fondness for, and a gentleness with, dogs. Complete confidence and affection must exist between dogs and keeper, and a man whose only idea of control is by coercion and fear is quite useless. I have found that many men who are supposedly dog experts, are not sufficiently sympathetic, and are apt to regard the dog too much as a machine. . . .
>
> The highest qualities—love and duty—have to be appealed to and cultivated. Coercion is of no avail, for of what use would this be when the dog is two or three miles away from its keeper? In fact, it may be said that the whole training is based on appeal. To this end the dog is gently taught to associate everything pleasant with its working hours.[2]

For a man whose experience with training dogs occurred in the first years of the twentieth century, Richardson was progressive. Compulsion and harsh corrections were once the presiding model of dog training in the military. (It seemed this was one of Richardson's teachings that was not so faithfully adhered to in the US military's early consultation of his manuals. This attitude would only start to change in the 1980s with a turn toward reward- and praise-based training, one where handlers would cull success from their dogs by relying on a positive reward system in conditioning.) Richardson was about one hundred years ahead of the curve in laying the framework for the modern-day handler. He preached patience, a respect for the animal, and appealed to the sensitivity in man as well as the dog. Dogs should not be "roughly handled or roughly spoken to." In his opinion even a lack of sympathy was grounds for dismissal. Even a strong dog, he warned, could "be easily thrown back in his training, or even spoiled altogether, by sharp handling."

Determining which fledgling handlers have the most potential is not always easy, even for the most experienced in the trade. Kevin Behan was never very good at picking out which of the handlers he was training would be the strong ones. Good at reading the dogs, yes, but he was never quite as good at reading the people.

Behan, a career dog trainer and author of *Natural Dog Training* and *Your Dog Is Your Mirror*, began working with his first dog, a poodle named Onyx, when he was only ten years old. But then, dog training was in his blood. His father, John Behan, was one of the most renowned dog trainers of his time. When the US military first started using dogs in the 1940s, they brought Behan's father in as a training expert to help prepare dogs and handlers alike. John Behan wrote about his time training dogs and military handlers during World War II in his 1946 book *Dogs of War*. But Kevin realized at a young age that he had his own way of handling dogs, one that worked and strayed far outside the methods his father employed. And over the course of his long career, Behan has trained thousands of dogs, from household dogs to police dogs and of course their owners and handlers.

But it wasn't until Behan worked with dog handlers in the Connecticut police department that he began to take stock of these handlers on the scale of their egos. Personally, he had always favored the quiet, introspective handlers over the loud bombastic ones, even if he recognized that there wasn't any room for passivity in handling dogs and so often dismissed anyone who appeared to lack voluminous confidence. But he soon realized that his initial impressions of these officers had skewed his expectations. Over time, Behan saw how the soft-spoken handlers proved to be the most intuitive, and when the occasion called for it, they exhibited an unexpected resilience, revealing an inner strength that he found surprising. The most talented handlers have to possess a dynamic aspect to their personalities. So, in the end what he would look for with these handlers was a balance.

It struck him as he watched these officers work—if a handler were to think of the dog only as a tool, this, Behan found, was limiting. But when a handler considered the dog a projection of his ego, that was even worse.

But if there's one thing *not* lacking in the dog-handling field, it's ego. The term "dog whisperer" gets thrown around a lot. Get a group of young handlers together, and there's bound to be some jockeying around who is the handler with the biggest, baddest dog, the one who hits and bites the hardest.

A good rule of thumb in gauging a handler on the job—Is he being too aggressive? Is he being too passive?—I found, is simply to watch the dog.

When Lackland Air Force base in Texas hosts its interservice Iron Dog Competition in May 2012, I join Chris Jakubin, who has brought along Mack and some of his handlers. The competition is designed to test a variety of skills over the course of the two-day trials—the very essence of the collective education a handler and his dog have developed together as a team, whether in training or during deployment. The course stretches across many miles and is meant to challenge the handler and the dog physically as well as mentally; it includes a low river crossing, an obstacle where handlers have to carry their dogs up and down a hill, as well as a basic obstacle course that includes an "injured soldier," a heavy dummy that handlers must carry or drag to "safety" while still managing their dogs and their weapons.

In addition to the competition there are a series of classroom seminars and a host of hands-on courses. In the San Antonio morning heat, I stand alongside a group of handlers who've circled around to watch an outdoor demonstration. The man leading the exercise is not a military handler but a private vendor. He is attempting to illustrate his theory that the way to maximize a dog's defensive drive is to heighten the threat at the peak of the dog's response. As he explains to the group, this extra push will elicit the "defender" in the dog, the ultimate "fighter."

The man invites a handler from the group to bring his dog onto the field and instructs him to hold the dog's leash taut. Then, like a bullfighter, the man begins to slowly advance on the dog and his handler, his face drawn into an expression of sheer aggression—mean and contorted. In one hand he holds a baton, in the other the red top to a water cooler that he brandishes like a shield. He is the aggressor picking a fight. If this dog is prepared to face this "attacker" he will exhibit the telltale signs: the strong, deep bark that says, "I am not afraid of you"; the straight back; the excited tail; and a forward lurching motion—all showing he is ready to engage this threat. But this dog's bark is high and shrill, and his tail is tucked in a downward loop, a half circle pointing to the ground. Instead of straining at his leash to get closer, he dances uncertainly from side to side. This dog is signaling fear, but the man continues to advance. And then the foul smell of excrement fills the air. The dog has literally just had the shit scared out of him.

Handlers might call this "melting the dog," meaning that a dog has been pushed beyond his limits. While it doesn't indicate necessarily that a dog's will to work has been broken, "melting" a dog is far from ideal and it's something handlers want to avoid. You can take a weak dog and build confidence, but you can just as easily push a fragile dog deeper into his insecurities. With the right amount of patience and attention a handler can work a dog through his fears and overcome his reluctance. But it's a fine line to navigate, pushing the limits of a dog's confidence, and a crucial one to maintain. An experienced handler can determine, just by observing a dog, whether he possesses the will to defend himself in a compromising situation, an assessment that can help protect not just the dog but whoever may be on the other end of the leash.

During his seminar in Texas, Jakubin shows the assembled handlers a video of just such a dog teetering on that line. On the screen, the handlers are conducting a routine traffic stop. Jakubin, in the role of the aggressor, is dressed like a bank robber: he's outfitted all in black and wears a ski mask, carrying a big black rubber baton. After refusing to heed the warnings of the dog handler, Jakubin "the criminal" advances on the dog. At first the dog tries to defend himself, starting forward toward Jakubin, but then he retreats, skirting backward, trying to hide behind his handler. Jakubin backs off, taking a few steps away and lowers his weapon. After another minute or so he advances toward the handler and the dog with his voice raised, giving the dog another chance to engage and defend himself. But again the dog shows a clear lack of confidence—he gives a few short barks but ultimately retreats. Jakubin pulls off the ski mask. He didn't need to be tough on the dog and there was no need to try again; he knew the dog was done.

When the video cuts out, Jakubin turns back to his audience and explains to his seminar attendees that what they just saw was a dog who didn't have the right kind of fight to be a patrol dog. But, he says, that's okay. Not all dogs are meant to be patrol dogs. It's no reflection on a handler's ability. Just because the dog had failed to pass this test, it didn't mean the handler had.

And this is where Behan's concern that a handler should not see his dog as an extension of his own pride comes in. Egos can be a problem. Egos can get in the way of judging a dog's true ability. Egos, Jakubin believes, should be checked as soon as handlers walk in the training arena; they don't make for good students or good teachers.

During another training seminar at Langley Air Force Base in Newport News, Virginia, I watch Jakubin coach a handler. She is working on a drill with her dog. The cool of the morning hours has simmered away in the humidity and her face is beet red, the edges of her hair are dark with sweat that drips down her temples. Most of the other handlers have given up for the day, already put their dogs up, and are now just milling around the yard, clustering in the shade. But she continues to struggle with the task in front of her, focusing on each note Jakubin gives, her face crinkling in concentration. Later, when the seminar breaks for the day, Jakubin is impressed: what the handler lacked in skill, she more than made up for in persistence. In this career, the handler's drive to learn is just as crucial as the dog's, perhaps even more important.

The next day, I find myself sitting on the picnic bench under the only shade in the training yard. The handler on the bench beside me has a hardness to him that makes me uncomfortable. He is good looking, like a really angry, muscle-inflated version of Matt Damon; he's done the majority of the shit-talking that morning during training in the small yard, and his tone rings more snide to me than supportive. I get the distinct impression that he has little interest in what I was doing here. But still he sits next to me on the bench. We sit in silence for a while, as a team works a drill over by the chain-link fence in the corner of the yard. And just when the quiet seems the most unbearable he starts to talk. He tells me how much he loved handling dogs, that he'd had the best job in the world. As he talks he stares ahead. Fuck all the lazy assholes in it for the quick promotion and the paycheck, he says. The day he had to trade in his dog for the position of kennel master was the saddest day of his life.

What he says reminds me of something Richardson wrote. It was his recommendation, in fact, that each officer appointed to the post of keeper be done so on a temporary basis, first having to prove himself during a probationary period and not fully integrated or assigned to canine-related duties until the "result of the man's work"—his aptitude for working with dogs—was proven.[3]

That same afternoon Colonel Alan Metzler visits the clinic, dropping by the Langley training field to speak to the handlers assembled. As he walks across the yard, the air shifts; all the handlers pop up from their seats on the picnic bench. If they were leaning into the chain-link fence, they stand up away from it.

Metzler is upbeat but intense; he moves with a tight decisiveness as he addresses the group. He is quick to tell the group to speak freely, to tell him directly what they need, what they would change if they could. There is a pause but then a few hands are raised. Some ask about funding, another handler suggests more training time and more special seminars like Jakubin's. The colonel nods, his head bobbing efficiently; he is a serious listener. And then Staff Sergeant Kaluza, the handler from the picnic bench, starts to speak. He wants to know if they could do more to weed out the handlers who are in the job for the quick rope-climb up the totem pole, the ones who are in it for the high pay, the ones who lack the passion and intensity of the diehard handlers. He is frank and deadly serious. He wants them gone.

Canine training can be a rough-and-tumble business. It takes a toll on the body. The resulting scratches, knuckle nicks, and bite marks—like scorecards or bedpost notches—are brands of the job and worn with pride. The badder the dog, the bigger the bite; the deeper the scar, the better the story.

On a training field one young handler pulls off his shirt and upends his bandages to reveal the bite he received the day before. In this case, the dog hadn't taken a temperamental turn; rather, it was the handler who'd made a move in the wrong direction during their bite-work training so that the dog, aiming for the protective layers, missed, and ended up raking off a good bit of skin right under the handler's rib cage. Because the dog's teeth only grazed the handler's side, the marks look more like scratches—angry red and all the deeper where the canines had pierced the flesh.

In the PowerPoint presentation Jakubin uses during the class portion of his seminar, one of the slides shows a particularly heinous dog bite. The label over the photo reads: "Super Epic Failure!!"

The skin in the photo is ripped so completely, it looks as though a crude blade had sliced a square patch of skin from the sweetest, fleshiest section of this handler's forearm. The blood pools in the wound, threatening to spill over edge; the rest of her arm is spotted with drops of red. Jakubin was with Staff Sergeant Ciara Gavin before she was rushed to the hospital. It's the worst dog bite he's ever seen.

Gavin worked in Jakubin's kennel at the Air Force Academy. She'd been partnered with a long-haired German shepherd who had a sweet temper. While this sweet dog had been competent in detection work, he never took to bite work, so Jakubin traded him to another base that was having trouble with a dog named Kelly, notorious for her volatile temperament and erratic moods. Not so fondly referred to as a "nasty little bitch," Kelly had bitten at least three handlers and sent them each to the hospital. When she came to the Air Force Academy kennels, Gavin became her handler. It was Kelly who tore that piece out of Gavin's arm.

Kelly's K-9 portrait hangs in the hallway of the Academy's kennel with the others. Her forehead is stout and square, her ears lean at a somewhat sharper bend, turning out at their own stubborn angle. The lids of her eyes have a reddish hue and actually seem to glow. There is no other way to describe it—the dog looks demonic. Gavin, on the other hand, appears almost angelic in a cherry red fleece; the softness of it seems to warm the space around her. Her brown eyes radiate kindness.

At best Kelly was merely unpredictable. Her moods changed suddenly and without warning or provocation; one minute Kelly was vicious and the next compliant, lying on her back offering her belly up for a scratch. Gavin would see the devil flash and then it would disappear again. And when Kelly went to that instant and ferocious place, snarling and bucking, it was like a rodeo, and wrangling her back down into submission was no easy feat.

There was nothing especially foreboding about the day Kelly bit Gavin. She and Jakubin were just trying to work the dog through the fierce possessiveness she showed for her toys, attempting to establish trust and consistency by showing the dog that if she released the toy she would get it back again.

Gavin was only standing behind Kelly, raising her arms and lifting the dog by the collar when Kelly whipped her head around, sinking in her teeth. It was the day Kelly beat Gavin at the rodeo.

It was six weeks before Gavin was able to use her hand again. When she returned to work, Jakubin put Kelly's leash back in Gavin's hand, and she took it without thinking twice. Gavin could have refused, but in her mind, picking up Kelly's leash wasn't a choice. Pure pride and ego kept her going. In the end, it was the good kind of ego that prevented her from letting her fear override her confidence. It's this side of ego in a canine handler that inspires persistence and the kind of commitment that separates a good handler from a great one. It was essential in the end that she get right back to work, to push through her fears of working with Kelly. It made Gavin a better handler.

Kelly eventually went to a different kennel. Gavin completed her career as an Air Force handler in 2008. And though Gavin is no longer an MWD handler, she will never forget that bite. Even from a distance the twisted lines of the scar shine a pearly white on her wrist. She saw Kelly recently. The dog seemed calm and under control. But for a few seconds, the old devil in Kelly showed through. When the dog growled and snapped at her new handler, adrenaline coursed through Gavin and her heart thundered as if it would never settle back down.

But as they say in K-9, it's not a matter of *if* you'll get bitten, only when.

I can feel the soggy Virginia heat on my face, but it's actually cool inside the enormous black bite suit I'm wearing. This luxurious damp is, I'm fully aware, lingering sweat from the bodies that had worn it during drills the day before, but I don't care. This suit is my big, bulky armor of protection.

The horses that had been grazing serenely just outside the fence the previous afternoon are now galloping in wide loops, stopping abruptly to shake out their manes and stamp the ground, their hooves setting off clouds of golden dust. Hurricane Irene is careening her way up the eastern coastline, and though it's hours away from hitting the area around Langley Air Force Base, the horses have caught wind of the approaching storm. Their restlessness and unease is palpable and does little to quiet the loud thumping of my heart. Still, they are more calming than the ribbing calls coming from the crowd gathered inside the smaller training yard to watch me catch my first bite.

"Catching a Bite" is exactly what it sounds like. It is essentially the act of becoming the animated human equivalent of a chew toy. And it's a crucial part of a handler's role in preparing his dog for patrol work. Bitework training is learned in stages. This is for everyone's safety—the dog's, the handler's, and the decoy's. (The decoy—a handler—plays the role of "perpetrator" so the dog can learn how to detain a fleeing suspect during patrol work.) If a decoy catches a dog incorrectly—turns the wrong way or keeps his body too rigid—he can really hurt the dog, or himself. The decoy will wear a bite sleeve or a full bite suit. Bite suits vary in size and bulk, but ultimately their weight is gradually reduced until the decoy is wearing something thin enough to hide under street clothes. This way the dog learns to associate the bite with a perpetrator, rather than with the suit.

The first suit I try on is huge. Two women handlers—the only other women besides myself in this group—do me a kindness, whether out of pity or female solidarity, and help me get into the gear. They hold out their arms so I have something to hang on to and work the zippers running down the side of the pant legs to squash them low to the ground, so that I can climb into them. Jakubin, who so far has been keeping a polite distance, looks relieved that I'm managing without his interference. The jacket is easier to get on but not easy to wear. It is very heavy and very large. This is when Jakubin steps in, shaking his head, and hands me a tack suit jacket, which is just as big but not as bulky and thick. It doesn't fit exactly but it's close enough. Under the weight of the jacket and the pants, I feel like I'm walking neck-deep through a pool, pushing against a wall of water. In a few minutes, I'm supposed to act the part of a fleeing suspect, and "run" away from a dog. I can hardly manage a respectable walk.

Handler Staff Sergeant Ted Carlson brings out the dog who's going to bite me, a slender Dutch shepherd named Rambo. From across the yard, I can hear Rambo's ragged panting, the high-pitched whining and the sound of his teeth smacking together as he snaps at the air in anticipation. The sight of me in the suit has ignited the dog's prey drive—the instinct that motivates him to chase and bite something into submission. It would seem that Rambo's prey drive is quite high. My brain knows that I'm safe, but my body doesn't—my muscles stiffen. It's a physical primordial response. It's fear.

Jakubin stands with me in the middle of the yard, adjusting my stance. Before leaving me there on my own, he offers one final directive. "If you get knocked down, don't move," he says. "I'll come and pick you up."

I hold my breath, shut my eyes, and wait for the blow. It takes Rambo under three seconds to clear the 25 feet separating us. I feel a spike of adrenaline as the dog makes contact, the force of his weight shoving me back as his open mouth locks around my arm. The sensation registers from dull to crisp, the trickle before the deluge as I feel teeth sink into me—and that sensation is pain.

To put the feel of a dog bite into perspective, it might be helpful to start with what's familiar—our own mouths. Per square inch, the human bite exerts 120 pounds of pressure. That's enough to do some damage—think Mike Tyson, who managed to tear away a piece of Evander Holyfield's ear with his teeth. Dogs have more teeth than humans, 42 of them,[4] but the big fangs, the canines, are the real damage doers. A dog's straight, muscular jaw is designed for meat eating, unlike the construct of a human's mouth and jaw, where the teeth move from side to side to better grind down on things that don't try to run when you eat them, like vegetables.

Different studies and tests have been conducted to try to measure the discrepancies in bite impact from the mouths of a variety of species. In an attempt to determine those animals who possess the most deadly powerful bites, the host of a National Geographic Channel series called *Dangerous Encounters*, Dr. Brady Barr, used a force-measuring device to scale an approximate bite impact among a range of different animals.[5] He found that lions and sharks use roughly the same force of bite pressure at 600 pounds per square inch. But were you to get an appendage caught in an alligator's jaws, you could expect something like 2,500 pounds of pressure to clamp down on your muscles, tendons, and joints, making it highly unlikely that you'd get your limb back in working order, let alone get it back at all.

Depending on the breed, dog bites boast considerable force, ranging from that of an American pit bull terrier at 238 pounds of pressure per square inch[6] to a bullmastiff, the breed with strongest bite, coming in at a recorded 552 pounds per square inch.[7] In training a dog to attack and detain a suspect, the objective is to get a full-mouth bite with a solid grip. The strength of the bite comes from the clamp of the dog's jaws. A weak bite happens when, for example, only a dog's front teeth catch the material, and that's not a bite that will hold for long. But the power of a dog bite depends on many things, from the obvious (how large the dog is) to the difficult to measure or predict with regularity (the dog's desire to bite). The military most often employs two breeds—the Belgian Malinois and the German shepherd. According to the Air Force, the average military working dog's bite exerts somewhere between 400 and 700 pounds of pressure.

I can't say for sure exactly how many pounds of pressure are coming down on my arm—Rambo isn't a very big dog, and I'm fully aware that what I'm experiencing is hardly pushing the limits of dog-bite pain. And because I know this implicitly, I grit my own teeth and force a smile, taking a few steps around the yard. But Rambo has got a good, full-mouth bite, and for that reason he remains fastened to me. Whenever I move, I drag him along with me. Jakubin encourages me to try to pull my arm away from the dog; the resistance excites Rambo, activates his prey drive, which in turn further ignites in him a desire to bite. I tug my arm for all I'm worth, but Rambo's grip seems only to get stronger.

We repeat this move of run, jump, and bite a few more times. When I take off the suit, a marking the shape of a dog's open mouth has already puffed pink and purple on my upper right arm, a swollen pinch where the dog's jaw clamped down on my flesh. Within an hour, that marking will billow into a righteous bruise of deep blues and greens. Compared to some of the batterings I've seen on arms far more muscular and experienced than my own, this mark is like holding up a paper cut next to a machete wound. That doesn't, however, keep me from regarding the bruise fondly over the next couple of weeks, proud as its coloring molts into withering shades of yellow and brown. When Rambo's imprint finally fades and disappears completely, I am sorry to see it go.

When Jakubin first became kennel master at the Air Force Academy in 2002, the dog program there was so new they didn't even have a kennel, so he and his handlers operated out of an old house on a remote part of the Academy's campus. The house is gone now; the area where it once stood is the site of their canine memorial. It's on the top of a little hill; the incline is slick in places where snow leftover from a recent storm still clings to the ground. A large tree with gnarly limbs had fallen on the ground and it serves as a barrier that closes off the memorial, making for a fitting, somber fence.

There's a small marker for each dog, a piece of stone bearing a bronze plaque with the dog's likeness etched in black. Jakubin walks toward them, his boots crunching on leaves and sticks. Ginger's memorial marker is on the exact spot where the old kitchen was, where she used to sleep. It's a peaceful place. Jakubin likes it here; if he could move the kennels back to this part of the campus again he would do it in a heartbeat.

He stands for a few quiet moments facing their markers, the sun somewhere above, almost warm. Jakubin's shadow falls behind him, the mountains in front of him, the dogs at his feet.

Even after a long career, losing a dog never gets easier. "That's the worst part of the job," he says, "is to see a dog go. I've probably become numb to it over these years and I still find myself thinking about the dog and shedding a tear."

Inside this world of handlers and their working dogs is a culture of dedication and sacrifice, even grief—all the things one might expect to find. But there was something else I encountered, something surprising.

Resistance to the idea of love.

THREE

the trouble with loving a war dog

They were the only four-foots who could be trusted to do a piece of work strictly "on their own." Each one knew his job and did it, not because he was made to, but because of the love which is the impelling motive for everything a free dog does for a man.

—Ernest Harold Baynes, *Animal Heroes of the Great War*

Everything is bright—the blue of the sky, the red-baked earth, even the glare off the many pairs of sunglasses is blinding. Kevin Howard sits in a collapsible mesh chair along with a few handlers from Chris Jakubin's kennels and two other former military dog handlers. They, like Howard, have volunteered to help with the day's training. The group is taking a lunch break from decoy work in the cold cavernous buildings on Fort Carson's immense training grounds in Colorado. Some of the handlers keep on their bite-training gear, whether for convenience or because the added bulk wards off the winter chill. While they wait for the next dog teams to come through the exercise, we pick at paper plates of pulled-pork sandwiches and coleslaw, using the open truck beds simultaneously for seats and tabletops. The conversation meanders from talk of Howard's recent scuba diving trip to the validity of canine PTSD. Howard has a raspy laugh and when he smiles, the small pucker of dip tucked snugly under his bottom lip bulges.

Howard says that a dog will not show a true preference for his individual handlers. He doesn't believe his dogs love him, nor does he believe that the emotion we call "love" has a place in working with dogs—affection maybe, but not love. Instead he feels a dog is driven by a will to survive and make puppies.

To understand dogs, he explains, you first have to understand that dogs exist with the dynamics of a wolf pack. Wolf pack speak is commonplace within the MWD program. The handler, Howard says, should be seen as the alpha male. He holds one hand up a little higher than the other to indicate the top of the pack where the handler, whom he refers to as a "benevolent dictator," the person in charge who rules with cementlike consistency, should be. The benevolent dictator's rules are hard and fast: if the dog stays within the preset boundaries, he will be rewarded and protected. If however, the dog breaks these rules, there are consequences, just as there would be in a wolf pack.

In Howard's view, it would be considerably worse for a handler to forget his position in the pack and treat his dog like a pet than it would be for a handler to show little or no emotional attachment to his dog. Treating a dog with too much affection is detrimental for an MWD, Howard says, because it ultimately undermines the dog's sole purpose, which is to serve.

This jives in part with the widely accepted theory that the domestic canine, or *Canis lupus familiaris*, is descended from the gray wolf, or *Canis lupus*. However, using a wolf theory of dominance is now commonly considered to be an outdated model for analyzing canine behavior. It doesn't stand to reason, as author Alexandra Horowitz points out in her book *Inside of a Dog*, that because dogs descended from wolves that all of their ancestors' attributes have transferred.[1] More limiting, she argues, is the "faulty premise" of the "pack." The real model of the wolves is not a pack, but a family. "In the wild, wolf packs consist almost entirely of related or mated animals. They are *families*, not groups of peers vying for the top spot." Breaking down wolf (and subsequently dog) behavior into a "linear hierarchy with a ruling alpha pair and various 'beta' and even 'gamma' or 'omega' wolves below them" is just too simplistic.[2]

But there's an appeal, conceptually, to this perceived organizing principle behind the pack structure. As Horowitz smartly observes, it allows us to suppose that, within this line of thinking, we are "dominant and the dog submissive."[3] And perhaps because they're influenced by the tiered structure of the military—military handlers still frequently teach, refer, or live by the dominance hierarchy of the wolf pack when training and working their dogs. And this leaves little room for the idea that dogs have a sophisticated set of emotions, or that they possess the ability to love freely or choose whom it is that they love.

Jakubin, who is standing nearby, nods along in agreement as Howard makes his case, which is startling given all he's said about the difficulty of losing a dog—his acknowledgement that with the loss of each dog there was real grief, real mourning. But he doesn't contradict Howard, nor do any of the other handlers. On this afternoon the consensus of the group is that in the relationship between working dog and handler, there is more function than feeling. They seem to readily agree that whatever is exchanged between man and dog, that thing is not love.

On Staff Sergeant Pascual Gutierrez's first day of K-9 school, one of the instructors told the class: "Your dog is a weapon. Your dog is not a pet. Do not get close to your dog. Do not grow attached to your dog."

Gutierrez is a handler under Chris Jakubin's command at the United States Air Force Academy kennels—all the guys call him Gutie. He's stocky but trim and fit. His brown eyes brighten easily as he's quick to smile and make jokes, but his pragmatic streak shows as soon as he begins describing the job of working with dogs. He's been a handler for four years, and that first-day lesson was one he accepted; he considers it an important bottom-line truth, vital to the integrity of being a good handler. Inside this instruction is a cautionary tale: a handler who is too emotionally attached to his dog is more likely to make an irreparably poor combat zone decision if he does so with his heart and not his head.

Staff Sergeant Pascual Gutierrez and Mack compete during the K–9 trials at Lackland in May 2012.

Like all handlers, Gutierrez readily acknowledges that the business of MWD teams is saving human lives, sometimes at the expense of canine lives. Gutierrez accepts that in a scenario where his life—or the lives of the men and women walking behind him—was to be weighed against the life of his dog, human life will always take priority. And it is this long-prepared mentality that he will be bringing with him when, in less than one month's time, he will be on his way to Afghanistan. It will be his sixth deployment, his third to that country, and his second as a canine handler. This time around he'll be going downrange with a relatively green dog, Bert, a Belgian Malinois with a high work drive. Bert is an aggressive, unpredictable type who likes to bite, and after spending 43 days at the Air Force's relatively new predeployment course, he and Bert were only now starting to mesh. Gutierrez is pleased; he feels that Bert has finally reached the point where the dog has accepted that he is his "dad."

This familial nomenclature is standard speak inside the military's dog training program—handlers refer to themselves as "moms" and "dads," especially when identifying the dog's point of view. During drills and exercises handlers are never "master" or "keeper," "handler" or "trainer"; they are always referred to in this parental terminology. It's a natural corollary. Handlers are responsible for their dogs in the most basic ways and, by virtue of their occupation, are primarily caretakers—they feed their dogs, bathe them, give them exercise, keep them in good health—so referring to them in terms of guardianship feels apt. But this terminology is one of many discordant details in defining what a dog *is* to his handler—weapon, comrade, soldier, tool, or, in this case, child. And however subtle, it shines a light on this contradiction internalized in the culture of the handler-dog relationship. And it doesn't help answer the question of why love would have to be selectively or summarily omitted from the equation.

But as Marc Bekoff, professor emeritus of ecology and evolutionary biology at the University of Colorado, Boulder, argues in his book *The Emotional Lives of Animals*, recognizing emotional expression in dogs is not applying what's human to animal; rather, it's simply "identifying commonalities and then using human language to communicate what we observe."[4] In his opinion it is "bad biology to argue against the existence of animal emotions. Scientific research in evolutionary biology, cognitive ethology [the study of animal minds] and social neuroscience support the view that numerous and diverse animals have rich and deep emotional lives."[5]

In the most extreme instances of purely utilitarian human-canine relationships, where the dog is stripped of his uniqueness and seen merely as an object, Bekoff believes people will distance themselves to the point where even the language they use provides a protective barrier. This is a defense mechanism that creates a necessary emotional separation. He cites the classic example of laboratory researchers who assign numbers to their animal subjects rather than name them, because "once you name an animal," Bekoff tells me, "you've formed a bond with him."[6]

Bekoff is not surprised when I tell him about Kevin Howard and his theory that dogs do not love their handlers. Bekoff reasons that military handlers might adopt a psychological distancing mechanism, knowing that in sending an animal to war there is the danger of the dog getting hurt, maimed, or even killed. And this is when, he believes, the idea of loving an animal that you're sending into war, and acknowledging that this animal loves you back, becomes very complicated.

When I ask Gutierrez to pinpoint what it was that cemented his relationship with Bert, he refrains from implicating "love" as a mitigating factor. So, what would he call that intangible thing: Bonding? Closeness? Affection?

"I guess you could say affection," he says. "But I think it's more of a, 'I'm the pack leader, now you're going to listen to me.'"

But even after he gives the credit of Bert's bonding to the "wolf pack," Gutierrez says with a sheepish sigh, knowing that he's about to contradict all he's just said: "At the end of the day you do grow attached and the dog knows it."

While animals' capacity for emotion might still be debated today, even Charles Darwin saw evidence to support the idea. A little more than a decade after he published *The Origin of Species*, Darwin produced *The Expression of the Emotions in Man and Animals* in 1872. The Father of Evolution's intent with this work was to show that animals not only had emotions, but also expressions much as humans do, along with other perceptible physical gestures. There were, he believed, visible expressions in some animals that were rendered in the animal visage that mirrored those of humans. For Darwin this was only further proof of the connective link of shared ancestry between man and nonhuman mammals.[7]

Darwin made thorough study of his subjects by examining not only animal behavior but human as well before coming to this conclusion. He pored over piles of photographs of human facial expressions—examining children, babies, people of many cultures, even traveling to an insane asylum—to look closely at the similarities present when expressing fear, agony, and affection. He conducted this study and wrote this book containing his findings in part to prove "his underlying theory that humans are an extension of the animal continuum . . . to show that animals have many of the same ways of physically expressing emotions as humans."[8] And though he may have had mostly anecdotal evidence to back up his theory, he was on the right track.

But when it came to dogs, Darwin was also content to rely on what he saw with his own eyes as proof enough that our canine companions reveal their emotions to us. And he didn't have to go further than his own backyard. One day while making his way through the yard, his dog trailed behind, fully expecting that they were on route to begin their lengthy walk, as it was part of their daily ritual. But Darwin had other plans and veered off to the greenhouse instead of following the path to the fence. The dog turned, and as Darwin wrote, "The instantaneous and complete change of expression which came over him, as soon as my body swerved in the least towards the path (and I sometimes tried this as an experiment) was laughable. His look of dejection was known to every member of the family, and was called his *hot-house face*. This consisted in the head drooping much, the whole body sinking a little and remaining motionless; the ears and tail falling suddenly down, but the tail was by no means wagged. . . . His aspect was that of piteous, hopeless dejection."[9]

Indeed, as Bekoff writes, "All mammals (including humans) share neuroanatomical structures, such as the amygdala and neurochemical pathways in the limbic system that are important for feelings."[10] Canine feelings are actually quite complex. And in fact, dogs are uniquely complex in that they have a startling emotional intelligence, especially as they relate to humans.

In 2006, Dr. Juliane Kaminski, a cognitive psychologist at the Max Planck Institute for Evolutionary Anthropology in Germany, conducted a study that sought to compare "the use of causal and communicative cues in an object choice task" between dogs, chimpanzees, and bonobos.[11] Footage taken of the same kinds of trials conducted during this study shows Dr. Kaminski at the Leipzig Zoo in Germany, her long brown ponytail hanging down her back, as she sits facing a chimpanzee. There is a plastic divide between them as well as a table. On the table are two banana-yellow cups turned over, bottoms up. The objective here is for the chimp to reach through two circular holes in the divide and find the food hidden beneath one of these cups.

Dr. Kaminski is there to help; she points to the cup containing the food. Her signals offer reliable and consistent information: all the chimp has to do is watch Dr. Kaminski and follow her movements, and she will find the food. Only she doesn't. The sweet face, with its deep wrinkles framed in wispy black hairs, hardly turns in the direction of Kaminski, even as the doctor speaks directly to her, conveying not just words but emotions, with her face as well as her hands. Each time the experiment is repeated, the chimp continues to make her own choices without acknowledging Kaminski's exaggerated gestures, often making her choice before the doctor even attempts to point out the food.

During another test, Kaminski is in a different room, and this time there isn't a plastic wall or a table, just two over-turned blue bowls on the floor. The experiment is the same, only now she is standing in front of a dog. From the moment the exercise begins the dog's eyes are trained on her face. And this time, when Kaminski points to the food, the dog's response is immediate: he moves directly to the blue bowl that she indicated, and the food is found.

The dog was able to use Kaminski's direction—what she calls "informed" gestures—while the chimpanzee did not. This experiment shows, she says, that the communication between human and canine is "in its essence a very cooperative interaction." For dogs, this kind of "following, pointing seems to be very natural, and it makes dogs extremely interesting." It is proof, she believes, of their extraordinary social intelligence, a grasping of something akin to a second language. They've learned "to interpret human communication which is different from dog communication."[12]

There is further evidence now that shows that dogs not only have the ability to read and register our gestures, but also to interpret the emotional expressions on our faces. At the University of Lincoln in England, Daniel Mills, professor of veterinary behavioral medicine, conducted a study using eye-tracking technology to better understand how dogs and humans interact with each other.

Humans reveal emotions more prominently on the right side of our faces. Which means that when we talk to each other, whether we realize it or not, we gaze left at the faces of our lovers, our friends, and our judgmental superiors in order to best assess their mood.

With this in mind, Mills set up his experiment by placing dogs in front of a screen onto which he projected images of human faces—some were smiling or frowning, while others showed no expression. Mills then used eye-tracking technology to determine what the dog's eyes would look at, if they looked at human expression at all. It turns out, as Mills discovered, that dogs also gaze left.[13] They were seeking out the right side of the human face—the "emotional" side. His findings provide strong evidence to support the idea that dogs read human expression—that they knowingly look and then decipher information from our faces.

But though these experiments show that dogs are uniquely in tune with humans and human emotions, they do not "prove" the existence of love. And for the most part, the study of the beneficial effects of the emotional exchange between man and dog have largely been one-sided. There have been quite a few scientific studies on what dogs do for humans—we know their company lowers our blood pressure[14] and greatly reduces the stress we feel[15]—but the study of the positive effect of humans on dogs is scarce.

One study that did examine the effect of the canine-human bond on *both* dogs and humans centered on oxytocin. A neuropeptide produced in the hypothalamus[16] linked to feelings of trust and bonding, especially between a breast-feeding mother and her newborn child, oxytocin is best known as the mammalian hormone of love. In 2010, researchers at the Karolinska Institutet in Sweden presented a study that looked at levels of oxytocin when dogs and humans were together.[17] What the study found is that after a "petting session" with their dog, owners experienced a boost in their levels of oxytocin. Perhaps even more interesting than the appearance of oxytocin in blood samples of the human subjects was that a similar spike in the hormone was also seen in the blood samples taken from the dogs—a finding that points to the fact that the bonding emotions really do go both ways.

Still, even Bekoff readily concedes that there is a lack of focus on *proving* the bond, and so the evidence is still largely anecdotal. But then, he wonders, why do we really need these studies? It's almost comical, Bekoff muses, to have to conduct scientific experiments for the things we assume would already have a strong empirical basis, like a dog's ability to love. The reason the studies don't exist, he believes, is because we don't really need them. The idea is backed by something far simpler—common sense.[18]

To believe that animals are without the capacity for the more complex secondary emotions—such as longing, jealousy, or shame—is an idea to which Bekoff takes tremendous offense. In his mind it's an arrogant and dismissive assumption by humans. Actually, the qualifying word he uses is "insane," and while we're on the phone together, his voice rises to very high decibels at the preposterousness of such limited thinking.

He poses it this way: "If you define love as an enduring and a strong bond—I love you, I miss you, I seek you out, I prefer you"—why, he asks, can't this be transferred to the dog? In other words, *of course* dogs love us.

Cold is slowly seeping from the Colorado ground through my many wintry layers into the backs of my legs. The frost of early morning is all but melted now, and when the wind relents, the sun is strong and warm against my back, a wall of heat that I lean into. My instinct is to keep my body loose and my movement soft and even, to project the very essence of calm. I'm attempting to engage in a courtship and the object of my attention hasn't quite made up her mind about me. But I am hopeful because the eyes that watch me carefully now are friendlier than they'd been the previous afternoon.

I had followed Jakubin into the back of the Air Force Academy kennels where each dog has his own separate quarters, a space of six feet by six feet, walled on all four sides by chain-link fence. As soon as Jakubin opened the door, a commotion erupted, and all the dogs were up on their feet. Some wagged their tails, clearly happy to see him. They took little note of my presence, all except for Boda, who, as soon as I set foot near her house, made it clear that I was an intruder, unwelcome and unwanted. She barked sharply and loudly in my direction, her growls becoming more beastly the closer I got.

Boda is one of Jakubin's misfit cases. She arrived at the Air Force Academy kennels with a superior detection record, but once they took her outside of a controlled training yard environment, her nerves began to show. Unexpected noises and unknown objects frightened her, and she shied from crowds, cowering in chaotic parking lots. Jakubin knew there was no way he could send this dog out on a deployment without a tremendous amount of work. So they were gradually trying to build up her confidence, trying to alleviate her fears.

Now I'm outside at Fort Carson, watching as Boda's handler, Staff Sergeant Robbie Whaley, runs a metal brush through her thick coat, sending tufts of fur into the air, like dandelion seed. Boda's velvety ears sink with pleasure. Whaley, in the midst of this focused caregiving, had overheard the chatter about handlers loving or not loving their dogs, but had chosen not to participate. Whatever had been said did not deter him from planting a kiss on Boda's muzzle; a kiss that she accepts without flinching.

When the grooming finally ceases, she turns her head in my direction. I want her to trust me, so I offer the very same gesture my father taught me at a young age, cautioning me, "Never force your hand on a dog." I rest my elbows on my knees and extend my open hands, palms to the sky.

Finally, she approaches me, ever careful as she takes a sniff and then a lick of my left hand, then my right. I don't touch her or speak. She hovers and then pushes her large face close to mine; I feel her nose cold on my cheek. I get a lick before she bounces back over to Whaley. Then a few moments later, she returns, her large nose sniffs my hair so close I can smell the cold air fresh on her coat. This time I don't hesitate to catch the scruff of her neck and reach up behind her ears to give them a good scratch. She leans into my hand and settles against me on the ground. I can feel her heaviness, her warmth. It is a peaceful exchange, quiet and complete. I have been accepted. I am friend.

A little while later Boda, emboldened by her shining coat, sashays around the group of us, weaving in and out of our circle, a pull toy in her mouth. The other handlers call to her, reaching out their hands to engage her in a game of tug-of-war. She hears them but ultimately denies them all, coming close but not close enough, at last bringing the toy to her handler—and only her handler—placing it at Whaley's feet.

Whaley looks down at her and smiles, convinced that this dog loves him. She in turn regards him, waiting and watching. There is expression in her face. It is a look of expectation and adoration. This is a face inviting play and she's chosen her playmate.

Driving out to Fort Carson for a second day of training, Jakubin takes the dogs and I hitch a ride with Jon Baer. It's just the two of us in his truck, no dogs and no other handlers. It's early, but he's coffee'd up and ready for another day with the dogs. A longtime friend of Jakubin's and a former Air Force handler, Baer was in the group yesterday and stood by during Howard's no-love-for-the-working-dog speech. And even though he hadn't said anything at the time, he believes that there's a lot more to handler-dog dynamics than simply dominating a dog.

When a handler is assigned to a new home station, the first thing he works on with his dog is rapport building. More important than establishing what some handlers like Howard call the "alpha," this is a time to connect with the dog, Baer says, and to let the dog know how close they will be as partners. He takes one hand off the wheel to cross his fingers, signaling the closest of close together. Those beginning stages of training with a new dog are not the time to give a lot of corrections, but the time to teach the dog to trust his handler. These exercises were the very first thing Baer did as a military canine handler when he was partnered to work with his very first dog, Benny. Baer and Benny were a team, training and working together for nearly three years. Benny was his favorite dog. "I loved that guy," he says. And then again, with more emphasis, "I *loved* that guy."

For each handler I talk to there's always one dog who stands out, one dog who ranks above the others as uniquely special. And talking about this dog is a lot like asking someone about his or her first love. For many handlers, there's also something memorable about the first dog: different than a favorite dog—and there's always a favorite dog. Sometimes they're one and the same but regardless, when the handler mentions this dog's name, there's a change in pitch and the inevitable smile that comes with remembering.

And this is where all the talk about establishing the alpha or composing a mindset where the dog is first and foremost viewed as a tool or a piece of equipment usually starts to veer off track. From everything I'd seen, the closer a handler is with his dog, the better they performed.

Which brings me back to Jakubin and Taint and all the things he's told me about how he feels when the dogs go. It poses a disconnect that I simply cannot wrap my mind around. Why couldn't something so plain just be called love? Almost a year after our afternoon conversation at Fort Carson, I would ask him the same question again. At first he gives me the same answer, but this time I argue with him. I point out that the ends don't meet, their purpose and their training are distinctly at odds, this idea that the dog is a tool *and* a partner. That you're supposed to bond with the dog to elicit better results but still somehow remain unattached.

He talks around an answer for a few minutes and I can tell he's getting frustrated. Whether he's annoyed with me or with the question I don't know, but he puts an end to our discussion by telling me to email him later and promises to send out my query to other handlers he knows to see how they feel. So I do, but he never does post the question. Jakubin did email me later after giving the idea more thought. His feelings, he wrote, were mixed:

A part of me says this is exactly how I feel and the other says this is totally opinionated based on each individual handler . . . it is definitely a controversial topic. Now you state, "you are not supposed to love your dog." Building that bond comes naturally. Me, I don't want to become attached but it just happens. I've cried every time I had to put a dog down. I couldn't really tell you if it was "love" or [because] the dog lived its entire life to give his life for me. . . . All in all there was some sort of attachment; handlers in general have trouble letting go . . . including me. With this being said I wouldn't have any trouble releasing my dog to protect me so I can go home

to my family . . . that's the life of a police/war dog nothing more nothing
less. . . .

There's a third perspective, one in which there is room for both love
and for the utility of sacrifice implicit in a military working dog's ultimate
role in war. In fact, according to Sean Lulofs, the most important *tool* you
have as a handler is the emotional bond you have with your dog. And that
bond, he says, whether it's built in minutes or years, is necessary to having
a successful dog. A dog, he says, has to trust his handler on an emotional
level.

One of the most admired traits of Lieutenant Colonel E. H. Richardson's World War I messenger dogs was that virtually nothing could keep
them from completing their task—not fatigue, not the temptation of food,
not the call of a friendly soldier. But it wasn't just a novel technique that
Richardson employed; it was his understanding of something more complex and deeply intertwined within the relationship between the dog and
his keeper—trust. As Richardson wrote, "It is safe to say, that if you can get
a dog to understand a certain duty as a trust, it will rarely fail you. In fact,
especially in relations to guarding duties, the dog will often rather lay down
life itself than betray its trust. . . ."[19]

Marc Bekoff believes that dogs have actually evolved over centuries to
expect this special bond with humans, one they do not share with other species. And that expectation, he says, is hardwired into who they are. It is an
egregious double cross to betray a dog, Bekoff says, because dogs implicitly
and unquestioningly trust the humans with whom they bond.

Konrad Lorenz, a preeminent zoologist and Nobel Prize recipient,[20]
wrote extensively on the canine's ability to bond to his human companions
and the responsibility it carries to the humans who make use of it. "The
fidelity of a dog is a precious gift demanding no less binding moral responsibilities than the friendship of a human being. The bond with a true dog,"
he wrote in his very popular 1954 book *Man Meets Dog*, "is as lasting as the
ties of this earth can ever be, a fact which should be noted by anyone who
decides to acquire a canine friend."[21]

Lulofs loved Aaslan, the dog who deployed with him to Iraq in 2004. And he has no trouble admitting it. But as much as he loved Aaslan, Lulofs has long since accepted the reality of the work he does, however harsh it might seem. The dogs go out in front closest to the danger. It's the nature of the job, he says, to put your dog at risk. But, as a handler—who's next in line to danger—that's your job, too, to take slightly elevated risks.

When he was on patrol with the Marines in Iraq, Lulofs would instruct them on what to do should he be critically wounded and Aaslan somehow made it impossible for them to help him. "If the dog tries to defend me from everybody, you kill the fucking dog. My life is more important than my dog's. That dog is a dog, I will cry for him, but at the end of the day, he doesn't have a family, he doesn't have kids." For Lulofs this is the one distinction that is absolute. "Even the softest, cuddly handlers that I know," Lulofs says, understand whose life comes first.

But when bullets are coming and a handler's dog is out in the open and unprotected, this mentality doesn't always prevail. Handlers have put themselves in harm's way protecting their dogs; some have even died trying to save them.

The moon cast an alabaster glow across the base, but then sometime around midnight the wind kicked up an angry bluster. A sandstorm swirled, drowning the sky; darkness swallowed up the night. There was no visibility; not even the strongest light could cut across the impenetrable black. It would mean a delay of the route clearance mission—and for that, Army Specialist Marc Whittaker was glad.

It was the Fourth of July, 2011, in Afghanistan. Earlier in the evening, Whittaker had woken with a bad feeling, a dread so strong that he wanted to refuse the assignment outright. But this of course was not an option. Still, the sandstorm filled him with a small hope; maybe the whole thing would be scrubbed. There was no way a medevac or any other kind of air support could navigate through the darkness and wind. The rest of the soldiers who had also roused in the middle of the night milled around, waiting. Whittaker and his explosive-detection dog Anax hadn't been stationed

at Forward Operating Base Shank in the Logar Province for very long; the
dog team had only been on a few missions since they arrived from FOB
Salerno in the Khwost Province.

Anax had noticed the drag in Whittaker's mood and, though the three-
year-old German shepherd wasn't prone to affection, he stayed close to his
handler, nuzzling his head under Whittaker's hand. In a matter of hours the
storm cleared, leaving behind gusty winds, but the threat was gone. The
mission was back on.

By the time the sun made its entry into the sky and the temperature began its rapid climb, Whittaker's unit had been walking for miles. He started
to sweat. Anax wasn't showing any signs of distress, taking the heat in stride.
They made it through the village to their destination without disturbance;
the roads were quiet and seemingly empty. All was clear and the resupply
convoy got the okay to move ahead.

At the outpost he, Anax, and the rest of their team—about 20 soldiers—
took a beat to catch their breath and rest in the shade, waiting for the convoy to catch up. They'd only been there a few minutes when a call came in
from a neighboring village that another unit had stumbled onto what they
thought was an unexploded ordinance. Whittaker and Anax walked over
with a Czech EOD team. It turned out to be a simple detonation, and the
Czech team made fast work of disposing of it.

By the time they returned to the outpost the convoy had already
made its drop-off and was ready for the return trip—the mission was
nearly over.

Whittaker's team pulled their gear back on and headed toward the village, this time choosing an elevated path, an alleyway that ran high along
the hillside giving them a clear, downward view of the main road and
the convoy. By now civilians were bustling about, busy with their early-
morning routines—getting to work, opening the shops, taking their children to school. Whittaker and Anax stuck to the center of the group as it
spread out. He watched the first few convoy trucks roll along the road, and
then he heard an RPG explode, followed by the sound of gunfire. The convoy was getting ambushed.

Whittaker heard orders coming in loud over the radio, instructing the unit to move from their position on the hillside, to go into flanking maneuvers and to engage the enemy in an effort to draw the fire away from the convoy so it could make its way out of the village.

Everyone began to run, moving fast down the hill over small rising walls and ditches, racing through the twisted alleys, closing the distance between Whittaker's unit and the convoy. Whittaker had his hands on his weapon while Anax, still hooked to his side on the retractable, kept pace beside him. The dog was just as amped as the rest of them, feeding off their anxiety and adrenaline, but the dog didn't make a sound, not a bark nor a whimper. The locals they passed were unfazed by the barrage of bullets and assault weapons, their faces serene and unafraid. A man rode by on his bike. It was as if they were operating on another plane of existence. The sounds of war had become so commonplace they were only background noises here, like the ringing of church bells.

They continued to run, feet and paws pounding on the ground as Whittaker and Anax neared the wall, the final obstacle remaining between them and the road. Bullets ricocheted off of the houses, echoing throughout the valley, making it impossible to determine the enemy's position. They jumped the four-foot drop to the road and into the line of fire.

They say that when bullets make a whizzing noise, you know they're close. When you can hear them cracking, they're even closer. As soon as they hit the ground, the sound of cracking flooded Whittaker's ears. He and Anax were stuck, pinned down in the wide-open middle of the road.

Without his body armor, Anax was exposed, and Whittaker instinctively threw himself across the dog, using his own body as a shield. If bullets were to hit them, they would hit his vest. But under his weight Anax squirmed, fighting his hold. He snapped his jaws at nothing, at everything and finally made contact, sinking his teeth into Whittaker's hand, three of his canines piercing through his glove and skin. A full-mouth bite, his jaw closing around the whole of Whittaker's hand—catching him near his thumb and down around his pinky finger. But in the heat of the commotion, Whittaker barely registered the sensation.

The barrage lasted two full minutes, and then the air shifted and Whittaker noticed the shots sounded different—it was his guys who were laying down suppressive fire, not the enemy. If they were going to move, they had to move now. He pushed himself up off the ground, ready to run, but his dog, who was always out ahead, wasn't even moving. Whittaker glanced back and saw that Anax's eyes were open; he looked as if he wanted to follow but couldn't. He was frozen. And that's when Whittaker knew something was very wrong.

He grabbed Anax by the collar and, giving up hope of reaching the others, dragged the dog to the nearest cover, a solid wall just a few feet away. Whittaker's hands flew along the dog's body, assessing him from head to tail. The dog was breathing, but he was whining and twisting in pain. And then Whittaker saw the blood on the dog's hind legs.

Fear set in. He didn't have his medical kit with him. He'd left it on the truck, still over at the dismount site. He pulled the bandages from his own medical kit, pressing gauze to Anax's wound to try to stem the bleeding. *This can't be happening. This can't be happening.* The thought hurtled through his mind again and again.

By that point, an air weapons team had been called in and the firefight was basically over. Whittaker finished wrapping the gauze around Anax's leg as best he could. A lieutenant got on the radio to let command know they needed an IV for Anax, as well as a helicopter to get him to treatment.

But the medic couldn't help Anax: he was occupied treating a civilian, a contractor riding in the convoy who had sustained a head injury when it was attacked. A medevac had already been called for the injured man and was on its way to the dismount site. All they had to do was get there in time and the medevac would transport Anax to a hospital.

The site was a mile and half away.

Whittaker took Anax in his arms and heaved him up, cradling the dog. He tried for one short, stilted step and then another, but as he trudged forward he could feel the dog's fur slide from his grip, the pair of them nearly dropping to the ground. Anax was just 80 pounds of dead weight in his arms. It was after nine in the morning and they'd been out in the hot sun for hours, having walked for miles. Whittaker was drenched in sweat. He was so exhausted he could not carry his dog more than a few feet.

The Czech EOD guys who had stayed with Whittaker and his wounded dog rushed to help. Stripping off their blouses they tied the fabric together, knotting their shirts into a bridge of cloth. Together they pulled the dog up, but with his wriggling and writhing his canine body slipped out of the makeshift stretcher, slowing their efforts to get him to the medevac with every step. Now Whittaker's panic was full blown; they weren't going to make it. Anax's eyes were glazing over, his gaze was distant—the dog was about to go into shock. Even if they made it back to the dismount site, he knew that the medical kit alone wouldn't be enough now; Anax needed emergency care.

Whittaker shouted at the lieutenant, "I need to get my dog on that bird! We have to get on that bird!" He yelled it again and again.

Then Whittaker heard the sound of a truck. It was an Afghan local. Whittaker heard the voices, the sounds of negotiation. The EOD guys managed to communicate the urgency of the situation, and the Afghan man agreed to loan them his truck. They piled in. There was the blur of movement, the jolt of the rocky road beneath them. They were moving, they were moving.

When they pulled up to the medevac site, the signal smoke marking its spot already billowed high in the air. Within minutes the helicopter was on the ground. They made it.

They just made it.

FOUR

beware the loving
(war) dog

The one absolutely unselfish friend that man can have in this selfish world,
the one that never deserts him, the one that never proves ungrateful or treach-
erous, is the dog. . . . And when the last scene of all comes, and death takes
his master . . . there by his graveside will the noble dog be found, his head
between his paws and his eyes sad but open, in alert watchfulness, faithful
and true, even unto death.

—George Graham Vest, September 23, 1870[1]

When Mount Vesuvius erupted in AD 79, the
volcano sent rushing waves of scorching toxic gases running at temperatures
estimated to have been as high as 570 degrees, smothering Pompeii in pum-
ice and ash. Death was virtually instantaneous.[2] As one surviving witness
to the eruption, Pliny the Younger, recalled a few decades after, "You could
hear women lamenting, children crying, men shouting. . . . There were
some so afraid of death that they prayed for death."[3]

The eruption claimed some 16,000 lives. What was left behind, revealed when the dust had settled, was a ghastly scene of horror and panic,
frozen in time. It's said one untethered dog was found among the bodies solidified in ash, standing resolute, squarely facing the approaching
danger. The dog was protecting a small boy, curled between the animal's

legs. Against all odds and the instinct of flight, this dog had remained with his boy.[4]

When it was exactly that man and dog first began their relationship is still being debated. Most scientists and researchers believe the dog originated around 40,000 to 50,000 years ago, while others have determined it was only somewhere between 12,000 to 16,000 years ago.[5] Also contested are the versions of how we met and came to forge such a strong friendship with dogs. For many years the prevailing theory was that dogs were the descendants of scavenging wolves who made early and convenient partnership with humans while picking off the trash along their villages. More recently, however, other ideas of how the dog really did become man's best friend have pushed their way to the forefront. The theory that seems the most sensible is articulated by Mark Derr in *How the Dog Became the Dog*. "It's fair," he writes, "to say that the humans and wolves involved in the conversion were sentient, observant beings constantly making decisions about how they lived. . . . They were social animals willing, even eager, to join forces with another animal to merge their sense of group with the others' sense and create an expanded super-group that was beneficial to both in multiple ways. . . . Powerful emotions were in play that many observers today refer to as love—boundless unquestioning love."[6]

Derr calls upon the December 1994 discovery of the Chauvet Cave, inside of which are the oldest paintings ever found, dated at 32,000 years old.[7] Perhaps more important is what was found on the cave's floor—two sets of footprints, dated at 26,000 years old.[8] They belong to an eight-year-old boy and a wolf. Little else could be discerned from the prints, for there are too few to determine where they went or why they were there, except that they were traveling together, in tandem, as friends.

The annals of dog lore are full of stories exemplifying canine devotion and the depths of their loyalty. There are great yarns that tell of dogs who, after accidental or untimely separations from their human companions, crossed the length of countries to be reunited. More extreme still are accounts, some thousands of years old, of dogs who went to remarkable lengths of sacrifice, facing death or, in the rarest of cases, committing suicide rather than be left behind in the land of the living, alone.

When King Lysimachus, one of Alexander the Great's ruling successors, died in 281 BC, his dog Hyrkanus dove into the flames as the man's body was being cremated during the funeral service.[9] A few hundred years later, a dog belonging to Titus Sabinus, the rightful heir to the Roman throne, remained steadfast after his master was jailed and then executed by the reigning emperor. First, the dog followed his persecuted master to jail, and then, after Sabinus's body was unceremoniously dumped in the Tiber, he jumped into the water and tried in vain to keep the corpse afloat.[10]

Somewhat more recent reports of dogs who were so forlorn after their owners died that they lived afterward in a perpetual state of mourning, made the canines into local, even national, celebrities. Greyfriars Bobby, a small Skye terrier, took up permanent residence in the cemetery where his owner, an elderly farmer by the name of Gray (known as Auld Jock), was buried in Edinburgh, Scotland, in 1858. When it became clear the dog was there to stay, the groundskeeper took pity on him and gave him food and shelter. Even during the most treacherous weather, it is said that the dog made every effort to remain by the grave, keeping his vigil going strong for 14 long years until he died in 1872.[11]

In the 1920s in Japan, a dog called Hachiko was renowned for a similar display of undeterred devotion. Hachiko would meet his owner, a professor at the University of Tokyo, at the end of every day at the train station. One day in May 1925, the professor suffered a brain hemorrhage and died, never making it home again to meet his dog at their usual time. But Hachiko continued his prompt meeting of the three o'clock train for ten years, until his own death in 1935.[12]

The noted dog author Albert Payson Terhune called these dogs "Professional Mourners" and suggested that the dogs behind these canine campaigns of loyalty were little more than opportunists who took advantage of public sympathy and free meals.[13] Yet even if the slant of these stories is too fanciful or, after being passed from dog lover to dog lover, details were exaggerated, these dogs were not just a passing phenomenon. Modern-day reports are too widespread to ignore or dismiss such abject devotion.

In the spring of 2011, terrible landslides ravaged the city of Teresópolis, Brazil; one photo of the devastation showed a brown dog next to a mound of red-clay dirt. She leaned against a fresh grave, one of hundreds lined in neat rows. The caption noted that the dog, called Leao, had reportedly been there for days, refusing to leave the side of her buried owner who'd been killed in the disaster.[14] A few months later that same year, inhabitants of the small village of Panjiatun in China decided to build a kennel by the grave of Lao Pan, a 68-year-old resident whose dog, a mutt with ears the color of butterscotch, had kept watch since his interment. Numerous attempts to coax the dog away failed, so Pan's former neighbors simply continued to bring him food and water.[15]

Known for their fidelity, their courage, and their capacity to love without judgment or duplicity, dogs have become an archetype: the iconic end-all be-all of a loyal and unselfish friend. It is this wholly emotional devotion we perceive on the part of a dog that makes any act of loyalty a heroic and indomitably heart-wrenching note in the narrative of war. There is plenty of battlefield evidence—testimonies of dogs leaping into bullet spray, braving poisonous gas, or ignoring the deafening roar of bombs to stay at the side of their handlers—to prove a canine's preternatural ability and willingness to protect and defend human life even when it comes at the expense of his own.

In the deep blue of a February night in 2010, in the Paktia province of Afghanistan, so near the mountainous Pakistan border, a group of US soldiers retired to their barracks, many of them preoccupied with the near-bedtime business of writing letters and sending emails. Others were already sound asleep.

Little else but dust stirred as a cool breeze swept through the compound. Then a growl rumbled, low and threatening. One of the dogs resting by the gate had caught scent of something she didn't like, and her warning caused the fur on the backs of the two dogs beside her to prickle in anticipation. Maybe it was the scent of the unfamiliar man approaching, or there was something repellent in the odor of the 24 pounds of C-4 explosives the intruder had strapped to his body. Or maybe the dogs just sensed that someone was coming to do their caretakers harm.

The dogs startled the man, who had crept into their compound wearing a stolen Afghan National officer uniform, but he made a rush to his target—the barrack's door. The dogs charged him. Target and Rufus sank their teeth into his legs, ripping and pulling at his shins, while Sasha bared her muzzle, barking and dodging in front of him, blocking his path. The commotion roused the soldiers inside and they called to the dogs to keep quiet. At the sound of the men's voices, the insurgent grew desperate and detonated his bomb.

So powerful was the blast that it rocked the barrack walls, knocking out an entire side of the building. The flying shrapnel and spray sliced through the air, injuring five men. There was chaos and smoke, but the men started digging in the rubble for the dogs until they were found. Sasha the puppy was so badly hurt she had to be put down. The other two dogs, Target and Rufus, were wounded, deep gashes stretched across their bodies flashing wet with blood. But these were not military dogs: they were strays who'd found their way onto the compound and had taken up a welcome but informal residence on the grounds. But to the soldiers who took them in, the dogs were more than just three Afghan mutts lying injured on the ground in front of them. They were comrades in arms, creatures who, in the minds of these soldiers, had just saved the lives of 50 men. Protocol be damned, all the medical resources at their disposal would be employed to try to save these dogs.[16]

Today's US military strictly prohibits the "adopting as pets or mascots, caring for, or feeding any type of domestic or wild animal" as it is written in General Order No. 1 Regulations issued by the Department of Defense.[17] But in the outer reaches of war, where regulations are slackly enforced, dogs and other animals are still taken in. The reasons are the same as they were centuries before: these animals quell the loneliness for home, and their company offers some much needed levity. Sasha, Rufus, and Target are more than just proof of this natural inclination dogs have to protect and defend; they are the latest in a long-standing combat zone legacy. War dog history is built on canines who, though their bravery and solidarity was unsolicited, offered it anyway, becoming the very first canine soldiers.

That was certainly the case in the United States during the Civil War. As early as November 8, 1862, *Harper's Weekly* published a dispatch from Fort Monroe, a military outpost located on the Virginia Peninsula that did not fall into the hands of the Confederates. A mastiff, described as having a "jetty blackness" save the "white breast and a dash of white on each of his four paws," had abandoned his Confederate "rebel"-jailer owner at Front Royal and followed home a band of newly released Union soldiers who had been taken prisoner. Jack, or Union Jack as the paper called him, proved himself worthy by leading the thirsty soldiers to sources of water and when one "sick and exhausted Union soldier was left behind, Jack staid [*sic*] with him for several hours until a wagon took him up." During his first cannon-ball attack, Jack ran *toward* the shell spray, barking as if he was chasing them down instead of retreating in fear.

Some eight years later, on September 2, 1870, the *Iowa State Register* ran a story titled "That Patriotic Dog" featuring the exploits of Doc, a dog with dark ears and dark spots, who accompanied the men of the 23rd Iowa Infantry as their mascot on whatever battles and arduous foot marches they endured during the Civil War.[18] Doc could be counted on to hunt down the occasional chicken and received no fewer than two war wounds—one to the foot, the other directly to the chest.

On Bastille Day in 1918, American Private Jimmy Donovan picked up a "gutter puppy" in the streets of Paris and brought the shaggy Scottish-Irish terrier to the front with him, calling him Rags. Donovan put Rags to work, training him to run messages pinned to his collar back and forth when incoming shellfire rendered easier communication impossible. In addition to leading medics to wounded soldiers in the field through smog and bullets, it was said the dog would, at the sound of incoming shells, flatten himself to the ground, signaling the danger to anyone around him. Along with the soldiers in Donovan's infantry unit, the little dog was gassed, and even lost an eye in battle.[19] Donovan was eventually fatally wounded, succumbing to mustard gas exposure. After he was injured Donovan's fellow soldiers made sure Rags traveled home with him, sneaking the dog on his stretcher and through field hospitals until they reached the United States together. Even after Donovan died in 1919, Rags continued to make his visits to the hospital, sleeping on Donovan's empty bed.[20]

Military service dogs started to edge their way into the war-front headlines during World War I. In October 1917, Mrs. Euphistone Maitland, secretary of the Blue Cross Society, told the *New York Times* about the heroics of the dogs in the trenches, their unflappable will to work, and their ability to pick the wounded men from the dead. "They know their men," she said, "and possess an instinctive love for them." Each dog, in her mind, had a favorite soldier for whom he showed preference. "Dogs," she said, "have been known to shield wounded men and so save the lives of the soldiers at the loss of their own."[21]

During World War II, the Associated Press sent out a dispatch from Guam island. "War Dogs Make Japs Miserable," the headline read. The report told of one of the Marine Corps' trained "battle-hardened devil dogs," a Doberman named Lucky. After a successful mission of uncovering "10 Jap snipers," Lucky was "found crouched close to his wounded handler in a gully near a concrete bridge over Asan River. . . . When the marines started to give first-aid to the wounded handler Lucky growled. But he let them work on his master. When the latter died Lucky moved to the side of the body and would not permit any to approach." The sergeant who finally had to pull the dog away with what the paper described as a "noose" said, "That's the way these war dogs are—one man dogs."[22]

On a December night in 1966, members of the Vietcong infiltrated Tan Son Nhut Air Base just outside Saigon, inciting what would be the biggest skirmish involving US canine teams—one that ultimately claimed the lives of three sentry dogs and one handler.[23] While patrolling a cemetery with his dog Nemo just inside the base the following evening, handler Robert Thorneburg, airman 2nd class, was attacked by Vietcong still hiding on the grounds. Thorneburg sent Nemo to give chase and the dog ran off ahead. The sound of shots was quickly followed by the sound of Nemo's yelps. The dog had taken a bullet to the face, and as the firefight continued, Thorneburg was also hit. Despite his injury, Nemo found his handler and maneuvered himself on top of Thorneburg, guarding him until help came. Nemo lost an eye to that bullet, but both dog and handler survived the attack.[24]

Forty-five years later, a black Labrador retriever named Eli would shield his young Marine handler, Colton Rusk, in exactly the same way during a firefight with the Taliban.

The two were inseparable. If you'd have glanced over Rusk's Facebook page in 2010, the first thing you'd have seen was Eli, a big black Lab with honey-colored eyes and a wide pink tongue.[25] With another click you could see more photos of Eli and Rusk, an infantry machine gunner, posing with the other Marines in Rusk's unit in Afghanistan, or sprawled out on Rusk's army-green cot, two bellies exposed, the air above them a mess of paws and arms. Handler and dog—both at the beginning of their military careers— appeared playful and fresh-faced, dark and handsome.

Rusk and Eli had only been in Afghanistan for a few months when, on December 6, 2010, Rusk was hit by Taliban sniper fire. He fell where he was standing. As the bullets continued to fly, Eli crawled on top of Rusk. When the other Marines rushed to Rusk's aid, Eli snapped at them, refusing to allow anyone to breach his protection, even biting one of the other men to keep him from touching his handler. The other Marines were able to distract the dog away from Rusk's body without harm coming to anyone else, but nothing could be done; Private 1st Class Rusk died that same day.[26]

In a way, military dogs are trained to be brave. They're exposed to rifle fire, machine gun fire, and the sound of explosions—simulated as well as live fire. They learn to navigate underground tunnels, climb ladders, and even scale walls. "The War Dog," Lieutenant Colonel E. H. Richardson wrote, "has to have all fear of explosions and firing, smoke clouds, water obstacles etc. eliminated."[27] But he also felt that the behavior in dogs that drove them to exceed even the highest expectations, and, say, cover their handlers' bodies during an attack, was an impulse of their intrinsic character, and a distinctly canine sensibility. "Apart from this trained courage," he continued, "we can all recall instances of natural pluck and real bravery in dogs, defending some person, or thing they valued, and believed to be in danger."[28]

It was an instinct that Richardson believed an adept handler might pull out of the dog during training, but not one that every dog possessed or even could be trained to feel.

As the sun descended, the desert air began to cool, its temperature no longer resembling the sweltering heat of the afternoon. The June night would be clear, offering good visibility. There was nothing remarkable about the smell of the coming night air, nor the feel of his gear, as Staff Sergeant John Mariana pulled on his Kevlar vest, just as he'd done time and time before. He looked down at Bronco, taking in the top of the dog's head with its marble rye blacks and browns. The dog looked up, returning his gaze with the dark eyes Mariana had found so reassuring during their eight months in Afghanistan.

Mariana and Bronco had been in-country since October 2010. The pair had carved out a well-honed pre-mission ritual that Mariana began by giving the eight-year-old Belgian Malinois an IV drip. The fluids would keep Bronco well hydrated while they were out on long missions. When the drip was done, Mariana ran Bronco through a few quick explosive-odor recognition drills—just enough to get the dog clicked into a working mindset. Finally, Mariana took hold of his weapon and sat with Bronco on the ground, waiting together until it was time. It was how they found their meditative calm before the storm of combat.

That night, Mariana and Bronco waited for the mission to begin, along with the Special Forces (SF) team they'd been with since November. Typically, dog teams are not assigned to a single unit for any extended period of time; they operate more like moonlighters, setting out from their main station for short stints on smaller patrol bases (PBs) and joining up with units for mission-specific operations. When a handler and his dog are assigned to work with Special Forces, it's a trial by fire, and the window for a handler to prove himself and the worth of his dog is only open for a short time.

Mariana looked like a Special Forces guy, tall and brawny, with a sleeve tattoo wrapping the length of his right arm. During the months of their deployment, his dark hair had grown out to match the beard on his face, full and thick as the sound of his New York accent. A thrill seeker, he was up for anything. On their first night with this new team, Mariana and Bronco had uncovered four explosives, three of them IEDs. They'd been with the same SF guys ever since, putting some 80 missions behind them.

Under the cover of dark the team began the first leg of their mission. As usual Mariana and Bronco took the lead, working out in front of the rest of the patrol. Bronco searched ahead off leash. They'd been moving steadily for about an hour and had entered a village. Mariana took off his night vision goggles, as he often did on a night like this one, preferring to let his eyes adjust to the natural dark in case he was forced to rely on his own vision.

When they neared the first objective of their mission, Mariana clipped Bronco back onto the leash at his waist to keep him close. Fully engrossed in his sniffing, Bronco had his head low to the ground. Mariana locked a careful eye on his dog, waiting, watching for the signal that Bronco was on odor. And then suddenly a man was standing just ten feet in front of them, catching Mariana by surprise. He blinked; the man was pointing an AK-47 straight at him.

The command that sent Bronco to attack burst from Mariana in pure reflex, as he popped the leash, freeing the dog from his side. Bronco bolted forward toward their attacker and Mariana raised his flashlight, flooding the man's face with blinding white light. The dog cleared the short distance between them, catching the man's upper torso with a strong bite. There was a blur of limbs and fur, but Bronco's teeth held their grip. The man struggled, fighting off the 65 pounds of dog that'd just attacked him. Then, Mariana saw the barrel of the rifle flash down toward Bronco's head.

A gunshot rang out, a single round fired. And then everything that had been happening entirely too fast for Mariana to comprehend began to slow, passing before his eyes in freeze frame. Mariana could see the force of the bullet as it hit Bronco; he watched the dog's head shake in a slow-wrenching wave.

As soon as the ring of the gunshot was over, time caught back up to tempo. There was a rush of movement; the scene around Mariana erupted in chaos. Within moments their attacker was no longer a threat. But Bronco was gone.

Mariana's mind raced. Bronco had run off, somewhere, but whether in pain or fear he couldn't be sure. He was certain Bronco had just taken a bullet to the head. There was blood splashed on the ground, and along with another soldier, Mariana rushed to follow its dark-spotted trail. His heart thudded, adrenaline pulsing through his muscles, ramping up, building into panic.

They moved quickly, Mariana calling out for Bronco—there was no need to keep quiet now. After a few yards the trail started to thin, becoming more difficult to see. If Bronco was still alive, his wound would likely be hemorrhaging blood. There'd be no way the dog could survive it. Then, about 100 meters out, the two men rounded the corner of a building and there was Bronco, sitting quiet and still. He was covered in blood but sitting all the same, waiting for his handler as if it'd been the plan to rally at this safe spot all along. Mariana flew to him, inspecting the wound. Bronco had been hit in the face: the bullet had entered on the left side of his mouth, going straight through, virtually dissolving the right side of the dog's muzzle, shattering the bone in the front part of his nose, and fracturing teeth along his upper jaw.[29]

They called in a medevac. Mariana pressed gauze to the wound, each cloth too quickly absorbing the blood. The passing bullet had done something to obstruct the dog's nasal passages and Bronco was having trouble taking in breath. He began to sneeze over and over, and with every sneeze came a new spray of blood as the force of air burst the clot that had just congealed. Though Mariana did his best to stop the bleeding around the wound, he realized there was little he could do. Bronco needed to breathe through his wound; covering it would suffocate him. Mariana could only mop up the blood.

After more than a few minutes of this, Bronco slumped to the ground, sprawling over on his side. Mariana's heart stopped. He stared hard into the dog's eyes, and then a terrible kind of relief washed over Mariana as he realized Bronco hadn't just bled out in front of him—he'd rolled over to offer his belly up for a scratch. He exhaled, marveling at the strength of his dog. "You little shit," he told him. "Don't do that."

But the lifted feeling was only temporary and guilt soon took hold. He pulled Bronco into his arms and leaned down over the dog's ear. "I'm sorry, buddy," he whispered. "I'm sorry." With one hand he massaged the inside of Bronco's ear, the way the dog liked it, trying to soothe and comfort him, reassuring him that he was safe. "If we make it through this," Mariana whispered, "if we make it home, I'm going to take care of you."

It seemed like hours, but within 45 minutes they were in the medevac. As they moved across the sky, Mariana allowed himself for the first time that night to catch his breath. He looked up. The stars were so bountiful and so bright they felt too close, like the lights of some floating aerial metropolis.

By the time they reached Kandahar almost another hour later, the first rays of morning light were showing. The medevac descended, but there wasn't an ambulance on the ground standing by as promised over the radio. Mariana scanned the area, but there was neither sight nor sound of an approaching engine. No one was waiting for them, and as far as he could see, no one was coming.

"Fuck it," Mariana said. He wasn't going to wait. Pulling Bronco from the floor of the helicopter, he hoisted the dog over his shoulders and began the 250-meter stretch from the landing site to the hospital on foot. Bronco rode along uncomplainingly, his furry side pressing heavily into the back of Mariana's neck. Exhausted, Mariana felt that at best his speed registered no faster than a walk. But in fact he was running with all the strength he had left.

When they reached Kandahar's main hospital, the staff inside the front door took Bronco and sent him on a stretcher to emergency surgery. However, they refused to let Mariana, who was still wearing his weapon, stay inside. Furious and frantic, he went back outside, pulled off his Kevlar and threw it on the ground. He was forced to wait. He didn't sleep; he didn't eat. A friend came to keep him company, bringing cigarettes. Though he rarely smoked, Mariana burned through almost the entire pack. Nothing helped.

Five hours later, the doctors finally delivered a groggy Bronco from surgery. Bronco was in stable condition and the prognosis was positive. Still, they could only do so much for a dog at the human hospital; they were going to transport Mariana and Bronco from Kandahar back to Bagram, one of the largest US bases in Afghanistan, where the veterinary technicians were stationed. Mariana asked for some blankets and set up a bed on the floor. Bronco's nose was so swollen that he was barely able to breathe. Mariana lay on the floor with him, taking the dog's head onto his chest, so he could hold the dog's mouth open.

When they finally got back to Bagram, Mariana was still wearing his bloodied clothes. He'd left everything of his own behind. The only things he had carried out of that night mission—gauze, IVs, toys, water—had been for Bronco.

In the two weeks that followed, Bronco underwent two additional reconstructive surgeries while in Afghanistan in an attempt to repair the damage. Sections of his nose had to be removed and replaced.

While they were in Bagram, Mariana never left Bronco's side, listening to his shifting, choppy breathing, always with one hand on the dog's mouth to keep the airway open. But even that wasn't enough, and within a few weeks Bronco and Mariana were sent back to the States, to the hospital at Lackland Air Force Base for more surgery. Soon after they returned from Afghanistan, the pair was separated.

The time apart from the dog that had saved his life wore on him, and Mariana dealt with it terribly. He was tormented with thoughts of bad, wicked things. It didn't matter that he was back at his home station and back with his family or that his wife was about to have a baby; he wanted to be with Bronco. Mariana was losing sight of himself.

It would be a long time before Mariana would see Bronco again. The dog wasn't able to do detection work anymore and would be retiring from service. Mariana had to fight to get the dog back, and even with the support of higher-ups, it wasn't easy—the battle spanned five long months. On the day they were reunited, the effect was instantaneous: Mariana felt the weight break and fall away like the cracking of a glacial crust of ice. He saw Bronco in the kennel and grabbed his dog, crying freely. In his joyful frenzy at seeing his handler, Bronco's nose, which would never be quite the same again, whistled like a teakettle.

This willingness on the part of a dog to protect his human companion is not, according to Kevin Behan, cognitive; rather, it's innate. Instead, Behan says, it's all part of the deep emotional bond they have with their humans.[30] That dogs are wholly emotional beings is a tenet Behan argues to the hilt in his 2012 book *Your Dog Is Your Mirror*. And because they are so keyed into this emotional connection, Behan believes the bond between a dog and a human can run so deep that it actually gets to the point of what he calls "fusion," where the dog perceives himself *in* his handler. And this über-attachment—or fusing—is only heightened by the stress of vigorous training, as well as what a team might experience while on patrol, especially during a deployment.

After working with those police dog teams in Connecticut, Behan began to notice something remarkable, something that at first he wasn't quite sure was actually happening. It appeared the dogs were able to anticipate a cloaked threat, intuiting danger before the actual danger came. At first Behan couldn't believe what he was seeing. It appeared that these dogs were able to sense criminal intent in people who weren't yet doing anything criminal.

After he got over his initial surprise, this behavior began to make perfect sense to Behan. It would be only natural, he reasoned, for the dog to pick up anything disquieting to his handler. It's all about the strength of connection between the handler and his dog. "They have this bond with this human, they feel so tight with this one human, that they feel in other humans, discrepancies."[31]

So emotionally close are they that there's virtually no barrier between them.

When a dog protects his handler, he is also protecting himself. This collective sense of "one" that Behan describes in the dog's emotional state is similar to a known phenomenon that occurs to men who go into battle together. Men in combat zones are known to form strong bonds—they meld from being a group of individual men to a single unit, embracing a shared will for all to live or die. It is this instinct and emotion that propels a soldier to throw himself on a grenade to shield his fellow soldiers.

Revered American war reporter Ernie Pyle, better known as the "fox-hole correspondent," spent years on the front during World War II and traveled throughout Europe writing and reporting on the soldiers he met and the war he experienced.[32] Pyle was killed by Japanese machine-gun fire during the battle of Ie Shima while reporting from the front on April 18, 1945. But sometime while he was in Italy from December 1943 to April 1944, he made this salient observation: "The ties that grow between men who live savagely together, relentlessly communing with Death, are ties of great strength. There is a sense of fidelity to each other in a little corps of men who have endured so long, and whose hope in the end can be so small."[33]

Over the course of a year, from June 2007 to June 2008, journalist Sebastian Junger embedded with the US 2nd Battalion in the Korengal valley of Afghanistan, where the fighting was at its most wild and raw. In his 2010 book *War*, he describes the intensity of the soldiers fighting at the tip of the spear together—facing the likelihood of one's own death as they watched their fellow soldiers bleed to death, alternating mind-numbing boredom with the adrenaline-pumping action of battle—and how it all culminated not in a slow massing of fear but in a "desperate bond," one that is ultimately "the core experience of combat." It is, he writes, a "shared commitment to safeguard one another's lives [that] is unnegotiable and only deepens with time. . . . What the Army sociologists . . . slowly came to understand was that courage *was* love. In war, neither could exist without the other, and that in a sense they were just different ways of saying the same thing. According to their questionnaires, the primary motivation in combat (other than 'ending the task'—which meant they could all go home) was 'solidarity with the group.'"[34] So it would stand to reason that a dog strongly bonded to his handler would, in the end, make for a better war dog. That the more "love" there is, the stronger the team.

When John Mariana talked about Bronco, he was adamant that the strength of their working relationship was based on a mutual commitment and a deep and shared connection. "He didn't work for me out of fear of me correcting him. He worked for me because he loved me and I loved him. And I really believe that he knew that."[35]

A loving dog makes for a formidable asset in war.

The day Marine Lance Corporal Matt Hatala was paired up with Chaney, his new IED detector dog and soon-to-be deployment partner, he went home frustrated, utterly convinced there was no way he could work with this dog. Chaney had been working with another handler and wanted nothing to do with this new Marine; the black Labrador retriever was 85 pounds of strong-willed stubbornness, and though he never became aggressive or mean, the dog simply refused to listen to Hatala, using his weight to cement his resistance. Chaney may have been heavy—literally hard to lift—but Hatala, who was strong and agile after his years of high school wrestling, could handle the dog's size. And with his Iowa upbringing he weathered the dog's attitude. Slowly, steadily, over the next couple of months of training Chaney became more trusting of Hatala. By the time they deployed to Afghanistan's Southern Helmand Province in October 2010, they were finally in sync.

Hatala and Chaney were stationed at Patrol Base Tar, a small expeditionary outpost that was once a private compound but had been taken over by the military. When one of the detection dogs there had been killed by an IED, saving the lives of three men on the patrol in the process, the Marines renamed the base after the dog. There were only about eight Marines at PB Tar and a couple of Afghan National Army soldiers. At night the Marines bunked in a mud hut. At first Hatala kept Chaney's kennel outside, insulating it as best he could by tucking hay around the bottom and wrapping a poncho around it. But the temperatures began to drop, and Chaney was soon sleeping inside, tied to Hatala's cot. After a while, trusting that Chaney would stay where he was supposed to, he let him off the leash.

Every morning as soon as he woke up Hatala would take Chaney outside to do his business. It was always early and most times they would catch the sun rising over the desert. It was his favorite time of day, calm and quiet. He would listen to the music his wife had burned for him and sent over on CDs, letting the sound of it flood his ears, and watch his dog. Hatala was growing very attached to Chaney; the dog had become his anchor, his best friend. The other guys loved Chaney too, and though it went against his training, Hatala never felt it was right to keep them from petting his dog. Why should he be the only one to benefit from his good company? They all had tough days, and Chaney was especially good at picking out who among their unit was in the darkest mood. The dog would seek out whoever it was and just nuzzle up next to him.

The Marines out at PB Tar took part in daily patrols—morning, afternoon, night—traveling back and forth between the nearby town and the base, checking in with locals and ensuring their area of operation was secure. Their small base was mostly surrounded by desert that was flecked with small remote farms. Further out, about 500 meters from the back of their compound, was a small town settled into an embankment. Houses lined the top and bottom of the ridge. Beyond that, there was only wide-open nothingness that stretched until a mountain range. The Marines had relatively good relations with the Afghans who lived there. The only thing that interrupted their missions was the massive Afghan dogs who would alert to their otherwise discreet nighttime presence. These outside dogs were large and unruly and never tied up. At night they roamed around in packs. Hatala and his unit would often hear them at the back of the base rummaging through the garbage.

On one afternoon patrol, Hatala, Chaney, and a few others were making their way through the town on the low side of the ridge. The patrol was spread out, their interpreter was in the middle, and Chaney was working off leash while Hatala and his friend, Lance Corporal Shea Boland, were out in front. Up ahead, Hatala spied one of the yard hounds come stalking toward them. The dog was well over 100 pounds, his coat a tangled mess of gray, his white underbelly and legs caked in dirt. The dog's back was arched; he was growling. They'd crossed into whatever this dog considered his territory, and he was coming straight for Boland.

They weren't authorized to shoot these dogs, so Boland threw a rock at him to scare him off, but the dog showed no sign of fear, and only skulked closer. A few feet behind Boland, Hatala readied himself to shoot if the dog should attack his friend. And then Chaney came out of nowhere and planted himself in front of Boland, hackles raised, his muzzle quivered; he let out a deep, savage growl. If the giant dog moved, Chaney moved to block him; he wouldn't let the other dog get any closer.

Keeping one eye on Chaney, Hatala motioned to Boland and the others and they slowly moved the patrol forward and away from the yard dog. Chaney stood his ground, snarling—his body always between this threat and the other men.

When they were finally clear Hatala called out to his dog, "Hey, hey. Chaney, here!" Chaney broke the standoff and trotted back to rejoin his handler. The other dog watched them for a while before losing interest.

Until that day, Hatala had never heard Chaney growl. Not once. Hatala had only ever heard him bark once or twice in all the months that they were together. That afternoon was the first and only time Hatala ever saw Chaney show aggression of any kind, but he'd revealed himself a dog to be reckoned with.

part ii

FIVE

a dog of many talents

The guard dog was incorruptible; the police dog dependable; the messenger dog reliable. The human watchman might be bought; not so the dog. The soldier sentinel might fall asleep; never the dog. The battlefield runner might fail . . . but the dog, to his last breath would follow the line of duty.

—Ernest Harold Baynes, *Animal Heroes of the Great War*

I have the leash in my hand. It's a retract-able, and I mindlessly click the button that controls the slack. Haus, the handsome German shorthaired pointer on the other end, looks up at me warily. He is not exactly a willing partner. We stand together at the threshold of a restroom at Buckley Air Force Base in Aurora, Colorado. There is a bomb in this bathroom—maybe, possibly, hypothetically—and it's our job to find it.

Haus is an experienced detection and patrol dog who has deployed five times with a solid record of finds. His body and legs are white and flecked with brown, save the one round patch of brown on his back, like a small, high-riding saddle matching his silky ears. I try to give him a look of reassurance and solidarity, belying the nerves that are spiking along my skin, but I must not be pulling that off because Haus throws a glance of clear concern and confusion back in the direction of Chris Jakubin and the rest of the group—the people this dog trusts—who are crowding around the entrance behind us.

I'm not sure how to begin so I turn to Tech Sergeant Edward Canell, Buckley's kennel master. "Just clear the room," he says. The smile on his face indicates that this is all the help he will be offering me. A host of faces press even closer together in the doorframe; I am being tested. The fluorescent lights of the bathroom are hospital bright and render the nerve-wracking effect of a big shining spotlight.

The bathroom is hardly a large space—a few empty stalls, a long counter with a few sinks, and a couple of urinals. I'm relatively confident I can do this. It should be easy enough; I have just spent all morning watching a handful of teams search the base chapel and a number of rooms in this building, sniffing out drugs and explosives.

I point my hand down to the seam where the wall meets the floor, mimicking the gesture I'd seen other handlers use. Miraculously, Haus puts his nose to the very spot I've indicated and follows as I lead us forward. "Seek," I tell him. I mean to give a clear, forceful command but my voice sounds hollow and small, making only a faint echo against the bathroom tile walls.

Haus and I move along with moderate precision from there, clearing the counter and sinks. Trouble hits when we get to the bathroom stalls. The dog follows my lead into the first stall and around the basin of the first toilet bowl, but having to hold the door open for both of us trips me up and he darts ahead of me, skipping a stall. When I pull him back, the leash gets tangled around his legs. I manage to free Haus the first time; by the time it happens again a minute later, we're a tangled mess. The door of the stall knocks into my back. I'm exasperated.

Haus gives up on me right then and there. He sits in the middle of the bathroom, turning expectantly to Jakubin, as if appraising my performance with a look that says, "Clearly, you can't be serious."

"Give up?" Canell asks, his eyes twinkling. I give one last desperate scan around the room, but nod. I can feel the heat rise in my cheeks.

Canell, however, does not let me go quietly. Instead, he walks me to the paper towel dispenser; it's your standard stainless steel container, with those brown napkins universally stocked in public toilets. There, as plain as day, is a sizeable piece of duct tape, hastily plastered above the keyhole of the clearly broken cabinet. It is out of place against the otherwise well-maintained and clean bathroom. He pulls back the tape and opens the silver compartment, revealing the "bomb." In my hurry to perform well—or get away from the crowd of observers—I'd breezed right by this painfully obvious visual clue. If I had been looking more carefully, it would've been the very first thing I saw coming into the bathroom. But I hadn't been using my eyes; I was relying on Haus to do the work and focusing all my attention on him. My clear inexperience, my confusion ran right down the leash to the dog. He knew the moment I gave up even as I was trying to hide it, and he exposed me by sitting in the middle of the room and giving up his search.

It was a fast but effective lesson. Haus didn't trust me, and he revealed not only my limits but also his own when I failed to give him the proper guidance. It's a lesson I only learned by doing, but it's at the heart of the folly of all the poor or misguided decisions made by those who do not understand how to work with dogs or who have never gotten close enough to see it for themselves.

Jakubin comes into the bathroom and relieves me of Haus's leash. The dog can't get away from me fast enough. Jakubin is amused. "Not so easy, is it?" he asks. His eyes are twinkling too.

If you know what to listen for, the sound is unmistakable. The attuned human ear can hear when a dog has found the sought-after odor usually long before he gives his final alert. And depending on the training and the kind of detection work, the dog will either sit at the source of odor or lie down to the ground. For obvious reasons, search-and-rescue dogs will bark. A practiced handler will recognize his dog's personal tells—the dog may twitch his ears or his movements may slow down and become more deliberate, or he may even have an "I'm definitely on odor" expression—but it's really the sound that is the big giveaway. It's the deep, staccato inhale and then the rush of a perfunctory and heavy exhale. It is the sound of satisfaction. It is the sound of discovery.

The canine nose is a masterful creation; all earthly schnozes[1] are not cre-ated equal, anatomically speaking. While the average dog has roughly 220 million scent receptors in his nasal cavity, the average human has around 5 million.[2] The canine sense of smell is a thousand times more sensitive than a human's. One of the best visual analogies of the dog's acute sense of smell is given by author Mark Derr in *Dog's Best Friend*: "Unfolded and flattened, the smell receptors from the average dog's nose could cover it like a second coat with hair dragging on the ground."[3]

Even the way a canine nose functions is more developed than ours. A dog's nose has four passages, two inner ones and two on the outside, almost like gills. The inner canals pull in the scent and then exhale to the outer, so that the exhaling air doesn't disturb the ground or source of the next odor, allowing always for the intake of fresh scent. Humans, in contrast, have just the two nasal passages, and what goes up comes back out again the same way. (We can of course draw breath through our mouths when we ingest or exhale oxygen, but it is not the best way to *smell*, although it is one of the best ways to use our sense of taste for certain foods—by orthonasal, or mouth, breathing. On the other hand, while dogs are great perpetra-tors of mouth breathing, they're not using it for scent. Though they have good reason to do so. Dogs actually pant through their mouths to cool off, whereas we humans sweat.) That always-damp and cool-to-the-touch quality of the canine nose also has its purpose; moisture that is "secreted by mucous glands in the nasal cavity captures and dissolves molecules in the air and brings them into contact with specialized olfactory epithelium inside the nose."[4]

It's not that we humans don't use our sense of smell, but as a sense it's powerful for very different reasons. Scent recalls memories and awakens our emotional subconscious. We associate different odors, good and bad, with people and places—and there's no accounting for taste in what we relish either. My father, for example, loves the smell of a good barn populated with fragrant livestock. As a family driving the New England interstates, we inevitably passed open pasture, and as we did, my father would lower his window to get his fill of the open air heavy with manure, while my sister and I groaned and pinched our noses. He was taking in the scent of his childhood on the farm and all the memories that came with it—we children of the suburbs were just smelling, well, shit.

Most people don't make a conscious effort to imprint particular or special smells, to file them away for later use—they register more like background noise, though invariably certain things punch through the ether, people and places we are reminded of by the power of scent. But perhaps we should take our lead from dogs and program our brains to catalogue smells in more proactive and useful ways. In one of the great old Disney movies, *The Parent Trap* (with Hayley Mills and Maureen O'Hara), when one of the girls—Susan, pretending to be her twin sister, Sharon—meets her grandfather for the first time, she sniffs the lapel of his jacket with such earnest investigation that he pulls back. "My dear, what are you doing?" he asks. To which she replies, "Making a memory." She puts her nose back to his tweedy chest, calling out the scents she identifies. "When I'm quite grown-up," she tells him, "I will always remember my grandfather and how he smelled of tobacco and peppermint."[5]

Making a memory of a smell, or imprinting odor, is exactly how a dog learns to seek out bombs, weapons caches, narcotics, missing persons, and, sadly, human remains. The process involves training a dog to associate odors with a reward. Dogs become visibly excited when they've discovered an odor they have been trained to detect. The less disciplined ones will cast their heads back, looking, waiting, and watching for the Kong (or tennis ball, or treat) they know is coming, too eager to contain themselves.

In this age of modern warfare and police work, dogs are trained to detect homemade explosives. These bombs are potluck-style concoctions, and while the recipes vary greatly, the ingredients are basically the same.[6] So each dog is trained on—or should be trained on—a handful of key bomb-making ingredients. This catalog of explosive scents includes TNT, smokeless powder, potassium chlorate, C-4 plastic explosive, detonating cord, and ammonium nitrate. And in order for military trained detection dogs to become certified, military regulations require that they meet a very high accuracy rate—explosive-detection dogs must hit 95 percent accuracy, and drug dogs must meet 90 percent accuracy. The key to this kind of training is repetition and reinforcement. Maintaining proficiency at such a high rate requires a minimum of four hours of explosive-detection training a week.[7] Whether or not this rate of accuracy also takes place in the arena of combat has not been proven and may be impossible to quantify.[8] This is at least in part due to the fact that there really is no way to assess how many bombs or bomb materials go undetected—unless, of course, they go off after a dog team has cleared an area. Whereas in a controlled environment, when planted materials are used in training, their hiding spots marked and known, those finds can be quantified and qualified.

A dog hunting for scent is like a linguist who, even when standing before the Tower of Babel (or more practically speaking, an international airport), can hear not only a cacophony of many tongues clamoring at once, but who can pull apart the sounds to find and comprehend the individual voices.

Imagine a leaf floating down a creek. Shiny and wet, it winks out from the moving water. At first the leaf spins in lazy, looping circles—around and around like a carnival ride. Then it meets with a new current, picks up speed, and travels much farther and faster than you thought possible. Powerful, unpredictable, this is the finicky prerogative of the wind.

A rocky, dry path in the desert doesn't much resemble a stream, but when the wind passes through the dust, moving around clusters of shrubs and bushes, you can imagine how the analogy of a leaf on moving water captures the movement of scent on air—the sensory path a dog must follow and all the obstacles in between. The shrubs would be like rocks in the water, parting the current and creating little eddies or pockets of scent. When a dog following scent across the desert floor comes upon a bush, he might pause and sniff around a little more, exploring the eddy created by wind, searching for a stronger pool of the odor he is tracking.

In order to harness the power of a dog's natural scent ability, a handler has to understand how a dog reads a scent trail, because it's the handler's job to assist the dog by tracking the wind. Because air is always flowing in the open space of the desert, all a handler needs to do is toe the earth and watch the dust lift to see which way the wind is going. Some handlers carry a spray bottle so they can punch a mist of water into the air and use that to detect the wind's intensity and direction. It's important that a handler has a good grasp on the direction of the wind because he needs to be able to "see" not what but *where* his dog is smelling.

The majority of the dog teams being dispatched to combat theaters are trained to find mortar shells, C-4, detonation cords, and pressure plates under the desert sand and brush: the components insurgents employ in their destructive IEDs. Pressure plates have become increasingly common. Insurgents bury these plastic disks, the size of dessert dishes, just under the surface of roads, and when the weight of armored vehicles rolls over them, the little plate clicks upward and a bomb or mine hidden within it explodes.

To find such deadly weapons, handlers and explosive-detecting dogs need to be prepared, focused. In addition to keeping watch on the wind, and on his dog, a handler must also keep his eye on the ground and the path ahead, watching for disturbances—wires, rock piles, things that do not belong—as well as any other sign of human interference, adding the keenness of the human eye to the power of the dog's extraordinary nose.

John Lutenberg has been training bloodhounds and other dogs to track and trail for decades. A former military dog handler, he's brought his dogs to Kenya to help officials there hunt down poachers, helped with searches for missing persons, and chased down escaped convicts with the FBI.

Lutenberg is tall and lean—a cross between Clint Eastwood and Henry Fonda in a pair of light denim jeans, green cloth bomber jacket, and a faded blue cap pulled low over his forehead. His voice rolls out in a soft, gravelly drawl. Weathered and creased, his face is that of a true outdoorsman.

This kind of trail work—the nighttime tracks on foot, the chasing down of escaped convicts from high-security prisons—has a dangerous edge. With only the narrow beams of flashlights and the helicopters circling above lighting the way, it would be far more hazardous work. But it isn't the middle of the night; there are no helicopters circling overhead. Instead it is a crisp Colorado afternoon. The sky is a brilliant alabaster blue, and the wind pushes the clouds by at such a clip that the sunlight flickers behind them like a dying light bulb. At Chris Jakubin's invitation, Lutenberg has come to Fort Carson to show me his bloodhounds.

Along with his fellow handler Terry Brown, Lutenberg brings Vicky from the back of their truck. At almost six years old, this dog's velvety coat droops from her body; her ribs show and her jowls swing. A signature feature of the bloodhound breed,[9] her loose skin flaps along her body with every long-legged move she makes. The dog with the greatest scent ability is, without question, the bloodhound. Where some breeds, like dachshunds, have 125 million scent receptors, and German shepherds have 225 million receptors, the bloodhound has on average 300 million.[10]

The way a trail dog like Vicky follows scent on air is different than how an explosive-detection dog might uncover an IED along a road, or how a combat tracker dog would hunt down an insurgent, by mapping out a path and tracking odor on the ground. Many of the same components are at play—following the wind, making sure the dog is on odor—but it is a different skill and the dogs are trained in distinct ways.

Lutenberg crouches down and pulls one long finger through the rosy dirt, drawing what looks like a triangle without a bottom, the point facing up. This is the scent cone, he says. Then he drags his finger across the dirt, starting at the base of the cone, and moves it from left to right, higher and higher until his finger, running out of space inside the cone, hits the top of the triangle at its smallest point. This is how the dog moves to catch the scent on the air—back and forth, closing in on her target until she lands right on top of it, right at the tip of the cone.

And this is how she will find Jakubin, who, acting as the runaway decoy, has gone ahead of us, marking the trail with little orange ribbons and finally positioning himself somewhere among the brush and trees where our eyes won't find him before Vicky's nose does. The scent moves along the air, and if there's wind, as there is on this afternoon, the scent pulls the dog away from the object it seeks, and so the nose could take longer to catch up to what the eyes might see first.

Trailing scent on air is fast-paced work; it requires endurance, a steady and constant fitness. As soon as Vicky is on the scent she is on the move and she is moving *fast*. Because she doesn't need to keep her nose to the ground, following scent with her nose in the air instead, she runs more freely. Brown, Vicky's handler, is keeping pace with her, holding onto her long lead and charging ahead of us on the uneven, rocky terrain. Lutenberg manages an equally brisk pace behind them.

When they finally reach the slight incline below Jakubin's hiding spot, where he is curled on the cold ground in the fetal position, Vicky makes a wide swing turn and dodges right past him, almost as if she didn't see him. But a split second later, she makes another sharp turn and bounds right on top of Jakubin.

Lutenberg maps out a replay. The wind was pushing to the right, tossing Jakubin's scent out and away from him. "She got right here," he says, pointing to the spot in the air where Vicky made her pivot. "And she smelled him: 'he's right here, he's right here.'" Lutenberg's voice rises in soft excitement as he imitates Vicky, or at least how he imagines she would sound were she able to talk.

Vicky, he explains, didn't *see* him because dogs use their noses above all else for detection, not their eyes.

It's a truism that adds yet another layer to the job when a handler works a trail—he had better be using his eyes and be prepared to stumble quickly upon a dangerous scenario, like when chasing an armed suspect. But even if dogs are nose strong, it's something of a mischaracterization to say that dogs have bad vision. There are endless articles with titles like "Dogs Have Terrible Eyesight!" One of the most popular misperceptions is that dogs are color blind—they're not, they do see color, just not as much color as we do. When we measure their eyesight the way we measure human eyesight, with 20/20 vision, we come to something of an egocentric conclusion, that dogs' eyes are inferior. But there are different ways to assess how dogs take in information with their eyes. Perhaps to put into context how dogs see differently than humans or cats or birds of prey, it makes sense to use the standard human eye system, but otherwise it seems a little, er, short-sighted on our part to assess and appraise their visual capabilities measuring on a 20/20 scale.

A dog's visual acuity (how well he is able to see defined details at a distance) is not as strong as a human's and not nearly as a strong as a cat's (eagles actually take the cake on this in the animal kingdom, seeing four to five times better than humans), but there's more to vision and interpreting information with one's eyes than acuity. And though a dog's eye may not be as sharp as our own, their overall ability to take in information with their eyes is perhaps much better than ours.

For one thing, most dogs (and it does depend on the breed) have a much wider, more encompassing field of vision at 250 to 270 degrees than humans (at about 180 degrees)[11] and even cats. For another, dogs see much better in low light and darkness than we do (dogs have what's called a tapetum lucidum, the part of their eye that acts like a mirror, reflecting twice as much light, helping them to see better in the dark.)[12] In fact, a dog's eye has more light-sensitive cells, called rods, in the center of the retina.[13] It's an advantage that Alexandra Horowitz explains well in *Inside of a Dog*: "While we might make out a match being brightly struck in the distance on a dark night, the dog could detect the gentle flame on the lit candle. Arctic wolves spend a full half of the year living in utter darkness; if there is a flame on the horizon, they have the eyes to spot it."[14]

In 2002, the department of zoology at Tel Aviv University conducted a study[15] to see how much a dog used its sight over its sense of smell when detecting explosives.[16] They took trained dogs and ran them through detection drills in different settings under varying amounts of light. What, they wanted to know, would a dog do if he had ample light and had been given visual cues as to where the scented object would be? Would he rely more on his nose or his eyes? The gist of their conclusion was that sniff over see always prevailed. Even "in cases in which dogs could have used both olfaction and vision, they chose to use only olfaction." It didn't matter how much light they had. The study's finding was, in part, that because dogs' eyes are more sensitive to moving objects than stationary when they're on the hunt, the nose is more reliable in seeking "prey" or, in this case, explosives.

So when we consider a dog's sensory prowess, we have to take into account not only *how* a dog sees but why. Perhaps they don't use their eyes because they don't need them. And in this way the handler and dog dovetail nicely together—one sees while the other smells.

Brown believes that 70 percent of his job should be devoted to reading the dog, interpreting her movements and her cues to make sense of the messages she gives him. In other words, if she tells him there's no scent, why would he continue to work her down that path? It's up to him to keep the dog moving to places where the scent is available.

Vicky wrestles around with Jakubin, her eyes hard to read buried under the soft wrinkles, but by the way her tail beats the air, it's clear she's pleased with herself. She did her job well. But there's no tennis ball or Kong for Vicky. The reward is the trail.

For a war dog, scent is perhaps the dog's keenest and most useful sense. Because of that, bloodhounds have been used during many wars to track and trail the enemy. Lieutenant Colonel E. H. Richardson wrote of the bloodhound's talent for tracking (and made note of at least one bloodhound employed as a messenger dog[17] during World War I), and the French sent bloodhounds to track the Vietcong in Southeast Asia but the dogs proved to be too noisy.[18]

But dogs possess other innate abilities that can be drawn out, honed, and sometimes manipulated to great success. Take for example a dog's sense of hearing. Most dogs can hear at a distance up to four times farther than humans, and their hearing ability overall is likely hundreds of times more powerful than ours.[19] The difference is most dramatic though when it comes to frequency, which means dogs are especially good at deciphering pitch difference in sound and equally good at recognizing this sound.

It is this combination of a dog's keenest senses, selecting the most amenable breeds for the tasks required, applied with special attention to the individual dog's suitability for war—judging the temperament, the will to work—that ultimately contributed to earning the dog a spot in successful missions again and again in war after war. To say nothing of their size, which allows them entry into smaller spaces, and their four legs, which carry them more swiftly to and from destinations.

But early use of dogs in war was often less about deploying a skillful force to serve and protect; the entrée of canines into warfare was something of a bloody affair. In all likelihood, these early war dogs took more lives than they saved, and they were notable not for feats of bravery but for the vileness and violence of their use. It was not their inborn supersenses or their natural intelligence that was put to task, but rather something more primitive, fierce, and undisciplined.

Take for example the dogs who ventured along on the journeys of Christopher Columbus. Though he did not have canines on his first voyage to the new world, Columbus brought them along years later when he returned to the Americas, calling his dogs "the most fearsome weapon of all."[20] In 1495, when the indigenous people of Hispaniola, the Taino, resisted his men, Columbus set his dogs loose. They attacked to kill and often disemboweled their victims.

The conquistadors used dogs in their warmongering to torment and instill fear. In one particularly vulgar description of Vasco Núñez de Balboa's exploits, a dog named Leoncico is said to have pounced on an elderly Indian woman, pinning her to the ground. When she pleaded for her life, the dog saw fit to spare her, though not before desecrating her by urinating on her as she lay on the ground. As the story goes, Balboa's soldiers wanted to kill her anyway and feed her to their dogs as they were running low on supplies. Balboa however, refused. "If Leoncico had mercy on her," he apparently replied, "I could do no less."[21]

Stories like these were actually used as shining examples in what were perhaps the first and most fervent arguments made for the integration of war dogs into the US military. Chief among these advocates was Benjamin Franklin. When he tried to convene a league of dogs—mastiffs and handlers—in 1755 as a defense against "Indian raids," Franklin cited Hernán Cortés, who, while conquering Mexico and Peru, employed "savage greyhounds to drag down and disembowel fleeing Aztecs."[22] Apparently Franklin, the enlightened man who brought the world electricity and bifocals, wasn't squeamish about dogs as vehicles for violence. When he made his case for canines, he invoked the savage dogs Cortés had dispatched as a model, arguing that these dogs should be "large, strong and fierce" and could be turned loose to "confound the enemy a good deal and be very serviceable."[23] Franklin's arguments did not garner much support.

Despite the failure of Franklin's attempt to rally support for a trained military dog force, dogs were otherwise a welcome presence alongside American soldiers on battlefields—some on American soil—centuries before their presence there was "official."

During the Revolutionary War, General George Washington exhibited a far more civil wartime etiquette where dogs were concerned. When his adversary's dog wandered into his territory after the Battle of Shermantown, Washington did not take the fox terrier in as a captive or bargaining chip. While his own dogs did not travel with him during battle, he was very devoted to them and was perhaps thinking of them when he had the dog sent back to his master, General William Howe, with a note from Alexander Hamilton (who was at the time under Washington's command). It read: "General Washington's compliments to General Howe, does himself the pleasure to return him a Dog, which accidentally fell into his hands, and by the inscription on his collar appears to belong to General Howe."[24]

But no commanding officer was better known for bringing his dogs on the battlefield than General George Armstrong Custer. From bird dogs to hound dogs, Custer traveled with an ever-changing and always growing legion of canines. And these dogs followed Custer wherever he went, including the battlefield (and there are many photographs of them together).[25] He often wrote of them in his letters home to his wife, Libby. In one such report in June 1876 he wrote of Tuck, a favorite dog. "'Tuck' regularly comes when I am writing, and lays her head on the desk, rooting up my hand with her long nose until I consent to stop and notice her. She and Swift, Lady and Kaiser sleep in my tent." During the Battle of Little Bighorn, Custer's dogs who were not properly detained followed him into the worst of the fight; like their master, they did not emerge from The Last Stand.

Lieutenant George A. Custer poses in Virginia during the Civil War with a dog. Custer was an avid dog lover and brought his dogs to stay with him on the front.
Courtesy of the Library of Congress, Prints and Photographs Division

Elsewhere during this time, canines of a variety of breeds were most often employed as sentry dogs to guard provisions, weaponry, and prisoners; they posed as a dual protection, both alarm raiser and deterrent. But it was in the trenches of World War I—the long stretches of open, uncovered ground in between troop encampments, marred by tangles of barbed wire and the enormous difficulties they posed—where the role of dogs evolved to become a more highly cultivated and respectable military asset.

Rescue missions were complicated and risky, communication between trenches often impossible. Even the bravest, most daring soldiers had little chance of recovering wounded men whose whereabouts were so uncertain. In the aftermath of these battles, armies would dispatch Red Cross dogs, known as rescue dogs, sanitary dogs, or mercy dogs. Four legs in this case were infinitely more valuable than two. These dogs were trained to move soundlessly, sniffing out the wounded and bypassing the dead. Despite the overwhelming odds, thousands of injured men were found and rescued in the dead of night. The larger dogs were trained to quite literally pull or drag wounded men, and they were preferred over horses because they posed a considerably smaller target. They were also swift deliverers of messages, reportedly carrying important information five times faster than the average soldier on foot.[26]

All tallied—including messenger dogs, mercy dogs, Red and Blue Cross dogs—upward of 75,000 dogs were on the ground in official war-related roles during World War I.[27] In September 1916, less than a year before the United States Senate would vote 82–6 in favor of declaring war on Germany, *Vanity Fair* ran an article titled "Dogs of Battle, Dogs of Mercy." The reporter describes the depths of the capabilities he saw among these animals:

> His task then is to lead the stretcher bearers to the spot where his find is lying. In this work the keen nose of the dog has been the means of saving many lives, for the wounded men not infrequently crawl into the thicket or other hiding place to get out of the way of shells or snipers, with the result that, hidden from sight, they are overlooked. Usually the ambulance dog carries at his collar or in small saddle pouches, a first-aid kit, by means of which the wounded man can succor himself if conscious, stimulants, and a pocket in the collar to receive any message that the soldier is able to write. Dogs in the trenches are sometimes provided with gas masks.[28]

But the messenger and rescue roles that dogs executed with such success during World War I would not be applicable to the front lines of World War II. It was a new war with different terrain, different tactics, and different weaponry. This would be, however, the war when the United States would, finally, officially get its war dogs.

The origin of the modern-day US war dog program resulted not from an order given within the military but rather from the efforts of a private citizen, a woman named Arlene Erlanger. As the story goes, within hours of the bombing of Pearl Harbor, Erlanger picked up her phone and made a fateful call.[29] On the receiving end of the line was Roland Kilburn, a noted reporter who at the time was working for the *New York Sun* and authored a column on dogs. Erlanger, a wealthy New York socialite and a longtime canine enthusiast and professional breeder, had long been aware of the United States' reluctance to integrate dogs into its military efforts. With war once again calling on the nation's doorstep, she wasn't about to let the opportunity pass by to change the canine status quo. "The dog game must play its part in this thing," she told Kilburn. The call that Kilburn later described as coming to his desk before "the echoes of the bomb blasts had hardly stopped reverberating through the Hawaiian hills"[30] started a movement that would change the war.

Soon after, Erlanger started Dogs for Defense. And after much haranguing, celebrity involvement, and negotiation, the War Department consented to the idea of dogs. The only question was, where would they get the dogs? At that time the US military had but a few huskies stationed in Alaska. If Dogs for Defense could provide the dogs, the US military would send them to war. And so the DFD appealed to the American public, asking them to give their dogs to a higher cause. The public responded with tremendous support, lending their dogs to the war effort, sending them off to the fight much the way they did their young men.

Not all the dogs who were offered for enlistment were taken—likely they were not the right size, or they did not possess the proper temperament. Or, in the case of one disabled woman who wrote offering her dog, a dependable companion who carried her groceries for her in a basket, the authorities sent her kind thanks for her gesture of patriotism but ultimately—and politely—refused.

Some people who put up their dogs for service later regretted and recanted. It wasn't always such an easy sacrifice as one letter reveals:

> In answer to your recent letter I wish to say that the Army may not have my dog. Her license number is 7220 and you can cross her off your list.
>
> The Army has my husband, two brothers-in-law and my father-in-law, the Navy has one of my brothers and the Government two more. I think that is enough.

My dog is the only protection left me. She is bodyguard and playmate for my two daughters and guards our house completely and faithfully each night. She sleeps in the children's room and I can sleep in peace, knowing that no person can harm them. After all, we owe the coming generations as much protection as we can give them.[31]

Still, the Army managed to pull together a robust legion, and in March 1942 it authorized the training of 200 sentry dogs. So successful were these dogs that by December of that same year, the quartermaster general came to the DFD with some news: they wanted more dogs, in fact, many more dogs for the Army, the Marines, and the Coast Guard—a whopping 125,000 of them.[32] In those first two years, the DFD would provide the US military forces with over 20,000 dogs of multiple breeds and sizes, all of them given by their owners in the service of a worthy cause. The cost of each dog was estimated at fewer than seven dollars.[33]

The military took its time figuring out which dogs were the best for service—which temperament, which skills, and which breeds fit the war dog bill. During World War II they finally settled on five breeds: German shepherds, Belgian sheep dogs, Doberman pinschers, farm collies, and giant schnauzers.[34] They would try to implement examples of past achievement, as well as experiment with a number of roles for the dogs—including mine dogs and even suicide dogs (a program that was modeled off the Russian tank dogs and was, thankfully, very short-lived and never fully executed).

Ultimately, the most effective dogs were the scout dogs. Their impact was nearly instantaneous. These dogs were reported to be able to detect Japanese soldiers at a distance of 1,000 yards "depending on terrain and wind condition" and were equally effective on "amphibious landings detecting the enemy on the beach and in the undergrowth."[35]

While in Sicily, a dog called Chips, who was part of one of the first K-9 detachments to go across the Atlantic to war, made headlines after overtaking an enemy den of Italian machine gunners, even surviving a shot to the face in the process. The three-year-old dog was cited by the quartermaster general for "courageous action in single-handedly eliminating a dangerous machine-gunnest [*sic*] and causing the surrender of the crew." The report noted that, incidentally, Chips was also "anxious to bite Hitler."[36]

Chips had been donated by the Wren family, who hailed from the pleasanter end of a nice, manicured neighborhood in Pleasantville, New York. In his suburban life Chips had earned himself something of a reputation. The large collie-shepherd-husky mix was notorious for chasing the postman and biting the garbage men. The family argued that it was his love for their eight-year-old daughter Gail that inspired his protective streak. He even followed Gail to school and lay by her desk during class, her teachers apparently either ardent dog lovers or, more likely, too intimidated to send the dog away.[37] But the temperament that made him an unruly housedog would, the Wrens supposed, make him an exceptional candidate for a war dog.

Chips would become the most famous war dog of World War II—he was awarded the Silver Star and the Purple Heart and met President Franklin D. Roosevelt and British prime minister Winston Churchill. When he met General Dwight D. Eisenhower, Chips bit him on the hand. After Chips returned home to the Wren family, they were immensely proud of their dog, but they saw a change in their pet—Chips was not the same. The rambunctious dog who'd once given chase to the neighbors shrank from the limelight of his newfound fame. As Mr. Wren would tell the *New York Times*, the dog suffered from battle fatigue: "He doesn't seem to wag his tail as much as before going to war."[38]

When it came time for the remaining war dogs to reintegrate back into civilian life in 1945, so great was the admiration for the dogs that the Dogs for Defense headquarters was inundated with adoption applications, receiving over a total of 15,000—a steady stream of requests that at its height reached 500 per day and stretched well into 1947.[39] But soon after the war ended, the dog program that had been started and built to great heights was no more. And while all would be mostly quiet on the war dog front until 1965, when the United States sent combat troops to Vietnam, those relevant lessons used to build the formidable World War II canine force were shelved and would need to be relearned.

Booby traps, land mines, trip wires, and the enemy's intricate tunnel system put American soldiers and Marines who made early entry into the Vietnam War at a tremendous disadvantage. During World War II mines and booby traps accounted for only 2 percent of casualties, but in Vietnam that number rose to 11 percent.[40]

From the beginning of their use in Vietnam, these canine teams gave patrols negotiating the froth and fray of the jungle an advantage against the guerilla tactics used by Vietcong. With a dog leading a patrol, such tactics lost their element of surprise. What human eyes couldn't detect was far more "visible" to the canine ears and nose. Within a year of scout dogs' arrival in Vietnam, they are reported to have saved over 2,000 lives.[41] After the dogs came to Vietnam, requests to have dogs accompany units on missions were so abundant that, sometimes, they were rejected only because there weren't enough dogs.[42]

Jesse Mendez, who headed up the scout dog program at Fort Benning in Georgia during the Vietnam War, described these dogs as "the only weapon system [the military] ever devised to save lives."[43]

If a soldier was injured on the battlefield during the Revolutionary War, say by the sharp end of musket's bayonet, his chance of dying was roughly 42 percent. During the Civil War—which saw the arrival of the Ambulance Corps and the swifter delivery of the wounded to surgery—the likelihood of dying from a combat-related injury dropped to 33 percent. The chance of survival didn't increase all that much over the next hundred years. During World War II, the mortality rate was 30 percent, despite the availability of antibiotics and blood transfusions. During Vietnam, even with helicopters to evacuate wounded men from the field, the death rate only dropped to 24 percent. However, the chance that a serviceman or woman would return home from Operation Iraqi Freedom or Operation Enduring Freedom in Afghanistan after being wounded is 90 percent or higher, the highest wartime survival rate in the history of American-engaged conflicts.[44]

While US wartime fatalities in Iraq and Afghanistan are at an all-time low—the result of the superior medical advances and the immediacy with

which they are administered after injury—the number of recorded casualties in a combat arena has steadily increased since 2003, as has the number
of amputees.[45] Even though the number of battle injuries reached an all-
time high during the troop surge of 2007, the number rose again the following year in Afghanistan. By 2011, the Department of Defense said the
number of troops who had lost limbs during wartime was, in that year, the
highest they'd seen in the conflicts.[46]

The role of military working dogs in these wars has almost exclusively
been devoted to combating IEDs—the single biggest threat to US troops
on the ground. IEDs are the most pervasive and pernicious weapon employed by insurgents in Iraq and Afghanistan, a weapon that has only became more widespread and complex as the wars in both of these countries
has continued. IEDs have claimed both limbs and lives, and in large numbers. But quantifying these numbers—calculating the human cost—is no
simple task. Getting the "correct figure," as Andrew W. Lehren wrote in
the *New York Times*, "depends on how you define the boundaries of the
war."[47] Operation Enduring Freedom, for instance, isn't limited to military
efforts in Afghanistan alone; the United States' efforts to stamp out terror-
ism stretches across the globe and includes a number of different countries.
The Department of Defense keeps track of US military casualties and as of
April 2014 the counts are as follows: During Operation Iraqi Freedom there
were 4,410 total deaths and 31,942 wounded in action. During Operation Enduring Freedom (in Afghanistan only) there were 2,178 total deaths
and 19,523 wounded in action.[48] How many of these deaths and injuries
were the result of IED attacks is even more difficult to parse out. But just
as they were in Iraq, IEDs were a "leading cause of death and injury" in
Afghanistan.[49]

Because IEDs are typically crudely made, the kinds of explosives used
and formed are something of a mixed bag. How much damage they do
depends on a variety of elements—where they are placed, how deep into
the ground they're buried, how many pounds of explosives are used, if it's
freshly made or has been sitting for days, weeks even. The list of mitigating factors is long. But in general, it's believed that in order for someone to

altogether escape the blast of an IED alive they must be at a distance of at least 50 yards. To avoid injury from the resulting shrapnel spray, the safe distance is estimated to be about half a mile.[50]

On May 25, 2005, the US military launched a new tactical campaign to reduce the number of deaths and injuries caused by IEDs. Called "5-and-25," it was adapted from the model British forces were already using with success in Northern Ireland. The idea was that when a convoy or patrol stops and dismounts from their vehicles, the first thing a unit does is clear a distance of 5 meters around the vehicle, spanning out until a 25-meter perimeter is cleared. And it should begin with a soldier's first step, for "in addition to bombs striking moving targets, patrols have been hit after being stationary for as little as four minutes." In the three weeks before the Army officially pushed out the 5-and-25 program, no fewer than 52 US service members were killed in Iraq, many of them by IEDs.[51]

As the rate of IEDs continued to increase, so did the Pentagon's efforts to counter them.[52] In 2006, the Department of Defense created the Joint Improvised Explosive Device Defeat Organization (JIEDDO): its sole purpose (and its many billions of dollars in funding) was to combat the IED.[53] Over the next few years, JIEDDO would spend upward of $19 billion pursuing numerous technological innovations—from handler sensors to aerial sensors to enhanced optics.[54]

In 2010 JIEDDO's director, Lieutenant General Michael Oates, gave a report on the organization's progress. After all the money spent, and all the tools developed during those years, Oates said the best detection ability US forces had against the threat of IEDs was a handler and his detection dog.[55]

Nearly two years later, on a sunny September day in 2012, the man who succeeded Oates as head of JIEDDO, Lieutenant General Michael D. Barbero, addressed the US House of Representatives Committee on Appropriations' Subcommittee of Defense in Washington, DC. In his calm, leaden voice, Barbero reported that the threat would not only persist, but become even more deadly in the future.[56] US forces were going to continue to operate in an IED environment; that was, Barbero testified, a reality of twenty-first-century warfare, and the country must prepare accordingly.

Not only had it surpassed artillery as being the greatest killer on the modern battlefield, but "the IED and the networks that employ these asymmetric weapons," Barbero said, "are here to stay—operationally and here at home."[57]

So while the United States may have taken its forces from Iraq and is already drawing down its troops in Afghanistan, the rate of IEDs is expected only to climb in the coming months and years—and not just in these battleground countries. Modern warfare's deadliest weapon is not only here to stay, but there's reason enough to think that the United States is not and will not be immune. In the past 20 years the United States has endured three massively destructive incidents where explosives were used to incite terror and cause mass casualties—in Waco in 1993, the Oklahoma City bombing in 1995, and the Boston Marathon bombing in 2013.

In truth, the battleground of bombs on American soil began many years before. And when it did, there were actually dogs trained to find them, protecting our homeland, even if few people knew about them.

At 11:30 on the morning of Tuesday, March 7, 1972, an anonymous caller phoned in to the Third Avenue headquarters of Trans World Airlines. The switchboard patched the call through to the secretary of a company executive. The voice on the line directed them to a locker, one of the 25-cent rentals in Kennedy International Airport's TWA terminal. The New York officials who searched the locker found two large Army duffel bags and a note demanding ransom in the amount of $2 million. If it was not paid, the note said, bombs planted on four of the airline's flights would detonate at six-hour intervals. The executive notified TWA security, and so began a 24-hour race against the clock that would set panic to skies and airports all over the world. The airline had thousands of passengers scheduled to fly their nearly 240 planes, and the task of finding the bombs in time seemed nearly impossible.

By the time officials determined the threat was indeed legitimate and put out an international call to all TWA flights for an immediate and mandatory bomb search, a host of planes were already airborne. One of these flights, a West Coast–bound Boeing 707, was already more than a hundred miles into its nonstop flight to Los Angeles. They'd only been in the air 15 minutes when the pilot, Captain William Motz, came over the intercom to tell the 45 passengers and the seven-person crew that they were headed back to New York, citing mechanical difficulties.

Motz landed the plane and taxied to a remote part of the runway, a good distance from the main hub of the airport. It was ten minutes past noon; if there was a bomb on the plane it was set to go off at 1 p.m. The passengers were hurried off the aircraft. The police, who were already waiting on the tarmac, rushed aboard. With them were two search dogs: Brandy, a German shepherd, and her handler, David Connally, worked the front end of the plane; another police officer worked Sally, a Labrador, toward the back. Inside the cockpit Brandy was nosing her way around a large black case marked "Crew." It was a nondescript piece of pilot gear, the kind of case that carried a flight manual. But after a few good sniffs, Brandy sank her haunches into a resolved sit. Connally knew they'd found the bomb and he signaled the others. The time was 12:48 p.m.

Detective William F. Schmitt of the police department's bomb squad called for all the officers to get off the plane. He cut into the case and quickly scanned over its contents—what he guessed to be roughly six pounds of plastic C-4 explosives with a fuse rigged to a timer. It was enough, he knew, to rip the plane to shreds. In a fast decision, Schmitt picked up that clunky, ticking case and carried it off the plane and onto the runway, moving quickly away from the crowd of people. Setting down the case on the ground, Schmitt disabled the bomb. The time was 12:55 p.m.

The very next day a bomb hidden inside another TWA plane in Las Vegas exploded. The plane, which was sitting idle and empty at the time, had been searched, but the bomb in the cockpit had gone undiscovered. No one was injured but a panic ensued. By noon that day, two of the airline's pilots refused to fly, and its business was down 50 percent.[58]

In response to the bombs and the public concern, a Federal Aviation Administration representative, retired Lieutenant General Benjamin Davis, sat in front of TV cameras and in a grave tone warned that his organization was now engaged in a "war for the survival of the air transportation industry."[59] By the end of that week President Richard Nixon gave orders to Transportation Secretary John A. Volpe to push into action, early, security measures that were already in development as part of the response to recent hijacking attempts made on American flights. Travelers would now be subjected to mandatory passenger and baggage screenings; airline and cargo facilities would now be off limits to unauthorized personnel. Nixon also ordered the secretary of transportation to create a force that included dogs. That same year, the Federal Aviation Administration started its Detection Canine Team Program.

It was that very program that is responsible for the two bomb dog teams patrolling the terminal in the Colorado Springs airport more than 40 years later: Colorado State police officer Mike Anderson and his dog Cezar, and fellow officer Wayne Strader and his dog Rex. These teams are part of the Transportation Security Administration (TSA) Bomb Dog Program that started here at this airport in 2005.

There's something about being followed by a big German shepherd and a police officer in uniform that makes my heart skip and my legs twitch with the urge to run. I'm pulling a smooth-gliding and nondescript black carry-on suitcase, possibly the most inconspicuous piece of luggage on the planet. And it's empty, except for the explosives packed inside. Technically speaking I'm not guilty of anything, but I am trying to act as normal as possible because I don't want anything other than the odor of the explosive material to tip off the dog, who's about to make a find on this piece of moving luggage.

I keep walking straight as I feel the dog team about to pass me. The dog's nose is barely a foot away from my suitcase and he's already picked up the scent. His body swivels with intense interest and that alone is enough to signal to his handler that there's something in my bag. The dogs make this find, as well as a series of others that day throughout the airport, without trouble. Anderson is especially happy with Cezar's performance because the dog is getting older and the handler has noticed he's started to slow down. Cezar is as big a dog as Anderson, who stands 6 feet 7 inches, is a man. Unlike military working dogs, Cezar and Rex live at home with their handlers—their careers together can span as long as the dog's working life. Both of these teams have been partnered together for over six years. Which is why Anderson is sad that Cezar isn't performing like he used to—it means that their work together will have to end.

On this December day in 2011, the terminal at the Colorado Springs airport isn't very crowded, and the few passengers sitting and waiting for their flights to board take great interest in the dogs—some point and smile, curiously, while a few eye the large Cezar warily. That visibility, Officer Strader explains, is a big part of the role they play in keeping the airport secure. Cezar and Rex do their jobs simply by being *on* the job, acting as a visual deterrent and inspiring any would-be criminal to think twice. Most of the time, Rex and Cezar search unattended bags or vehicles left without a driver by the curb. In addition to their post at the airport, they also respond to any bomb threats in the city.

The dog program that was born out of Brandy's heroic find in 1972 evolved under different agencies, and after 9/11 the canine program was transferred to the TSA, which would become part of the Department of Homeland Security (DHS) the following year. It's expanded significantly since. There are now over 900 canine teams working in 120 airports nationwide.

After conducting an analysis of the Customs and Border Protection Canine Program from April 2006 to June 2007, it was determined that the dog teams, while accounting for only 4 percent of overall agents, were responsible for "60% of drug arrests and 40 percent of all other apprehensions in 2007."[60] In other words, this program was a rousing success.

Despite the influx of K-9 security presence in airports and mass transit systems around the country over the last decade, the majority of airports rely almost entirely on scanning machines. So officers Anderson and Strader don't use their dogs to check the majority of the luggage they encounter; it's not part of their job.

Since 9/11, airport security under the TSA has depended heavily on a series of electronic scanners and full-body imaging machines that have stirred controversy over the years, not only for their invasiveness, but also for their ineffectuality. During a July 2011 congressional hearing convened in front of a House Oversight and Government Reform subcommittee, House members listened to testimony offered by TSA representatives, the former director of security at Tel Aviv Ben Gurion International Airport, and an inspector with the Amtrak Police Department's K-9 unit, among others, in order to evaluate the current state of US airport security and DHS policies. Subcommittee chairman Congressman Jason Chaffetz, a Republican from Utah, led the inquiry and did not mince words as he kicked off his opening remarks, citing a litany of concerns—chief among them that, since November 2001, there had been 25,000 security breaches at US airports.

From there the hearing unfolded in high drama, especially when explosive-detection dogs were brought into the discussion. Proponents of canine detection teams went head to head with those advocating machines. Among the many issues that were hotly debated: invasion of privacy, the longevity of million-dollar machines that proved ineffectual, and the cost of Alpo.

During the height of this inquiry and testimony, Chaffetz invoked the Pentagon's conclusion, with its $19 billion price tag, that dogs were the best bomb detectors. He then leveled a challenge at TSA assistant administrator John Sammon:

> You're suggesting that the whole body imaging machine is a cheaper alternative than using the K-9s. I tell you what, let's do this. I would love to do this. I would love to do this. You take 1,000 people and put them in a room, I will give you 10 whole body imagining [*sic*] machines. You give me 5,000 people in another room and you give me one of [the] dogs, and we will find the bomb before you find your bomb.
>
> That is the problem. There is a better, smarter, safer way to do this. And the TSA is not prioritizing it. And if you look at who those lobbyists were that pushed through those machines, they should be ashamed of themselves, because there is a better way to do this and it is with the K-9s.[61]

But though there is nothing yet that proves technology has outmatched or outdone a canine's ability to detect odor—especially bomb detection in a combat arena—or even that they could, scientists and technology developers and their vendors have long tried to re-create and out-design Mother Nature's canine nose. In security or defense settings, groups of private contractors and researchers at universities are racing to do this, at the behest of the military.

When dealing with IEDs or landmines, the priority for these projects is to eliminate the risk to human life. Imitation might well be the most sincere form of flattery, but when it comes to detecting bombs, these attempts have proven to be lacking, and their results have fallen hopelessly short of expectations.

In the mid-1990s, the Defense Advanced Research Projects Agency initiated its "Dog's Nose Program" to make the bionic version of a dog's nose, and backed the venture with $25 million. As *Discover Magazine* reported in its September 2001 issue, two companies were in the running to develop this technology. Each took a slightly different approach.[62] The first, run by a neuroscientist at Tufts University, sought to create a "true electronic nose, capable of distinguishing a large variety of smells." The other, partnered with Nomadic, Inc., focused on two particular materials used in explosive making (TNT and DNT) and created Fido, the first "artificial nose capable of sniffing out a land mine in the real world." But results were mixed. As one of the Tufts researchers said in 2001, what they produced was "probably about a factor of 10 times less sensitive than the best dogs, but about par with the worst dogs." Hardly a glowing appraisal, and hardly a ringing endorsement for the mechanical answer to the dog.

Even now new iterations of Fido persist—the latest version, Fido X3, was recently launched, advertised on its website as the "next generation of threat detection." But its promoters are no longer trying to sell these devices as viable *replacements* for a canine, but, instead, as an additional resource for base detection work. Amy Rose, the product sales director at the sensor manufacturer Flir Systems, the company that makes Fido, told the *New York Times*: "We see our technology as complementary to the dog. Dogs are awesome. They have by far the most developed ability to detect concealed threats." But, Rose continued, "dogs get distracted, cannot work around the clock and require expensive training and handling."[63]

Army dog handler Staff Sergeant Taylor Rogal has had experience with bomb dogs, but he's also worked with the electronic bomb-detecting gear—handheld devices. Most soldiers, if they don't have dogs with them when they conduct searches, will use sensors like Fido. But Rogal says they have a reputation for breaking easily or being too sensitive to humidity and sand, which can render them ineffective. Rogal would rather put his trust in a dog—even a dog who's tired, thirsty, or hungry and has had a bad day.

When Rogal was deployed to Qatar in 2009, he and his detection dog, a German shepherd named Teri, worked security at the gate to their base. One time while they were on duty, a civilian drove onto base and Teri gave a standard search before they let him through. But then, to Rogal's surprise, Teri paused and sat. He was on odor. Teri could be a stubborn dog, but Rogal knew that this was the dog's serious, no-bullshit response: there was something in that car. So Rogal called it in.

When EOD came to investigate, Rogal's squadron commander, Lieutenant Colonel Gregory Reese, came to watch. It was a nerve-wracking few minutes for the handler, who was worried he had shut down gate access for nothing. But he trusted his dog. And while there wasn't a bomb, Teri's response was still a good one: EOD confirmed there was explosive residue in the car, as the driver, a contractor who worked with explosive materials, hadn't cleaned up the car properly. The find was a testament to the dog's powerful nose. The lieutenant colonel was impressed.

Rogal felt lucky to have a commander who supported the dog teams—one who would weigh this support against his reputation one day when a vendor came out to the base touting a Fido sensor. The man was wearing a Polo shirt and had a briefcase slung over his shoulder, sorely sticking out. He was selling his product hard to the men in the group gathered around him, promising that these little handheld sensors would soon be all the detection help they needed. Rogal stood watching from off to the side with another handler when he noticed Lieutenant Colonel Reese had come out to see the vendor's pitch.

To demonstrate the effectiveness of his sensor, the salesman took out a sample of C-4 and pressed it against his thumb. He walked over to the bathroom trailer wall and pressed the same thumb against the side of the building. After that he pulled out Fido and ran it over the trailer wall. A ding sounded; the minuscule amount of explosives had been detected.

Reese chuckled and told the vendor their dogs could do that and just as fast. The vendor scoffed. Reese called over to the handler next to Rogal. "Go grab Hhart," he told him. The handler came back with Hhart, his search dog, and walked him over to the trailer, following a standard search pattern. As soon as they hit the spot with the thumbprint, the dog sat.

The vendor was visibly taken aback, shocked that the dog had performed so well and so quickly. It was clearly not what'd he'd been expecting. Reese, on the other hand, just kind of gave him a satisfied smirk. His confidence in the dogs had paid off.

Being a handler, Rogal knows that he comes to this debate with a bias. But when he thinks back to standing guard on that gate, watching Teri give a fast and clear alert on just residual odor alone, there's no question in his mind which he would chose if given the chance. All Teri did that day was stick his nose in the car, and that, Rogal says, took just two seconds. And for Rogal those extra seconds could mean the difference between life and death.[64]

It was raining, or at least it had been. The morning ground was wet and muddy. It was spring 2010, the rainy season in Kandahar province, Afghanistan, and Staff Sergeant Justin Kitts was up early. He washed his face and brushed his teeth using bottled water, as there was no plumbing or electricity. Their base, Strong Point Haji Rahmuddin, was small and remote; outside the makeshift gate and beyond the safety of the military-constructed Hesco border was open farmland and grape fields.

The day's mission was pretty standard. Kitts's unit had orders to travel to a nearby town and meet with a few of the locals. Every now and then, as part of their efforts to build better relationships with the people of Afghanistan, the Army sent in soldiers to see if the locals needed anything. The soldiers packed their pockets with candy to hand out to the children who lived there. But they were also hoping to find people who could become reliable and friendly sources of information on the Taliban and to gather new intelligence and reports of suspicious activity in the area.

Along with 20 other members of the 101st Airborne and an Afghan interpreter, Kitts geared up and prepared his detection dog, Dyngo, to accompany them. To keep from being easy to track, the unit avoided the shorter, more direct route on a hardened surface road. Instead, they rambled through a grape field, its earthen-packed walls, each about waist high, covered in tangled vines. Hopping over them slowed down the patrol but made their movements less predictable.

The gray weather started to clear as they walked through the grape field. The sun came out and then, suddenly, so did the sound of gunfire: it was an ambush. In this field they were exposed, so Kitts, Dyngo, and the rest of the unit ran for the cover of some higher walls that flanked the main road, the sound of their boots pounding the ground. Once they reached the road, the soldiers spread out along the front wall and took aim with their guns, while a few others stayed behind them, covering the wall on the other side of the grape field and laying down suppressive fire. The unit called for air support, but they knew it would take a while to arrive. In the meantime they would have to hold their ground yet also find a way to move out of their vulnerable position.

Kitts took Dyngo and looked for an exit route. He started down the road to the left, sending Dyngo up ahead, watching the dog carefully as he put his nose to the ground. When Dyngo was about 30 meters out, Kitts noticed the change in the dog's search pattern. Dyngo began taking in deep, sweeping breaths. There was something there. Kitts shouted to Dyngo, calling him back.

The others in the unit, pulled back from the left side of the road, were still trying to return gunfire at an enemy they could not track or see. Kitts pulled Dyngo down against the walls, keeping the dog low and close to him for cover. Suddenly, the enemy shot two RPGs toward them. The first went over the back wall and exploded in the field behind them. But the second flew into the wall, destroying a chunk of it just ten feet from where they sat.

The explosion registered a deep shock to the ground and the noise was deafening. Dyngo began to whimper; it was a high whining sound the seven-year-old Belgian Malinois rarely made. Kitts knew his dog was not reacting to the noise or the chaos—it was the pressure from RPG blast that scared him, the shock wave causing real pain to Dyngo's sensitive ears. Dyngo collapsed to his stomach, his limbs limp, his ears flattened. The dog was afraid.

Kitts instinctively reached out his hand to break off a branch from a nearby tree and pushed the branch under Dyngo's nose. The dog latched onto it and began a nervous, mindless gnawing—the canine version of hand wringing. Kitts pulled on the branch and they played a little game of tug-of-war. Dyngo was usually so calm, unshakable. Even when they took helicopter rides, as they frequently did, Dyngo never minded the noise. Unlike some of the other military working dogs who were easily frightened by the chopper's noise or balked at the strong, rough winds kicked out from its fast-beating blades, Dyngo always hopped on happily and pushed his muzzle as close to the window as he could so he could see what was happening on the ground. To see him unhinged, to see this normally calm and experienced dog under duress, filled Kitts with dread. But soon the release of energy from playing with the branch calmed Dyngo and also settled Kitts's own rising nerves.

The incoming gunfire was still distant and intermittent, so the leader of their unit asked Kitts to clear the right side of the road, hoping that this could help them work their way farther from the ambush in that direction. Despite being shaken, Dyngo followed Kitts's instruction to "seek," trotting along, working quickly, sniffing over patches of dirt, over clusters and clumps of road and grass. When Kitts saw Dyngo slow, once again growing more intense, more deliberate, the handler called the dog back even before he had time to give the final alert. Kitts didn't need to see it—there was no doubt that Dyngo was on bomb for a second time. Now the unit couldn't move left or right, they were trapped on the road. The only way out was back through the grape field.

It seemed like forever, but it was only a few more minutes before the air support arrived. Soon there was no more enemy fire and the grape field went quiet. The enemy had retreated. It was now safe for them to retrace their steps through the grape field.

An EOD team arrived to remove the bombs. Buried nearly two feet deep in the ground were two yellow jugs, each packed with 50 pounds of explosives, cunningly hidden only 200 meters apart. The attack had been a setup. The Taliban had deliberately flushed them out of the grape field and onto the road, where their path was boxed in on both ends by IEDs. Everyone in that patrol had been in the kill zone—not once but twice.

If it had not been for Dyngo, they might all be dead.

Today little flecks of white color Dyngo's muzzle just below his nose, as if he's just lifted his head from sniffing powdery snow. His soft amber eyes have a tired, well-worn quality, but they still brighten with interest when someone he likes walks into a room or when—especially when—it's time to work. He has a stout and sturdy body and large head with an expressive face. Dyngo is a dog who smiles.

As a younger dog, Dyngo had a reputation for being a little hellion and something of a biter. But Dyngo is beginning to slow down. He's changed over the last year; two back-to-back deployments have taken their toll. Even though you can see that his body aches, the dog still loves to work and works to please.

Over their six-and-a-half-month deployment, Dyngo accompanied Kitts on 63 missions. And during all those missions, Kitts only fired his own weapon twice. Once was that day in the grape field. The other time during a routine patrol was to protect Dyngo. Kitts had seen a yard dog out of the corner of his eye. The dog, mangy and gaunt, his hackles bristling, had caught wind of Dyngo. The closer they got the deeper and more threatening the yard dog's barking became. He wore a metal chain around his neck, but Kitts could see that it was broken and nothing was keeping

Tech Sergeant Justin Kitts and his MWD partner Dyngo take a break in the shade while they compete in the K-9 trials hosted at Lackland Air Force Base in Texas in May 2012.

him tied down. When the yard dog charged at Dyngo, Kitts raised his nine-millimeter and fired, killing the other dog instantly.

There is a closeness between Dyngo and Kitts that has remained intact, even after Dyngo was paired up with another handler. Despite spending six months apart, Dyngo is still tuned into Kitts's every movement; his eyes and nose follow him like the point of a compass always bobbing to north. Kitts, now a tech sergeant, is an instructor at the Marine Corps predeployment training course in Yuma, Arizona, working to teach other handlers on their way to war, sharing his experience.

Like so many other handlers who've bonded with the dogs they deploy with, Kitts wants to adopt Dyngo. He feels a sense of ownership and believes he is the best one to take care of him when the dog is ready to retire, just like he had to care for Dyngo after that day in Afghanistan. When they'd finally made it back to their patrol base after the ambush, Dyngo was exhausted and nervous. The dog had lain for days without eating, heavy-lidded and melancholy. Kitts had been patient and had given him room to recover, refusing to work him until he was rested. In just a few days, Dyngo had come around, starting to act like his old self.

Even though they were both stateside again, Kitts would still have to wait for the chance to bring his former partner home. At least for another seven months—or however long the dog's next deployment will take. Dyngo already has orders to go back to Afghanistan and back to war.

Marine IEDD Chaney mugs for the camera.
Courtesy of Corporal Matt Hatala

Lance Corporal Trevor M. Smith, a Marine dog handler, taunts Grek, a combat tracker dog, who replies with intimidating snarls while they train together at Combat Outpost Rawah, Iraq, on December 3, 2008.

Photo by Lance Corporal Sean Cummins

MWD Dyngo takes a break in the shade after he and his former handler Tech Sergeant Justin Kitts ran through an obstacle course at the Department of Defense K-9 Trials at Lackland Air Force Base in Texas on May 5, 2012. Dyngo and Kitts deployed to Afghanistan together in 2011.

US Air Force Staff Sergeant Joshua Fehringer guides MWD Suk across the obedience course at Cannon Air Force Base in New Mexico on August 15, 2012.

Photo by Airman First Class Xavier Lockley

IEDD Molly keeps Seaman James L. Louck company at a new Afghan Uniformed Police security post in the village of Regay, in Musa Qal'eh district, Helmand Province, Afghanistan on February 1, 2012.

Photo by Sergeant Earnest J. Barnes

Staff Sergeant Pascual Gutierrez carries his dog, Mack, down a hill at Lackland Air Force Base in May 2012.

Staff Sergeant Robbie Whaley plays with MWD Boda after giving her a good grooming at Fort Carson in Colorado in December 2011.

MWD Turbo stands with his handler during a training exercise at Yuma Proving Ground in March 2012.

While on foot patrol a group of Marines found Layla (above) when she was a puppy, but because of IED risk, taking her on patrols was too dangerous, and they decided to trade her for some cigars to the Marines of the 1st Battalion, 8th Infantry Regiment. Here she is with her Marines from the 1/8 at Shir Ghazay Patrol Base in Landay Nawah County, Afghanistan.

© *Rita Leistner/Basetrack*

Layla relaxes in the arms of one of the Marines who took her in during their deployment to Afghanistan.
© *Rita Leistner/Basetrack*

Marine Sergeant Charlie Hardesty works with MWD Turbo during a training session at YPG.

US Air Force MWD Luck goes through an obstacle course on March 8, 2010, at Hurlburt Field in Florida.
Photo by Staff Sergeant Sheila Devera

Marine Lance Corporal Joshua Ashley takes a knee with MWD Sirius during a nighttime training exercise at YPG in March 2012.

Combat Tracker dog Lex—who loves attention—enjoys some free time with his handler, Marine Lance Corporal John Peeler.

the road to war leads through Yuma

Entreat me not to leave thee, or to return from following after thee: for whither thou goest I will go; and where thou lodgest, I will lodge: thy people shall be my people.

—Book of Ruth

The drive out to the proving ground from downtown Yuma—a stretch of two-lane desert highway that runs approximately 30 miles—seems endless in the predawn pitch black. During daylight hours, this road is populated by snail-slow farming tractors and leisurely retirees—the snowbirds who make Arizona their home during the winter months—caravanning around in their mobile homes. Every once in a while, the sickly sweet stench of the cabbage fields that line the highway blows into the car.

But now, just past 4 a.m., this road is desolate and very, very dark. It is the first time I make my way to the training site that is home to the Inter-Service Advance Skills K-9 (ISAK) course, an intense, three-week predeployment program in a remote part of the Sonoran desert that prepares dog teams from all branches of the military to go to war. About an hour's drive from downtown Yuma, the Yuma Proving Ground (YPG), a military base in southwestern Arizona near the California border, stretches 1,300 square miles. Each year, this immense area—larger than the state of Rhode Island—tests over 10,000 artillery, mortar, and missile rounds. The only other place in the world where you can get such a concentrated amount of explosive material together in one place is a combat zone.

Something so large shouldn't be quite so hard to find—but maybe that's part of the problem. My prayers to come across road signs are wasted, for the simple reason that such signs do not exist. Directions that tell you to "turn right at the jump site" are particularly tricky for someone who has no idea what a jump site looks like, let alone possesses the ability to find such a land marker in the dark. (The giveaway reveals itself more clearly in the light of day: a line of port-a-potties. Or, if I'd had the skills to drive while staring straight up, it would be the men parachuting from the sky.)

I know I'm finally in the right place when I come across the course's only real distinguishing mark—a bright yellow caution sign, bearing the black outline of a dog, posted at the entrance to a dusty gravel parking lot. Just beyond that sign is an aluminum-roofed hangar. A wide, sparse building with high ceilings, it is the ISAK course hub, and home to course manager Gunnery Sergeant Kristopher Reed Knight's office, a men's room, some lockers for the students, two classrooms, and a folding table that holds a microwave and a coffeemaker. An ice machine just inside the front door is clearly labeled with a sign that says, "For Dogs Only." Over the next few days I become familiar with this place and its quirks, like the two old backseats that once belonged inside of a van and offer the only seating outside the classrooms. If you sit on one, you have to take care to balance your weight in the middle or the seat will tip heavily to one side, ejecting the sitter from his perch. I fall over enough times that I decide it's just safer to sit on the floor.

There is the faint but ever-present smell of dog, mingled in with the odor of burned coffee and the jar of shared peanut butter or the remnants of whatever food has just been warmed in the microwave; wafts of leftover pizza, oatmeal, chicken. Every once in a while a bag of homemade elk jerky gets passed around, and the chewy meat emits its own pungent, gamey fragrance. There is, depending on the time of day, the aroma of fresh sweat and unwashed uniforms.

Posted on the wall outside of Knight's office is a chart of desert snakes arranged in order of how quickly they will kill you. They appear more frightening still, given how their markings make for easy camouflage against the desert floor. The poster is the most colorful thing in the hangar aside from the dozens of neon tennis balls that litter the floor. Even coiled in two-dimension renderings, the snakes look malicious—a reminder that there are more than buried explosives training aids to be found in the desert.

But as I walk across the parking lot for the first time at 4:50 a.m., it's dark and cold and the only light shining in the parking lot comes from the open door of the hangar. Marine Sergeant Charlie Hardesty emerges. He's on his way to the training field adjacent to the hangar to join the physical training (PT) course, where the dog teams are already hopping over and under a series of obstacles in full gear, handlers and dogs alike. Hardesty is the lead instructor at the ISAK.

We walk up and down the length of the training field where the March 2012 class of handlers are doing their morning PT. Their faces are obscured by their helmets, and in the dark it's difficult to pick apart the dogs and see which handlers belong with which furry body. There are calls of encouragement, shit talking, and laughter. It's so cold their breath hangs in clouds in front of them.

A chorus of howls sound nearby. They do not belong to the dogs. I glance at Hardesty and he smiles, a wide, mischievous smile. "Yep," he says, reading my mind. "Those would be the coyotes."

The last handlers to go through the course lift their dogs over the practice wall, and the teams head back toward the hangar. By now Knight has arrived, and he and Hardesty stroll together through the parking lot, talking through the plans for the day. Hardesty is on his way to plant explosives for the first tactical training exercise. The sun is starting to rise and with it the temperature. There is a full day ahead for these handlers and their dogs, a day of looking for bombs.

For an instructor who teaches handlers to search for explosives outside the wire, Hardesty is dependably cheerful. Born and raised in a conservative Catholic home on a cattle ranch in Smoot, Wyoming, he possesses a

Sergeant Russ and MWD Uudensi, with spotter Staff Sergeant Joseph Tajeda training at YPG.

certain kind of purity of purpose that, along with the *Leave It to Beaver* way he curses, makes him seem wholesome.

Each afternoon, after the day of tactical training is over, Hardesty stays to work the dogs and the handlers who need (and are willing to accept) the extra help. He does this instead of heading home to tinker with his pickup truck—a rickety vehicle he's taken to calling Betty White because "it's old, it's white, and it just won't die." Like most Marines he doesn't tolerate laziness, and though his patience might fray from time to time, neither the long days nor any amount of poor showing on behalf of the dogs or their handlers dampen his positive attitude. Except for once.

Army Sergeant Dontarie R. Russ and his dog Uudensi, a tawny German shepherd, are running a detection drill with instructor Army Staff Sergeant Lee McCoy. So far this handler has been a standout in the class.

Tactically Russ is tighter than many of the other handlers working through these exercises; he downs to one knee before rounding corners and manages his weapon with experience. On this particular afternoon Russ is doing well. "Fucking awesome," in McCoy's words. But when Uudensi starts to alert on human odor (which in the job of finding explosives counts as a false response[1]), Russ begins to founder. Rather than calling the dog off the distracting scent and moving forward with the search, Russ jerks the leash and gives a flat verbal correction. Uudensi has lost his focus and, ignoring his handler, continues his frantic scratching at the ground.

Hardesty, watching this unfold beside McCoy, steps in. "Be firm, Dad."

Russ attempts to call the dog off again, but the tone of his voice is unchanged. If anything he sounds even less concerned, almost apathetic. In a flash, Hardesty advances fast in Russ's direction, his voice suddenly harsh and loud. His even temper erupts. "We're not fucking around here," he yells. "Call him back like your life depends on it!"

Russ is flummoxed; beads of sweat have taken over his face. When he short arms the Kong throw for his dog a minute later, he gets even angrier at having to retrieve it. Seeing Russ struggle, Hardesty's storm passes as quickly as it broke. Lowering his voice, he coaches the handler through. The command for the dog to "come" needs to be absolute, Hardesty tells him. The dog's urge to respond to his handler has to be stronger than the dog's desire to alert on odor, and stronger even than his desire to get the reward he attaches to alerting on odor. In the heat of the search, when a handler needs to call the dog away from danger, that dog must respond without delay.

I couldn't tell what triggered Hardesty's reaction—maybe he just didn't want to put up with a piss-poor attitude. But Hardesty also knows what's waiting for Russ and Uudensi after they leave Yuma. He knows better than most what happens when you don't keep your eyes open and pay attention.

In retrospect, that painted red rock sitting outside the entrance to the compound was a dead giveaway, but at the time, their team was getting shot at, and in their rush to take cover they hadn't noticed the Taliban's tip-off to the danger inside. Neither Charlie Hardesty nor the British paratroopers he was with had seen that rock for what it was.

The men of this British Air Regiment had begun their mission at dawn. It was January 2010, and the frigid temperature propelled them to move faster across the river that morning, as they made their way through the desolate fields up to the main market some 5 kilometers from their patrol base.

Hardesty and his combat tracker dog Robbie were with them. The dog team had joined this regiment at the start of their deployment, and Hardesty found himself more at home with the Brits. These men had seen their fair share of firefights and were marked by a gritty approach that Hardesty found appealing. That they'd requested a combat tracker dog team—a job that required nerve, a lack of hesitancy, and a willingness to engage in swift-footed manhunts—meant they were willing to take risks.

Today their mission had two parts. The first was to reach out to the Afghans who lived in the area, to find new friends and identify potential enemies. For this they had invited the village elders in the area to a *shura*, a meeting over tea and bread, to discuss news of the Taliban.

The area they were in was wide open and rural, populated by clusters of different compounds; each set of compounds was roughly 200 to 300 meters apart. Intel had gotten back to their unit that there might be Taliban living in one of these compounds. So, while the *shura* continued on, Hardesty and Robbie pushed out with a smaller team under the command of British officer Pete McCombe to patrol the other compounds and complete the second part of their mission.

Earlier in the day they'd seen some children playing outside of a compound, but the inside looked inexplicably quiet, so they marked that as their target and made their way over. But as soon as they started to cross the field in that direction they started taking gunfire. The enemy was stationed somewhere across the field in a neighboring compound; they'd seen the soldiers coming and had no intention of letting them get any closer.

Hardesty and the others started to run, Robbie galloping alongside of them keeping tight to his handler, and they didn't stop until they passed through the open door of that empty compound and out of the range of bullets, taking cover behind its walls.

Once inside, the first priority was figuring out exactly where the enemy was. McCombe yelled to one of the other men to climb up onto the roof of one of the smaller huts. But the guy was having trouble hoisting himself up on top of the wall.

The soldiers always carried a ladder, 30 pounds of collapsible aluminum that they would unfold as a makeshift pathway, enabling them to get across canals and ditches. McCombe started to get pissed and told him to take the "fucking ladder" and tossed it over. But no one caught the ladder; it hit the ground, falling right on top of an IED. The explosion launched the ladder some 40 meters back into the air, a tail stream of shrapnel spray sailing out behind it.

The blast knocked Hardesty to the ground. Rock and debris slapped against his face—and then the lights went out. When he opened his eyes, it took a few minutes for the scene to come back into focus. Whether he was out for seconds or minutes he couldn't tell, but as soon as he came to he knew something was very wrong with his ear. There was no sound coming in on one side; it was completely muffled. All he could think was, *It's gone. It's gone.* He brought his hand up to the side of his face, found his ear intact but touched it over and over anyway, overwhelmed with the sensation that it had somehow detached from his body.

He could tell his dog was still by his side without even having to look. He knew Robbie was staying close to him, he could feel him. The dog had remained relatively calm during the blast but looked up at Hardesty, eyes round and fearful, as if to say, "Holy shit, man. What the hell just happened?"

And that's when his eyes fell on McCombe, who was lying on the ground completely still. The shrapnel had hit him square in the face and made a bloody mess of his eye, knocking him unconscious. Hardesty moved toward him, and as he got closer he could see McCombe's body kick into survival mode—springing back to work on its own before his mind was fully conscious. McCombe drew deep, gut-dragging gasps of air back into his lungs. The medic was instantly at McCombe's side, wrapping the wounds on his face, setting up an IV to give him morphine. But when Mc-Combe finally came to, finding his eyes covered sent him into a panic and he started fighting the hands that were trying to help him.

"I can't see! I can't see!" he shouted and tried to tear the bandages from his face. McCombe had been a boxer back in England, and he was solidly built and strong. It took four men to hold him down, to keep him from fighting the medic off.

Shrapnel had hit Hardesty as well, a few small pieces entering the back of his head, another few under his plate carrier. But with all the chaos and adrenaline he barely noticed. He took a quick few moments and gave Robbie a more thorough check to make sure he wasn't injured. There wasn't any bleeding, nor were there any apparent breaks. The dog had been low enough to the ground that nothing hit him, and while Robbie continued to brave the sounds of the nearby bullets, Hardesty could see the loud noise had unnerved him.

They had called a medevac for McCombe and had started to make a plan for their exit when someone shouted, "Freeze! Freeze! Freeze!"

The blast had shaken the compound and the ground beneath it, shifting the sand. A circular pattern of what looked like another buried explosive revealed itself just behind Hardesty, less than five feet from where he had fallen after the initial explosion. When they ran a metal detector over it, the machine let off a shrill beep: it was another IED.

Outside the firefight still raged, but it was still too dangerous for the unit to remain in the compound where there might be more IEDs. They marked the bomb's position so they could safely avoid it during the evacuation. Some of the guys in their unit went into the field, settling into a ditch to lay down some supporting fire. They yelled back and forth to each other across the field while Hardesty took the metal detector and swept the rest of the compound so the Quick Reaction Force could come in to get McCombe.

It took them nearly a half hour to safely evacuate, after which they had to walk the 5 kilometers back to their operating base. McCombe lost his left eye, and another guy, who was standing just to Hardesty's left when that IED exploded, lost his arm. It would be two weeks before Hardesty got his hearing back.

They would find out later that the explosives had been sitting idle for several weeks. As the ground compacted over time and rain fell in the compound, the earth around the IED had changed its shape. As a result, only 7 of the 20 pounds of buried bomb had blown up, and the blast had exploded straight up, rather than an IED's typical outward-shooting trajectory. If things had gone differently, more than just pieces would have been gone.

You would think having an IED explode in front of him like that, ripping away at his friends, would make a handler hesitant, afraid even, to go back out on patrol. But for Hardesty, it had the opposite effect: "After that I kind of said screw it, 'cause if it's my time to go, it's my time to go. We don't have control over squat. You think you do, but we don't. Tomorrow you could get in a car accident—you're dead. It's that simple, it's that silly, it's that sad and stupid, but that's how fragile life is."

His voice hasn't entirely lost its upbeat turn; it's just quieter and more contemplative. "Crazy stuff happens in combat. You do things and you think to yourself, it's not as simple as being a farm boy from Wyoming anymore."

By the spring of 2012, the marines have reduced their use of the combat tracker dog, and there's only one tracker team coming through Yuma during that March class. Hardesty sets up special drills for this team to train on—their job is much different than a bomb detection team.

Hardesty is standing at the entrance to the "mosque" in the K-9 village, just one of the 90-some-odd structures that make up one of two massive training sites at YPG. The village was originally built and modeled after a satellite image taken of an actual Iraqi village. It is staged with considerable detail for authenticity; the huts are built from organic materials, mud and clay, just as they would be in the combat theater. Inside the village are a wide market lane, a number of alleys and courtyards, and a cluster of huts that forms its own kind of maze. Many of the buildings have two levels with access to their rooftops. In its entirety this training area stretches over nearly 80 acres.

Today Hardesty is going to set a track and then give the handler a mission, a story with all the information that handler will need to pick up that track. That story goes like this: rumors are spreading that locals are cooperating with US forces, alerting them to areas where explosives have been planted. Tension between village leaders and the Taliban is growing. Intel led Marines to find a bomb planted inside the village mosque—thankfully before it detonated—but the insurgent who planted it there escaped undetected. US forces believe that this man has likely taken refuge in a nearby cluster of huts, but the streets are crowded with people, loud with the bustle of the day. The tracker's job is to find him.

I chew on this information and look out over the huts a short distance away. It's time to think like the enemy—which route would he take and where would he hide? I can feel a pair of eyes on me. Hardesty is watching me expectantly. It's me; I'm the insurgent.

In about an hour's time Marine Lance Corporal John W. Peeler and his combat tracker dog Lex will be hunting, or rather tracking, the insurgent—me—down. The task is pretty simple to lay a track, leave a scent on the ground. But there's more to it than just walking from one place to the next. Hardesty wants to make sure Peeler and Lex get to conduct the most realistic search possible—and taking on the mindset of a Taliban insurgent is key. How would this person assess the scene in front of us? How would he navigate the rolling mounds of rocky desert and the cluster of small one-room dwellings made of bleached brick with flat roofs?

Unlike explosives detection, for which a search dog must be able to identify several odors, a combat tracker dog is always following new and different odors. Each track is a new scent, the odor of the suspect they are chasing. It is essentially a fast-moving manhunt in which dog, handler, and the team working with them must stay close together. It's a footprint-to-footprint search in which a team has to abandon whatever abundance of caution they might otherwise consider to push fast and far outside the boundaries of relative safety. This means closing in on the gap between human bodies and unexpected danger—booby traps, trip wires, the enemy lying in wait.

After seeing the success the British were having with their combat tracker teams in their other counterinsurgency efforts in Kenya, Cyprus, Malaya, and Borneo,[2] the United States took interest in the idea. And by 1968 the first ten American tracker teams were sent into Vietnam.[3] The business of tracking is now a sparingly used skill because today's modern warfare has other means of hunting down the enemy—air support, unmanned drones—that are favored over riskier options that stretch manpower thin on the ground.

As we walk, I twist around to see what kind of imprint I'm leaving behind. Far from pressing distinct impressions as you might walking through snow, I can barely make out the pattern of the underside of my shoes, and their markings are faint against the pebbly ground, crossing paths with whoever else has been out where we were. But my track—whether visible or not—is quite strong. Aside from footprints and whatever odor we emanate in our wake, our trail is mostly made up of skin cells. It is a little unsettling to think that we unknowingly cast off epidermal flakes everywhere we go. It's like Hansel and Gretel, only instead of bread crumbs, it's microscopic flesh droppings.

After the track sets, Peeler and Lex walk over the small wooden bridge near the mosque. A Southern boy, with a thready accent to match, born and raised in Blue Ridge, Georgia, Peeler grew up around lots of dogs and horses. He has a fair complexion and soft blue eyes. Somehow the mustache on his face doesn't read ironic or comical. He's only been a handler for about a year and partnered up with Lex for about half that time, but he is completely self-assured when it comes to his dog. One of the course instructors had complained that Peeler was too cocky, but to me his excess of confidence reads more quiet than that. He has a settling of self that makes him, at 24 years old, seem older.

Hardesty feeds Peeler the story about the runaway insurgent and then outlines the objective: find the bomber. Peeler kneels down to Lex and pulls the harness onto his back, a ritualistic preparation that signals to the dog that it's time to go to work, it's time to hunt. The change in Lex is instantaneous; he looks energized, ready to go. Next, Peeler hooks the long leash around the back of his neck, behind his back and under his arms so it rounds to the front. He is wearing gloves and lets the leash slip through his hands as fast as Lex will pull it, lacing it through his loosely closed hand like a zip line, until he decides Lex has gone far enough; then he finally grasps and holds the leash, applying a certain amount of resistance.

It's a technique Hardesty calls opposition reflex, and it's unique to tracking and trail work. Putting tension on the leash, and adding that extra pulling sensation, only fuels the dog's drive to push harder. It's all about the reward; the toy the dog knows is waiting for him at the end of the track. The dog knows from doing this time and time before, Hardesty says, that if he pulls hard enough and smells that odor on the ground long enough, he's going to get his reward.

Unlike in IED detection work, where military handlers have had great success working their dogs off the leash, in combat tracking it's essential that the handler and the dog maintain a taut-leash tension between them. In tracking, Hardesty explains, the amount of odor you're following is very small and is supersensitive. Giving a dog a correction or command at the wrong time could too easily throw the dog off the track.

Peeler begins by scanning the ground and finds his starting point—a spot where I gave a good dig in the ground with my heel. He directs Lex's nose to that spot, and with a perk of his ears the chase is on. Lex's nose is working hard; the sounds of his panting, inhales and exhales, are audible: he is a dog intent, moving with a controlled frenzy. For a tracker dog, Lex has a deliberate style and works at a moderate pace. While Lex ambles a little ways away from the path we tracked, Peeler is looking at the ground, holding his position and only allowing Lex to pull the slack of the leash. A tracker dog handler has to not only focus on his dog, but he must scan for signs of disturbance as well as other clues along the way.

Hardesty and I follow the pair from a distance; I don't want to get too close to the dog so that Lex can focus on the scent trail I've left on the ground. After some fast moving, we make an abrupt stop. Lex lifts his head and Hardesty gives me a nudge. "Dog cast his head up," Hardesty whispers,

Lance Corporal John Peeler and his combat tracker dog Lex at YPG in March 2012.

explaining that this is a sign to the handler that his dog has lost the scent. Peeler peers at the ground hard, and his expression is inscrutable. The ground is a maze of messy earth: each patch looks nearly identical, and if he sees anything noteworthy among the scuffs and pebbles, he doesn't reveal it.

But, as the moments pass, Peeler remains calm and unhurried and pulls Lex back a few feet and to the left, to the last spot where the dog was really pulling him on scent. They hold there, steady almost still for a few breaths, the leash between them taut. Within a few seconds Lex's nose hits the ground and they're back on the move, this time even faster than before.

And Lex doesn't stop moving until we reach the spot where I had kicked out another small divot to mark the end of the track. Hardesty had planted a tennis ball, Lex's reward, on the same spot. Peeler whoops to praise his partner on a job well done, and Lex takes his prize and hunkers down inside one of the small huts out of the sun.

A combat tracker dog handler not only has to put a lot more trust in his dog, but he has to be very knowledgeable about the art of tracking. Before Hardesty's deployment to Afghanistan in 2009 to 2010 with tracker dog Robbie, he took a visual man hunters course as part of his training. He learned that people leave nearly a field guide's worth of information behind them as they move from place to place. All the trained eye of a good tracker needs is a start point; once he has that, he has a good chance of not only finding the individual but sorting out his intentions and his plan of action. Even watching the way a person moves their feet can reveal a telling amount of information about what that individual is going to do before they do it. And if you apply all that observation to terrain in an area where there is no pavement, Hardesty says, "Those tracks, that'll tell a story right there in itself."[4]

The following week, I leave another track across the gravelly Yuma desert, but this time I'm walking by myself. There's no dog following me. Instead, I'm following the dogs. When the sandy path gives way to a paved road, finally the steps come faster, easier. The only thing behind me is a big white pickup truck driven by the veterinary technician assigned to the night's ruck march. In the truck, Captain John Brandon Bowe is riding shotgun. That I am still somehow ahead of the truck is nothing to be proud of; it's their job to keep up the rear in case any of the dogs (or handlers) are injured or become too fatigued to finish out the eight-mile ruck march. If anything, I am the reason they are going so slow.

They pull up alongside me. Bowe, a Marine and executive officer of the Military Police Instruction Company and the ISAK course's school director, leans out the open window and calls over to ask me how I'm doing. "You know," he says, his eyebrows crooked with concern, "I won't think any less of you if you don't do it." We are barely 20 minutes into the ruck. There's miles of tougher ground still to cover, including the incline leading to the tower, the site that marks the midway point. At the top of the hill the teams will break for a short rest and the handlers will water the dogs, take their temperatures, and collectively catch their breath.

I feel the sweat trickling down my back and chest. I look at the backseat; it's empty, inviting, air-conditioned. My fingers are cramping but I tighten them around the big red gun in my hands and shake my head, declining the captain's offer. He gives me a dubious look but assents and I push ahead of them on the road, willing my unwilling muscles to put some distance between us.

At least Staff Sergeant Christopher Keilman was rooting for me. "You tell them to go fuck off," he'd said earlier, when a couple of the course instructors had joked that I wouldn't make it through the first mile. An Air Force handler and instructor for the ISAK course, Keilman has dark hair and a lean frame, serious and sincere. I felt grateful that his upbeat attitude was contagious.

This evening kicks off with the big ruck that would lead straight into the K-9 village, which is when the nighttime mission—meant to be as close to the soon-to-be-very-real assignments these dog teams would be assigned downrange—would begin. It was the second night of "nights," the third and final week of the ISAK course when training begins every day just before sundown. Tonight would also be the last night of "hand-holding" before the students and dogs would run drills without the instructors walking alongside them—when they were to be tested and evaluated on all they have learned.

When, a week before, one of the instructors had asked me if I planned to go on the night march with them, I'd said yes. It was Keilman who took that opportunity to press me further to see if I'd "gear up" with them as well. I hesitated for the briefest of moments, knowing there was only one answer I could give. "That's fuckin' badass, man." He whooped at this. "Hey, yo," he called out to the other instructors, letting them know I was "gonna kit up and do the ruck." There was an exchange of raised eyebrows.

Keilman helped get me into the gear, tightening the Velcro shoulder straps of the Kevlar vest while also cinching the ones that wrapped around my rib cage, trying to get the snuggest fit he could manage. He apologized when it still brushed so low it tapped against my hipbone. (The plate carrier, which belonged to a male instructor, weighs somewhere between 15 and 20 pounds.) I can still fit my backpack over the vest, which contains, among other things, my notebooks, warmer layers (layers I would have no need for), and four bottles of cold water (weighing around 12 pounds). Next Keilman handed me the red rubber training rifle (solid and heavy, it weighs roughly seven pounds); shaking his head, he quickly corrected my instinct to keep my fingers hovering over the trigger. Apparently, this was bad. When I relaxed my arms and let the rifle go slack, allowing it to point downward at my toes, he scolded me. "You can't let it hang down," he warned. This was also bad, as it increased the likelihood that, were this a real gun with real bullets, I might quite literally shoot myself in the foot. "You have to keep your weapon at the ready," he said pulling the gun's barrel upward. I adjusted my grip to keep it straight, my forearms instantly twitching.

After doubling up some of the magazine clips on my vest, Keilman took a step back to look me over and, seeing no other room for improvement, shrugged and hopped off to join the other instructors who were already outside. His pep talk and show of solidarity had been fortifying but brief.

Outside the dogs were fidgety while their handlers tugged on leashes to keep their line formation. The teams stood in two rows flanking the left and right of the road. Each dog team had to keep a distance from the team ahead of them—about six feet or so—as the dogs need their space from one another, mostly to keep the more aggressive dogs from fighting. Some had their muzzles on. There had been a couple of dogs struggling during the course and I pick them out—MWDs Jeny, Jessy, and Turbo—knowing watchful eyes would be swept in their direction all night. Everyone was in full gear, an expectant energy prickled in the air, boots shuffled, the dogs were twisting, ready to move. Finally, Tech Sergeant Justin Kitts shouted over the din of low chatter and the jostling gear: the ruck had begun.

And then I begin to feel the actual weight of what I am doing—it's as if the vest and backpack are straining to meet the ground, threatening to take me with them. All together I'm still only carrying about half the weight the handlers are—their packs and plate carriers average around 70 pounds, bearing extra water for their dogs, who are attached to their handlers' sides by the leashes they keep strapped to their waist. The troop is moving at a rigorous clip, a speed that, even without the gear, would have registered for me as a steady jog.

I stop to adjust the straps on my pack and look up. I'm alone and already trailing behind.

About an hour into the march, modest relief comes on a teasing breeze, one that promises that a more temperate night is on the way. A good sign for everyone, including the dogs, as many of them, whose home stations are in cooler or more humid climates, are unaccustomed to steady exercise in such dry heat. Kitts is even hoping for rain. But after tonight, after Yuma, steady heat is what awaits these teams in Afghanistan or Iraq. Up ahead the sky is turning a buttery orange; the silhouettes of the handlers and their dogs blacken against the horizon, moving like upright shadows.

Keeping a brisk pace behind the last handler, Knight has brought along his dog Max, a Belgian Malinois puppy he's training privately. Max is tireless, tenacious, and a favorite playmate of all the instructors. He noses his way into the classroom during briefings to drop a slobbery tennis ball on unsuspecting laps, poised for the chase. While the other dogs are in work mode tonight, focused and marching in synch with their handlers, Max is off his leash and bounds ahead of Knight, dipping on and off the road, his big ears flopping out of rhythm with his wild, young-dog energy.

"Look at him," Knight calls over, unabashedly proud of his rambunctious charge. "He could do this whole march at that pace and *still* not be tired."

Knight's deep baritone rings in the space between us. At 40, he is barrel chested and gives off an air of impenetrability, projecting the very essence of the prototypical, badass Marine. It's a deadly kind of calm that smacks

*Marine Gunnery Sergeant Kristopher Reed Knight wrestles with Max, a
Belgian Malinois puppy in March 2012.*

of testosterone and is communicated more with the look of his dark eyes.
Though he doesn't say so, I suspect Knight is walking the eight-mile ruck
with Max tonight to keep an eye on me. A thought that comforts and
slightly alarms me.

When I had first arrived in Yuma, I'd called Knight from my hotel
room. It took a few minutes before I was convinced that he'd still been
expecting me; after giving me a flat "Yeah, okay," he went directly into fast
and to-the-point directions. When I started to say my good-byes he cut me
off to ask what kind of cell service I had. I named my provider and he made
a snorting sound. "Yeah, you won't get shit for reception out here," he told

me. I pointed out there wasn't much I could do about that. "Well," he said. "Don't get lost." And then he hung up.

Knight does not have a reputation for being a warm, fuzzy type. He's known instead for the lengths he'll take to enforce his high, uncompromising standards. Before arriving in Yuma, I'd heard a story about a handler from Buckley Air Force Base who'd had orders to fill an instructor position out at Yuma under Knight's command. But when he had found out that she had no outside-the-wire experience, he called her and told her not to bother coming. In his mind, without having done it herself, she couldn't offer anything worthwhile to handlers on their way to war and therefore was no use to him. Supposedly the movers had been there at her house, packing her stuff while this conversation took place, but it hadn't mattered. He didn't want her, so she wasn't coming.

He's not Jewish, but Knight wears a Star of David on a thick gold chain around his neck. He met his wife while he was training dogs with the Israel Defense Forces in Israel in 2006. He loved Israel and loved the handlers he worked with there, loved the way they handled their dogs.

Knight was raised on the outer cusp of a wealthy suburb of Cincinnati. His father was white, "a redneck" who drank too much, so Knight lived much of his childhood being raised by his black mother's parents. Knight adored his grandfather, a generous and patient man who taught his grandson the value of self-reliance, a quality that Knight has cultivated in himself to an almost obsessive end.

If there's one person I don't want to see me struggle through this march, it's Knight. Right after I put on the gear, he'd passed me in the hangar and watched me pop a stick of gum into my mouth. "Huh," he smirked. "That gum's not gonna save you."

But now that we're moving, Knight is my only company. He shouts again for Max, who, like a tiny gazelle, pops back into sight from behind a sloping mound of sand, his pink tongue flapping out of his mouth to the side, his eyes alight with adventure.

When Knight deployed to Afghanistan in 2009 with his dog Brahm, he was the senior officer in charge of three other Marine dog teams—another

Specialized Search Dog team, a combat tracker team, and a Patrol Explosive Detection Dog (PEDD) team. He and his fellow handlers had been called out on a mission to Forward Operating Base (FOB) Castle in Khan Neshin, Afghanistan, located about 150 kilometers south of Camp Leatherneck, in Helmand Province.

After they'd been on-site for days and had yet to be assigned any missions, Knight had begun to wonder what the hell they were doing out there. He remembers that during the day, the temperature was so high, holding out his hand into the sun was like sticking it directly into a hot oven.

Frustrations had been building, and not just because of the baking temperature. Knight had already had trouble getting enough water for their dogs from Command, and there was no air-conditioning or special shelter for their use. Instead the handlers had to get creative about how to keep their dogs from overheating. There had been so little shade that the men had dug holes in the ground under their own cots so the dogs could try to keep as cool as possible.

On one afternoon, around midday, a young lieutenant runner jogged over to where the canine unit had been setting up their gear. He told Knight that he and another handler would need to pack up everything and be ready to leave with a convoy in 30 minutes.

"Well," Knight told him, looking around at all the stuff they came with, "we've got quite a bit of gear here. Where are we going?"

But the younger officer had no answer. Knight suggested that he find out. The lieutenant made a call. "You'll find out when you get there. It's need to know," he told Knight. No mission had been discussed at their early morning meeting and the request had come with almost no detail, not where they were going or for how long. Given the hour, it was already too hot to work the dogs. It wasn't quite noon and the temperature was already approaching 130 degrees. The dogs were panting, salivating around their mouths. The heat in the air was deadly.

So without more information Knight refused to budge. And, after another series of back-and-forth that included speaking to the lieutenant

himself and a strong attempt to convey that his need to know was a matter
of safety for his dogs, the reply had been the same: no further information.

That wasn't good enough for Knight. He told them he wouldn't be going and that none of his men or their dogs would be moving either.

His rebuff had not gone over well and it prompted the major, whose
orders Knight had just refused, to come out to confront the dog teams himself. A heated confrontation ensued and escalated until, finally, the major
was shouting at Knight through an open window of a vehicle.

As he stood there and listened, Knight had prayed that this man would
actually come out of the vehicle, that he would put his hands on him and
initiate physical contact, because at that point all Knight wanted to do was
snap his neck.

In the end the confrontation was venomous but contained, and afterward the major sent over two officers who read Knight his rights for
refusing a mission in a combat zone and for disrespecting an officer. Knight
signed the statement, though nothing ever officially came of it. After that he
called for a flight off the FOB. Before the whole episode was over, a lieutenant colonel finally got involved and tried to diffuse the situation. He had
asked Knight to stay with his dog teams, but Knight declined.

It took four days for their ride to come and collect Knight and his dog
teams, and they sat, stagnant and disconnected from everyone else on the
FOB. They had become pariahs. When the bird landed, they had to pick
up and carry all the gear they'd brought—a month's supply for the four handlers and their dogs—the 400 meters to where the helicopter was waiting
in the dark. They were not permitted to put lights on, so they had to move
everything in the pitch black. No one helped them. Knight bit his lip, did
not complain, and they left.

The way Knight remembers it, after they left with their dogs, that same
unit would suffer a lot of casualties during the war. But, he says, those guys
were a bunch of cowboys, guys who didn't want to listen to reason, guys
who didn't even try to work with his team or his dogs.

As far as Knight was concerned, shame on them.

"You ready for this?" Knight asks me with his sly-dog grin.

I don't know what you would call it—a hill, a modest incline—but as the midway point of the ruck comes into view all I can see is a mountain, a big, insurmountable rise in the earth coated in slippery pebbles and loose sand. I watch a couple of handlers shoot up to the top, pushing themselves through the worst of the steep, their dogs panting but bullying their way up alongside them. No one falls down. I'm in no hurry to be the first. I just shake my head in Knight's direction as we take the first few steps and try to laugh as if I am having the time of my life, but I am breathing so hard the noise I let loose sounds more like a horse choking.

"Here," Knight says, holding out Max's leash. The young buck of a puppy is making wheezing sounds similar to my own, but unlike me he's actually yanking hard to race to the top. I cannot keep pace with this dog. I shake my head again. I am starting to question Knight's motives, wondering if the instructors had taken bets on when I'll pass out and we'd just hit his payout mark.

But Knight won't let it go: he puts the leash in my hand and pushes my shoulder. "Lean back," he tells me in a low voice. And suddenly my addled brain catches on—Max, beautiful, inexhaustible Max, so desperate to get to the other dogs, is going to pull me with the force of a tractor-trailer all the way to the top. I use my weight to counterbalance his tugging and all I have to do is hang on and lift my feet. We smoke past the other teams trudging their way up the hill on either side, hurdling with the grace of a tiny tornado through the middle of the road.

At the top of the hill the handlers have broken off into separate pairs, maintaining a few feet of modest but necessary distance while they rest. The group is quiet for once, and it feels symbolic to see them joined not en masse, but each handler with his or her dog, just as they would be on a mission, a team of two. Staff Sergeant Robert Wilson kneels in front of his dog Troll, taking his temperature while Bowe looks on. Peeler is sitting on the ground, his pack slumped up behind him still strapped onto his shoulders, and he leans back into it, his weapon flat across his bent knees. Lex is on the ground by his ankles, the sides of his body moving as he takes in each deep, rapid breath. Lance Corporal Eddie Garcia is about two yards down the slope from Peeler, his dog Lubus curled on his side against him. Lance Corporal Joshua Ashley is one of the few still on his feet, standing to the left of the truck; he's holding his gun at the ready. His dog Sirius has taken position by Ashley's boots. Hardesty and McCoy make the rounds and check in on the dogs, watching the handlers as they take rectal temperatures of their dogs, water them down and bring them in turn to the orange coolers placed around them for a nice, long drink. Most everyone keeps on his gear.

And then the day is gone. The sunset's blushing oranges have burned down into the horizon and a dusky purple rises to color the sky. My eyes adjust to the dark as the chem sticks that each handler has put on his back, or has tied to the bottom of his helmet, begin their neon glow. The break is over, the ruck is back on.

Packs lift and the descent begins. Max's leash stays with Knight; our trick to get me to the top won't work the same on the way down. The dogs don't seem to have any trouble picking their way along the slant of the hill. I watch the camo-clad legs of the handlers and copy their side-to-side steps, trying to grip the hill with the bottoms of my feet.

From the base of the hill the dog teams start the walk back to the K-9 village. My bones and joints are already protesting the movement. I hope for numbness. While we walk one of the dogs defecates, and the smell smacks into us, overwhelming as it lingers on the air.

"That's one thing I'll never get used to," Knight says, shaking his head hard as if he can forcibly toss the stink of it from his nose. His eyes are watering. There's little in life that bothers him, but that smell is one of them. That, he says, and seeing small children get hurt. Something he saw too much of in Iraq. While he had been on tour, an Iraqi man had brought his young son in for emergency treatment. They'd been riding on the man's motorcycle and the small boy had tumbled off as they were driving. When Knight had seen the boy, his body was lifeless, his face drained of color, and the blood gushed from his head. Knight said he could barely stand to look at him.

Behind the braying bravado, the crass jokes, and the don't-fuck-with-me eyes, Knight is a man who cares deeply about what he does. Almost a month after the night of the ruck march, Knight would find out that the Air Force intended to start its own advanced course and would be pulling not only its students from the ISAK program, but also its instructors from the course. That meant Knight would lose Staff Sergeant Philip Mendoza, Kitts, and Keilman all at once. On top of this news, other changes were weighing on his mind—pending budget cuts loomed over the whole of the Marine Corps, threatening the ISAK course's funding. That night in April he calls me from his car while he waits for the new class to finish up their ruck. Our conversation rounds a corner, and it is like a tight coil inside of Knight springs out of shape, launching, directionless.

He is sick of others in his field doing the bare minimum, the people who just put checks in boxes. The only ones who get hurt are the handlers, kids he says that, without the proper training, will be sent to fight a war, to offer a service they're not capable of delivering. To him it's like using a weapon that's missing parts, or a gun without any bullets. Knight's voice grows louder and louder, angrier and angrier. "We're just going to send them into the wind and pray it doesn't come back on us. That's not the right way to do it."

The overflow of his frustration has something underneath it—not weakness exactly, but something more straining. It feels like helplessness.

"If the fucking mothers of America knew what their kids were over there trying to do, running at half speed at best, looking for 40-pound and 200-pound bombs," he said, "they'd be disgusted. They'd break their own kids' leg so they couldn't go."[5]

At the end of the ruck march, the instructors stand together behind the open doors of their trucks and the golf carts that everyone calls gators parked at the edge of the K-9 village. They are waiting for the dog teams to get ready for the night's "missions"—the drills that will extend well into the morning hours. The taillights and the glow from the car interiors cast a hazy, purplish pale over them, and I can make out the approving grins that meet me as I limp my way over to them. Keilman asks me how I feel.

My bones ache. My knees, which have been reduced to unsteady knots, wobble, and my shoulders scream for mercy—it's like the places where my joints ought to meet no longer want to hold together. But my face stretches into a smile so big it is beyond my control. Keilman smiles back and tells me he's proud, raising his hand to give me a high five.

Knight and Max are waiting for me to walk the final yards—about the length of a football field—back to the hangar. But in a moment of adrenaline-fueled mania, I offer to take Hardesty's pack up to the office for him. As he helps hoist his 70-pound rucksack over my much smaller backpack, I teeter, my hips nearly giving out. But I smile the smile of delirious triumph and suck whatever air I am able to harness into my lungs. I can do this, too, I tell myself. By the time I make it over to Knight I know I've made a terrible mistake. After taking one look at me he knows it too, and pulls the pack off my shoulders and carries it the rest of the way.

There is one phrase a handler must know forward and backward. It is as much a mantra as it is an instruction. "Where I go, my dog goes. Where my dog goes, I go."

This is the line Staff Sergeant William Stone repeats as he delivers his Spotter's Brief to McCoy. Stone says this part fast, rushing the words that culminate in one of the most important things he will communicate to a commanding officer before a mission. (They teach the handy acronym YMCA—You, Me, and Course of Action.) It's a monologue the handlers have rehearsed endlessly these last few days at ISAK. The message is: See this dog here with me? We are not to be separated.

This is followed by instructions on how to handle the dog—if the dog is a biter, if he is protective of his handler—as well as the location of the Kong and the muzzle the handler carries on him at all times. Handlers also carry a card that they give to the medic before a mission. It lists basic emergency care for anyone who might be able to administer life-saving measures if the dogs are injured downrange. Things that even a medic might not know, like, for example, that dogs require more morphine than humans.[6]

Stone is about to patrol the market lane in the ISAK's K-9 village. The dog teams only have a few days left at Yuma, and the following evening they will begin the course's final exams, or FINEX. Earlier that evening I'd walked the dusty market lane with McCoy and he showed me where he'd set up the plants. "Tonight's the rude awakening," McCoy says.

It is the last night for practice, the last night to make mistakes. The instructors have purposely set the teams up for failure, giving them more difficult exercises to jar the handlers out of bad habits and complacency.

At one of the huts, McCoy has set up a trip wire drawn loosely along the base of the wooden doorframe. It is so menacingly obscure it all but disappears in the darkness. And while the teams won't encounter a trip wire during FINEX, if they pay attention and use what the instructors will show them tonight, they should easily deal with the tests during FINEX. McCoy steps back and looks at the wire, crossing his arms. He knows this is still the crawl phase for the handlers, but tomorrow, he says, they'll be running.

In the Urzugan Province of Afghanistan there is a ten-mile-long thoroughfare known rather notoriously as IED Alley. During McCoy's deployment to Afghanistan with his Specialized Search Dog Spalding, a chocolate lab, they had regularly patrolled IED Alley.[7] One day, after they received reports that there were IEDs on the road ahead, McCoy and Spalding pushed out and started doing a search with the Afghan National Army guards working with them. After a while McCoy saw that the dog was tired and needed a rest. No sooner had he grabbed Spalding and turned away than a bomb blew up. The blast knocked McCoy clear off his feet and Spalding onto his side. They'd been only 20 feet from the explosion.

McCoy has a vague and throaty southern accent and a very deep tan. He's a little older than the other instructors, and when McCoy expends his advice to the handlers, he does it in a fatherly kind of way, stern and soft altogether. He's eager to show every intricate part, to make sure they understand exactly how it all works—the wires, the proper way to enter and exit a building, how not to get lost in cordon search or in the maze of the K-9 village's alleyways.

For the night missions the handlers are using NVGs (night vision goggles). The handlers have theirs clipped to their helmets. Hardesty shows them how to balance them over their helmets, weighing them down with batteries to keep them from sliding out of place. The NVGs are small and black, essentially half a pair of binoculars. The flap around the eyehole is malleable, soft black rubber, and it closes out all the light. After a few blinks a fuzzy picture comes into view, in which everything is colored in varying greens: shades of neon lemon and lime.

It's one thing to see through NVGs, it's another to actually know how to use them. It's McCoy who takes the time to demonstrate how to adjust them and pick out the trip wire. At first it's barely visible; it lies flat in the dark. If you didn't know it was already there, the wire would be nearly impossible to see. But with a twist of one of the filters and a push of the infrared button, the wire pops into view, glowing white hot, like a thin thread of crackling electricity. There is no way anyone could miss it. It feels like magic, a secret defense like Superman's X-ray vision—the ability to unveil otherwise invisible dangers.

But that wire in McCoy's lane nails almost all the teams that come through that night, and they all have their NVGs. Lance Corporal Phil Beauchamp, a young Marine from Walnut Creek, California, later admits that it was in McCoy's lane where he had problems.

Loud music blasted from the intercom system throughout the village, and there was a bonfire raging in an oil drum, with its flames blazing more than ten feet into the air. The blast simulator, rocketing off the noise of erupting mortar shells, sounded constantly. This combined chaos was designed specifically for this night of training. It created an added layer of stress that threw Beauchamp off. He sighs and says he "died" twice within five minutes. He kind of laughs and when he does, his cheeks pull up and the thin wisp of a mustache bristles above his lip.

That night though, he and his dog lost their groove. "My dog was pissing me off, and I was getting pissed off. As soon as you lose your attitude everything goes downhill. And the dog loses his attitude, too, when you lose yours. And I believe in that," he says, his brown eyes serious. "You know, everything that you feel the dog feels."

Lance Corporal Phil Beauchamp and his MWD Endy at YPG in March 2012.

They were doing pretty well until McCoy's lane, but after that trip wire, Beauchamp got frustrated and just lost it.

But just like McCoy said, failing this time is the whole idea.

Few of the handlers coming through Yuma arrive ready to hit the ground running—neither do their dogs. Some of them have deployed before, but others are new handlers, some of them just a couple of months out of Dog Training School. Some haven't picked up a weapon, a real weapon, since basic training; others have never even held NVGs before, let alone been trained on how to use them properly. They're meant to learn it all here in three weeks.

And they are meant to make mistakes. The handlers' frustration during drills is palpable, and there is a lot more than tactical training going on. The instructors are imparting life lessons in the most base sense of the word: humility in the face of failure; lessons on patience and tolerance; how to accept that some things cannot be rushed; how to accept that it might be your time; how to not be so afraid of getting hurt or dying that you worry yourself into failure when failure is not an option. If you fail, they teach, you die. And if it's not your time then, well, you still could be risking the lives of the people following behind you—the people who trust that when you say it's safe, that it is truly safe to walk this road.

McCoy, Keilman, and Hardesty take the time to coach each frustrated handler, especially the handlers who take out these frustrations on their dogs. There is no room for this. Stay positive, stay gentle, stay patient. Do not rush. Do not breach doorways. Do not let your dog breach doorways. Each time a handler crosses that threshold and trips the wire, McCoy presses them as to why they were moving so fast. Were you given a time limit? he asks. Their answer is always no.

Which is what McCoy asks Stone, when he and his dog Atos go through the lane and set off the trip wire. Take your time, McCoy tells him. But Stone seems unconvinced. "Even if we're in a hard knock?" he wants to know.

McCoy is adamant. Even in a hard knock, he tells Stone. Even, he says, if there's all types of crazy shit going on, you—the handler—have to be firm and careful. You have to do a thorough search before crossing any door seams.

"Yes, sir. I'm not gonna die anymore," Stone says, making a stab at self-deprecating humor. But as far as McCoy is concerned there isn't any room for jokes. He tells Stone a story about what happened to six men from the 1st Battalion, 75th Ranger Regiment when he was with them in Afghanistan. The regiment didn't want to use the dog guys. And one day, when they came under enemy attack, these six soldiers ran into a building. They made it over the first threshold, he says, but the second threshold had a trip wire. All six were buried alive. All six died.

Stone is reinvigorated, ready to go again, and gives McCoy a loud, firm "Yes, sir!" before he and Atos move forward onto the next section of the lane. McCoy instructs him to clear the building while skipping the courtyard, then to come out, hook left, and clear the left side of the lane. As Stone searches, it's clear he's taken McCoy's words to heart. There are the sounds of a washing machine door banging and the clamor of the dog's nails scraping the wall as he sniffs high toward the ceiling. They are in this part of the lane for a long time, which doesn't upset McCoy. But when Stone breezes through a corner, he stops the handler. Clearing a corner should be simple and methodic—high, low, square, deep—he tells Stone, that way you don't miss anything. If Stone had taken the time to do this, he would've had the find even faster. McCoy shakes his head. A lot of people try to do short cuts, he says, "and short cuts get people killed."

Despite the many likely hazards waiting for them in a war-zone, most of these handlers are excited to get downrange. Some are at the beginning—their next deployment will be their first deployment, while others are on their second or third. Still others have deployed as many as six times. The high number is surprising, especially given how young they are. If they aren't actively excited to go back, then they don't seem to mind it. If they've been to Iraq, they're looking forward to a tour in Afghanistan. They want to go.

The reason why so many of handlers join up in the first place varies. A lot of them cite 9/11 or talk about doing their patriotic part, serving their country. Others have relatives, fathers or grandfathers, who served, and they're just following in step with a family legacy. For others still, reaching the combat theater promises a more complete sense of purpose—it is the place where they can put into practice all their training, all their hard work with their dogs. Many of them don't want assignments working base patrol—manning military base entry and exit points, or conducting traffic checks. As far as they're concerned, these jobs are rote, boring. As far as they're concerned, these jobs aren't the fucking point.

Keilman did his stint as a handler in Afghanistan, and he hadn't liked the country or the culture; he hadn't found any beauty in the landscape. His seven months were all with the same Special Forces team. For most of the time he was there, he and his team lived without air-conditioning or

regular showers. He said they were constantly locking horns with their partner force and working with Afghans whom he felt had not just resented, but
hated them. Still, he smiles when he talks about it. The guys he was with
made the difference to him. They became his family. "Some of the worst
times are the best," he says.

Combat has its own intoxicating allure; battlegrounds are their own
kind of conquerable new frontier. It's an idea that journalist Sebastian
Junger comes back to many times in his book *War*. "War is a lot of things,"
he writes, "and it's useless to pretend that exciting isn't one of them. It's
insanely exciting."[8]

For handlers the draw of deployment holds more than just the satisfaction of seeing through a successful mission with your dog, or saving lives—
combat zone life is a rush. After Lance Corporal Joshua Ashley and Sirius
arrived in Afghanistan, Ashley would tell his older brother that going out
on a mission was the best adrenaline high he'd ever had.

The intoxicating thrills of war aside, going downrange is the most in-
tensely intimate time there is for a K-9 team. Combat-experienced handlers
like Knight say it's the best time for the dogs, because they're with their
handler upward of 20 hours a day. And it's the best time for a handler to
learn everything he can about the dog.

Even Chris Jakubin, who never deployed to a combat zone or worked
outside the wire in either Iraq or Afghanistan, admits that he has mixed
feelings of gratitude and envy when he thinks about what it would have
been like if he had deployed to war. When he talks about this hole in his
otherwise vastly extensive dog-handling experience, his voice is regretful,
even as he acknowledges that it may well have been a blessing.

Kitts describes being downrange with Dyngo as unlike anything he's
experienced on assignments here in the States. It's where the trust a handler
has in his dog is truly tested. By the time a team finishes all their training
and gets downrange, the handler has to have confidence that his dog can
and will find explosives. He has to trust his dog with his life. To walk outside the wire without that mentality could easily thwart a handler's chance
of surviving. He remembers the first time he went outside the wire, the

very first step. His stomach was full of butterflies, but for him it was like stepping out onto a sports field. Once he and Dyngo started working, everything fell into place and the nerves died down.

But inevitably doubt can creep in and take hold of a handler. Knight says he's had students who've come to him to express fear about deploying, fear about being blown up. But there is no room for doubt with this job, Knight says, and what he tells them is: "Don't cry to me about it."

Hardesty more readily admits that theirs is a daunting job. And a little bit of fear, he says, is healthy. But he agrees that if a handler is just straight scared, it isn't the job for him. A handler leading a patrol has to be mindful of his job and all the responsibility that comes with it. A handler has to accept that when he and his dog clear a path, there are lives on the line. "It's not about you," Hardesty says. "It's the guys coming up behind you. You're leading the way. You're the one making it clear or safe for everybody else to travel. That's a huge responsibility. If you aren't humble and honest with yourself and what you're really capable of, then you need to get the hell out of the way and let somebody else do it."

Sometime in the wee hours of that March morning, after the ruck, after the missions and hours of chaos in the K-9 village is nearly finished, the EOD crew comes around to collect and lock away the explosive materials, their headlights cutting through the black. After a night of dark, the white streams of light are blinding. Somehow I feel wide awake. Hardesty and Kitts stand around waiting for EOD to wrap up, playing songs from their cell phones, faces lit with incandescent blues and whites. Hardesty plays a twangy Johnny Cash song and I hold up my iPhone, offering Bob Dylan's "Girl From the North Country," the version he recorded with Cash in 1969. Compared to the dizzying music and the simulated noise of AK-47s and RPG blasts that have been sounding all night, this melody is oddly jarring. Hardesty smiles at the sound of it, nodding his approval. The voices—Dylan's young and sweet, Cash's deep and aching against the strum of guitars—fill the space around us.

The song breaks and then lifts the night of war practice hovering in the air—the shouting, the rushing of bodies, the adrenaline. I feel suspended between worlds, between the green halo of NVGs that still clot my vision when I blink and the cars that would deliver us home parked just a few hundred yards away. The sensation fades further as embers in the oil barrel die out, but the reality of what this preparation was all for, that place they'd all be going, is palpable. Tonight that distance between here and there was pulled in closer, tightened like a stitch along a loose-fitting seam. Yuma is the place between places, somewhere between here and war.

A satellite image fills the screen at the front of the room. The map is colored in shades of slate browns and grays; the higher land is darker and stands out like veins on the underside of a leaf. There are red dots on the image, marking places of significance: rallying points, targets, and safe houses.

Hardesty is in front of the classroom at the podium. He's giving the group orders for the night's mission. It's approximately one klick long, and each dog team will have an hour to carry out their task. In between the scripted instructions Hardesty interjects little reminders—check the wind, he tells them, and the ambient temperature.

"What happens when the temperature gets warmer?" he queries the group, but then answers it for them. "The odor spreads out. The colder?" he asks. "Depending on the wind, you could be 100 meters from odor tonight," Hardesty tells them as he looks around the room. But then he smiles at them. "It's gonna blow your mind."

Tonight the teams are only to use white light inside the buildings. If they turn on their lights outside he warns them they're going to light it up like a Christmas tree. These handlers have to get used to working in the dark with their NVGs, and they have to learn how to maneuver comfortably with their dogs when there is no light.

"What happens when you are in a unit that says no white lights?" This time Hardesty scans the room expectantly; he wants an answer.

"You're screwed," Beauchamp says from his spot in the back with the rest of the Marines from II Marine Expeditionary (MEF) based at Camp Lejeune in North Carolina. This group of Marines—Ashley, Peeler, Beauchamp, and Garcia, having all come from Lejeune together—is the most colorful and raucous of the bunch. They're always laughing, joking, giving a play-by-play of their weekend, pieces of what they remember after a night of heavy drinking.

Hardesty fixes them with a hard look. "What are you going to do?" he repeats. No one speaks out of turn this time. "Adapt and overcome," Hardesty says. "Right, guys?" Then he warns them to be careful working the dogs off leash; there will be donkeys and coyotes roaming the area tonight.

There's a graveyard marked on the laminated map being passed around the room. Master-at-Arms Seaman Raymond Jones, the youngest handler to come through the March course at YPG, has been peering at the map with rapt attention. He's not only young, but he looks it too, with a string-bean frame. Hardesty mentions the graveyard again and Jones's face blanches; he asks, probably without thinking, "Is that a real graveyard, a real one?"

Hardesty rolls his eyes—the "graves" are built out of plastic, nothing more than overturned kiddy pools. But he is deadpan. "Yes, that's where we take all the teams that fail." Everyone laughs, and Jones looks embarrassed but somehow still unconvinced. I wouldn't realize until later, months later, the double meaning in Hardesty's joke. I don't think any of us did.

In the constellation Canis Major you will find Sirius, the dog star. It is the brightest of all the stars in the night sky. The ancient Egyptians tracked the Dog Star, using its position to determine the rising of the Nile so that each year they would know when it was time to seek shelter on higher ground.[9] It is fitting, then, that on this mission into the desert, I will be following Ashley and his dog Sirius. It is the last night of nights at Yuma.

The air is warm, balmy even. When he's clear on his instructions, Ashley begins by giving his pre-mission brief to Kitts and McCoy. He tells them his call sign is going to be "Shrek," and Beauchamp, who is acting as Ashley's spotter, chimes in with his chosen sign, "Gingerbread Man." (He briefly considers but ultimately decides against using "Donkey.") Sirius stands close to Ashley, looking up at the cab of the SUV as if he's listening to all of this, and then out again into the distance as if he's assessing their target from here. I hear my name and realize I will also be assigned a call sign—"Princess Fiona." Tonight I am a part of this unit.

And tonight all bets are off. It's FINEX, final exams, for the dog teams; all the work of the last three weeks is about to be tested. Instructors are observing from a distance and communicating only through walkie-talkies. Kitts drives the truck and McCoy rides shotgun, filling out the FINEX evaluation sheets on a metal clipboard. Hardesty sits in the back. The air in the car is a jiggling mix of something like parental anticipation, confined frustration, and midsummer-night mischief. Sitting in the car for eight hours observing from a distance is proving tedious. The instructors are wound up; there's more than a passing grade on the line tonight.

These are the last hours they will have with their students, the last time they can impart any lessons to them, the last hours in which to convey helpful instruction—to say the thing that might stick, the thing that might keep them from getting blown up. Tomorrow they have to let them go, and away they will go to the real thing. Someone else will have planted bricks of C-4 just like the ones stacked behind a wooden board in a hut in the palm grove—except finding them won't be an exercise for the dog teams; it will be life or death.

Ashley, Sirius, Beauchamp, and I set off, taking the road that leads away from the kennels. All the lights across the area have been cut specifically for tonight—a mandatory blackout. This means no headlights on cars, no white lights of any kind allowed in the vicinity. Again Yuma's night sky is flush with stars, and again somehow the moon is out of sight, nowhere to be found. I'm beginning to wonder if Yuma has no moon. Ashley sets a confident pace. He, Sirius, and Beauchamp are moving quickly, talking their way through the path ahead, deciding which route to take from the road up into the palm grove that we are meant to search. They are both using their NVGs. I hold mine tightly in my hand but I'm reluctant to use them.

Instead I train my eyes on their feet, watching the heels of their boots so I can follow their exact steps rather than forge my own route.

I've decided to shadow Ashley and Sirius in part because I've kept close watch on their tactical training throughout the course, but also because I trust, from what I've seen so far, that Ashley will do a good job. We won't, for example, spend 20 minutes heading in the wrong direction (as one team does), and I'm certain my presence won't ruffle him. Ashley's self-assuredness is evident and is so seemingly unshakable it borders on arrogance. And I choose to follow them because I know, with Beauchamp as his spotter, this team of three will be fun.

The palm grove comes into view, and Ashley takes a knee, scoping out the target, instructing Sirius to down. The dog drops beside him. His obedience to his handler is quick, and their communication is easy and smooth. Sirius keeps his eyes trained on his handler as Ashley radios to "base command" and waits for the area to be "cleared." A few explosions

Marine Lance Corporal Joshua Ashley and his partner, MWD Sirius, look for buried aids during a training exercise at YPG in March 2012.

sound, followed by bursts of light. In tonight's exercise, this is achieved by hitting the button to the remote-controlled blaster from the SUV. The booms are simulated but powerful. Ashley gets the okay from Kitts to move forward.

We leave the road and move onto uneven ground. Beauchamp starts turning back to make sure I don't pitch and fall, cautioning me to watch my step. I squint and squish my eyes, trying to pinch whatever light I can out of the night, and I realize I'm not going to make it far without the NVGs after all. My depth perception shifts as I close one eye and open the other into a world of green. I stumble and drop, and my uneven footsteps make sounds as the bottom of my shoes scrape against the sand and stone.

The palm grove is the only irrigated spot at YPG's K-9 course and as we approach, it lifts in front of us like a mirage, lush even in the dark, the palm fronds bending with the wind. The huts inside are squat, square structures that, in the daytime, are orange and dusty, just like all the others in the nearby K-9 village. Here, they feel almost tropical.

Earlier in the day I watched Hardesty and Kitts stack explosives, little blocks that resemble oversized sardine cans, using them to completely fill the bottom of a window frame. In the dark I'm disoriented; I can hear Beauchamp, Ashley, and Sirius moving around, but I worry that I won't be able to find them. It seems only too easy to get turned around in this filtered nighttime world, to lose entirely one's sense of direction, even in the small palm grove. There's the sound of trickling water and the ghoulish white of the night sky reflecting in enormous puddles that break up the ground.

Ashley works methodically, his voice low and melodic as he coaxes the dog through the search, while Beauchamp calls out helpful directions—reminding him of doorways, letting him know which directions are clear. And then Ashley sends Sirius into the hut with explosives, his body taking up the entire length of the doorframe. Sirius moves under the "hot" window and his response is swift. The dog lowers his haunches, his hindquarters sinking in slow motion until his tail finally meets the ground. He casts a look back at his handler. They've found it.

"This is Gingerbread Man," Beauchamp says into his radio. He alerts the instructors that they have a positive response, identifies the location of the hut, and requests EOD backup.

Kitts's voice comes back over the radio. The find is good, the first part of the mission complete. Ashley and Beauchamp relax and walk down a deep slope and back up the road toward the K-9 village. The next leg of the mission includes a cordon search of a building with low beams and plywood walls where the bats will fly so low that everyone has to duck their heads. Kitts and McCoy are waiting outside when we arrive. McCoy comes around to Ashley. "You did good, man," he tells him. "You did good."

Ashley and Sirius pass that night of FINEX with 100 percent. And this is the memory that comes to my mind later, months later when the unthinkable happens.

SEVEN

the fallen

If there are no dogs in heaven, then when I die I want to go where they went.

—Will Rogers[1]

Lance Corporal Joshua Ashley arrived in Af-
ghanistan in May 2012, two months after he and the other handlers from the March class finished their stint at the ISAK course at Yuma Proving Ground.

He wasn't the only handler from II-MEF to deploy to Afghanistan. But it didn't take long before the teams scattered—going out on different missions, assigned to different units. In mid-July a few of them crossed paths at Camp Leatherneck and, for a brief intermission, were together again. They sat around the same fire smoking Cuban cigars, catching up, sharing their stories. Ashley talked about how much he loved deployment, how satisfying it was because he was doing what he came to do. He'd already signed up for reenlistment. It was the last time the guys from II-MEF would see him alive.

On the night of July 18, 2012, Ashley and Sirius, assigned to a Marine Corps Forces Special Operations Command (MARSOC) unit, were patrolling along the Helmand River. Ashley was following Sirius, wading through a canal when he stepped onto a pressure plate and set off an IED. The force of the explosion blew him backward. His unit called a medevac and cleared the area as quickly as they could; they managed to get him to Camp Leatherneck, but he died the following day.[2]

Ashley's was not the first fatality the handlers from II-MEF endured during their 2012 summer tour in Afghanistan. On July 16, Lance Corporal Kent Ferrell and his PEDD Zora, a German shepherd, were on a foot patrol. Zora walked up ahead of her handler as they cleared an alley; a combat engineer was also with them. A grenade came sailing over the wall like a bird, and they watched as it landed on the ground in front of them. The engineer veered sharply and started to run. Ferrell yelled for Zora. She came toward him but the grenade exploded. Shrapnel went flying, a shard struck the engineer in the elbow, but Zora, caught between the engineer and the explosion, absorbed the brunt of it. She took five or six pieces—one to the neck, two to her face, and two directly to her chest. The marks were so small they could hardly make out the entrance wounds. When Zora reached Ferrell a few moments later, she lay down next to him and died. It took less than a minute for her to go.

The vet who performed the necropsy said a piece of shrapnel had nicked Zora's heart. Even if the vet had been there the moment it happened, there would have been nothing he or anyone else could have done to save the dog.

Because handlers and their dogs are never separated—*"Where my dog goes, I go. Where I go, my dog goes"*—Ferrell had traveled back to Camp Leatherneck with Zora. He was there when they brought Ashley in to try and save him. So Ferrell, who had lost his dog, was there to become a surrogate caretaker to Sirius, the dog who'd just lost his handler.

As the flight crew prepared for takeoff on the C-130 that would deliver Ashley's body back home to his family in the States, Ferrell and Sirius stood together on the tarmac during the night of the ramp ceremony at Bastion Airfield on the main British military base northwest of Lashkar Gah, in Helmand Province. A crowd of servicemen and women came to pay their respects.

It was quiet, unearthly quiet for an airfield. Someone in the mass of mourners watched Sirius from afar. He saw the dog was in distress. And when the ceremony finished—Ashley's body gone, boarded on the aircraft—the tarmac emptying of people, Sirius kept turning back to look at the plane.

While 2010 and 2011 saw record losses for canine handlers, 2012 was proving to be an especially brutal year for the military working dog community. The losses that started in April 2012 continued through the summer, almost without pause.

On April 12, Marine Lance Corporal Abraham Tarwoe was killed in action. Two weeks later on April 26, Army Staff Sergeant Dick A. Lee Jr. was killed in action. In May, two handlers were killed "during combat operations": Marine Corporal Keaton Coffey on May 24, and, six days later on May 30, Navy handler Petty Officer 2nd Class Sean Brazas was shot in Panjwai, Afghanistan.[3] There was a brief respite in June, and then Ashley died on July 19. Two days later, on July 21, Petty Officer 2nd Class Michael J. Brodsky succumbed to the injuries he sustained from an IED blast on July 7.

During those same months, military working dogs Fibi, Zora, Nina, and Paco were all killed in action in Afghanistan. There were also canine wounded: Layka, a Belgian Malinois Air Force dog, lost her leg after being shot protecting her handler[4]; and JaJo, a German shepherd and part of the Army's Tactical Explosive Detection Dog (TEDD) program, was seriously wounded along with his handler by an IED explosion during a ground patrol on September 15 (no limbs were lost).[5] And then there were the dogs and handlers who made it back, whole in body but not so in spirit.

For the most part, when it comes to K-9 it doesn't seem to matter what branch handlers serve—they're all part of the same community, and in a combat theater, they are all searching for the same bombs. Word of injuries and death travels quickly.

It's Kitts who calls in July to tell me that Ashley was killed. "We lost another handler," he told me. "You know this one." Ashley had been Kitts's favorite student. Three days later Kitts is again the one to deliver bad news; he texts me to tell me that Brodsky has died. "Three students in three months," Kitts writes. "How many more friends do I have to lose?"

When Hardesty heard about Ashley's and then Brodsky's death, he was still teaching at Yuma, working with a new class of handlers, running them through the same tactical drills, getting them ready to go on to the deployments that were awaiting the group. He texts me to make sure I've heard the news about Brodsky. I reply that I have and ask him how he's holding up. "Praying for a better tomorrow," he writes back.

One night during that summer while Hardesty and I talk on the phone, I ask him if he'd lost very many friends to these wars. He says that he feels lucky; he'd known quite a few people who've been injured, some of them pretty badly, though he says for the most part he hadn't lost a lot of people close to him.

"But," Hardesty clarifies, "I guess that depends on what you think of as 'a lot.'"

I tell him one sounded like a lot to me. "Well, then it's been a lot." He kind of laughs as he says this, but the sound is sad.

News of the recent losses had been hard for all of the instructors out at Yuma. The only slight consolation was that neither Coffey nor Brazas was killed because they had failed to learn and apply the lessons of their training. One thing ISAK can't teach is how to dodge bullets.

The night Tosca and Wrinkle died there was a knock at the door. It was July 31, 2011, Army Veterinary Specialist William Vidal's second night in Afghanistan, and he'd barely been in-country 48 hours. The voice on the other side of the door told him to get ready, a body was coming. He roused and dressed; this was part of the job, and he'd known that going in. Vidal's first act in Afghanistan would not be as healer, but as undertaker.

Earlier that night, three MARSOC Marines stationed in Western Afghanistan had died in a fire.[6] It had started in their living quarters and quickly burned out of control. The bodies were brought to Bagram Airfield by plane; there were enough servicemen on hand to give the fallen Marines honors, so the group formed a line, passing the bodies from one set of hands to the next.

One of the litters coming off the plane was draped in an American flag like the others, but it clearly held a body that was much smaller than the rest. Vidal and the others in the Army's 64th Medical Detachment (Veterinary Services), Captain Katie Barry and Sergeant Alyssa Doughty, placed the small black body bag into their truck as some of the soldiers and airmen gave a final salute to their fallen comrade: Tosca, a Belgian Malinois who had died in the fire alongside her handler, Marine Sergeant Christopher Wrinkle.

The veterinary team brought Tosca's body into the examining room and opened the bag. Vidal could barely make out that what was on the table in front of them had once been a dog: Tosca's distinguishing features had been all but erased; only the collar remained intact. Captain Barry removed it before they zipped the bag back up. She cleaned it later, after conducting a necropsy, so she could return it to the Marines who'd brought the dog to them. A single thought ran through Vidal's mind: *Welcome to war.*

Early the next day, one of the Marines from Wrinkle's unit was waiting for the vet team. He was grief-stricken. Wrinkle had been his best friend and he'd come to make sure that Tosca's remains made it out of Afghanistan on the same flight as Wrinkle's body.

Vidal took him down to the incinerator, but when they got there they were told the machinery needed cleaning and that it would be 24 hours before they could manage another cremation. But that would be too late. The Marine pleaded with the technician, begging him to hurry along whatever it was that needed doing. He said it was for his best friend and told him how Wrinkle had run back into the fire when he heard Tosca barking, and died trying to save his dog and partner. They belonged together, he said, and the man finally relented.

The Marine cradled Tosca in his arms and gently surrendered the dog's body into the incinerator. He sat and waited for the four hours it took for the flames to finish their work. He didn't move from his post once the entire time, so that the dog would never be left alone. Vidal found him sitting there later with Tosca's urn held tightly in his hands. He made it back in time to get her on the plane with Wrinkle and they traveled home together.

It rained the day of Wrinkle's funeral in his hometown of Dallastown, Pennsylvania. Poured, actually. Reporters said there were two coffins in the church. The handler and his dog were buried together at the Susquehanna Cemetery.[7]

When someone dies, it is customary in the Jewish tradition for a living person to sit with the body, to act as guardian from the time of death until the time of burial. The Talmud says that during these brief hours before a body is laid to rest in the ground, the soul hovers in a space between this world and whatever lies beyond. The job of these guardians, called shomrim, is to comfort that soul by reading psalms and prayers aloud while keeping watch over the body to prevent any kind of desecration. It is a practice that I find reassuring; it makes death and whatever comes right after seem a little less lonely, and that's likely the true service the shomrim provide—a consolation for the bereaved the deceased has left behind. As the poet and undertaker Thomas Lynch writes, the rituals we "devise to conduct the living and beloved and the dead from one status to another have less to do with *performance* than with *meaning*."[8]

Captain Barry, Sergeant Doughty, and Specialist Vidal, the veterinarian team stationed at Bagram Airfield, are the ones who waited with wounded or dead dogs and comforted their handlers until the flights came to take them home from Afghanistan, no matter the hour, day or night. They acted as the shomrim for the souls of the departed dogs.

Tosca and Sergeant Wrinkle were the first combat deaths that Vidal had ever experienced. During the opening stint of his yearlong deployment in Afghanistan, much of what he encountered treating military working dogs seemed extreme. It wasn't the deaths that had come as a shock. He was used to treating sick dogs, but Tosca had been a healthy dog. As far as he could reason, she was the victim of circumstance. Her death was sudden and violent, and it was this he found so jarring. As the days of his tour turned into weeks and then months, this all started to feel routine. Seeing dogs get blown up became normal. So Vidal numbed himself to it.

Vidal hadn't known Tosca or Wrinkle, but Captain Barry had. That night as they viewed Tosca's body she was transfixed by the tortured corpse—the thing that no longer resembled a dog. What, she wondered, must the Marines who died in that fire look like? She couldn't drive the thought from her mind.

Barry had dealt with a lot of tough cases with the dog teams she treated during her deployment in Afghanistan. She'd seen a lot of bad, bloody things. But that night was the only night she went home, sat on her bed, and sobbed.[9]

Marine Sergeant Adam Cann was the first dog handler killed in Iraq. He was the first handler killed in action since the Vietnam War.

It was the first week of January 2006. A crowd bustled outside the police recruiting station in Ramadi, Iraq. Cann and his dog Bruno were on duty along with Corporal Brendan Poelaert and his dog Flapoor. The two soldiers stood alongside the walls of the building, eyeballing the crowd in front of them, keeping a tight rein on their dogs since there were so many people milling around. They posed for a couple of pictures; Bruno reared up on his hindquarters, teeth showing, mugging for the camera while Poelaert watched from the side.[10] But then Cann's eyes landed on someone who gave him a bad feeling. He pushed his way through the crowd to confront the man. It's said there was a scuffle, a deafening noise, and then only darkness.

When Poelaert came to, he was on the ground. His arm pulsed in pain; one of the ball bearings from the suicide bomber's explosives had hit his arm, crushing the bones at the point of contact. He looked around frantically until he saw Flapoor. Somehow the dog had managed to keep upright, staggering only a few feet away. Poelaert could tell his dog was trying to get to him. The dog was in shock: his eyes unfocused; blood ran in a fast current, flowing from his chest.[11]

"I got to get my dog to the vet!" Poelaert shouted. Shrapnel had hit Flapoor, piercing the dog's stomach and puncturing a lung. The impact of the blast had been so powerful and had hit with such force that ball bearings had lodged inside Poelaert's weapon.

Eventually Poelaert and his dog were carried out of the chaos and to surgery. They would recover, as would Cann's dog Bruno, who was also wounded in the blast. Cann did not survive.

Sometime later Flapoor came through the ISAK course at Yuma with another handler. The instructors remembered him because the dog was so petrified of explosions. One day while the dog teams were in the training field, a sonic boom sounded and Flapoor took off, streaking away in fear. They chased after the dog and found him curled up in a van, shaking. Three months later the dog died of heart failure. But Flapoor wasn't an old dog; his heart just gave out on him. Later, when they cremated him, they found shrapnel in the ashes leftover from that day in Ramadi.[12]

Cann was one of 58 people killed in that 2006 bombing,[13] just three weeks shy of his twenty-fourth birthday. He wasn't even supposed to be on patrol. He had just finished a mission but when he returned to base he saw his friends, handlers Poelaert and Sergeant Jesse Maldonaldo, with their dogs and he decided he wanted to go along with them. The others told him he didn't have to do the extra work, but Cann had insisted.[14]

After he died, the men on his base in Iraq set up a memorial, an upright slab of pocked alabaster concrete that reads "CAMP CANN" in large, rust-colored, stenciled letters. It bears his name and the date he died; someone has sketched a likeness of Cann and his dog Bruno onto the rough surface. It has the look and feel of a tattoo, the shading and shadows of ink on hard skin. Scrawled off to the side, in quotation marks, is "This bites for you." When the United States pulled its troops out of Iraq, the Marine Corps shipped the memorial back to Camp Pendleton, Cann's home station in California. It is now the first thing people see when they drive up to the K-9 office.

This tradition of military handlers memorializing their fallen is both old and well kept—as is commemorating the fallen dogs among their ranks.

Marine Scout dog Kaiser, an 85-pound German shepherd, was the first dog killed in action in Vietnam. Kaiser and his handler, Lance Corporal

Alfredo Salazar, were leading a patrol when they were hit with artillery fire and grenades. The dog was hit, his handler was not; it's said Kaiser returned to his handler's side, tried to lick his hand, and then died. The Marines carried his body back to camp, buried him under the shade of a tree near their tents, and renamed their base after the dog. A red sign mounted on a wooden frame was painted with large, yellow block letters:

CAMP KAISER: THIS CAMP IS NAMED IN HONOR OF KAISER A SCOUT DOG WHO GAVE HIS LIFE FOR HIS COUNTRY ON 6 JULY 1966 WHILE LEADING A NIGHT COMBAT PATROL IN VIET NAM.[15]

In Afghanistan at Camp Leatherneck, near the dog kennels, there's a placard with the dark outline of a handler kneeling beside his dog. In black are the words, "From a Few of the Finest."[16] Next to it is a painted wooden cross; "K-9 MWD" is marked in black against the wood's pale yellow. Small rectangular panels bearing the names of the dead dogs hang from the arms of the cross. When the wind blows they move, almost like wings. In front of the cross is a small wooden podium, the top of which is made of three framed photos of fallen handlers.

If a dog is killed in action, he is memorialized and eulogized by his handlers and kennel masters at their forward operating bases in-country or at their home stations, often times both. These ceremonies are executed with the utmost dignity and respect. The loss is the loss of a fallen comrade, nothing more and nothing less. Open displays of mourning are appropriate, accepted.

Journalist Ernie Pyle made a note of this culture that embraced mourning canines after spending time with one dog in particular who was on the front lines of World War II. Pyle described him as a "beautiful police dog" that belonged to "the headquarters of a regiment I knew well." Sergeant, as the dog was fondly called by the men around him, was not only much beloved but highly intelligent; the dog had learned to run for cover when a raid flew overhead, and the men in this regiment had even dug a special foxhole just for him.

Sergeant was in his foxhole when "shrapnel from an airburst got him." The dog's injuries were beyond treatment, so the soldiers had to put him down. Six other men died in that same attack, and while Pyle's account of this day is short, it is revelatory. "The outfit lost two officers, four men and a dog in that raid. It is not belittling the men who died to say that Sergeant's death shares a big place in the grief of those who were left."

Even outside the intensity of combat theater, kennels hold formal memorial services for their dogs when they die; handlers eulogize their partners, making full mention of their service with gratitude and respect. If you walk into a military working dog kennel on any base in the United States, you're sure to come across at least one wall commemorating all the dogs who at one time or another called the site home. Like the one on the walls of the US Air Force Academy kennels in Colorado, like the one that Barry, Doughty, and Vidal had up in their clinic in Bagram.

On one of the first days that I was out at the ISAK course in Yuma, I noticed that Tech Sergeant Justin Kitts was wearing a black metal bracelet on his right arm. When I'd gotten close enough to take a better look, I saw that it was a memorial bracelet, with the name Sergeant Zainah Creamer, the first female handler killed in action. She died on January 12, 2011, in Kandahar Province. Kitts had been in Afghanistan with Creamer, and they had trained together at the beginning of their deployment. The day she was hit, he and Dyngo were being helicoptered back to FOB Wilson following a mission. The pilots gave him the news. Creamer had stepped on a pressure plate. "The waist down was gone," Kitts remembered. A medevac had come, but she had lost too much blood, and by the time they had gotten her to Kandahar, it had been too late. Her dog, Jofa, had not been hurt. Kitts wore the bracelet always, he said, removing it only when he showered.

In recent years, the advent of social networks has opened up a new vein for a more accessible and immediate way to memorialize fallen handlers and their military working dogs. On one hand, these accounts—on Facebook, MySpace, and other networks—held by handlers killed in action, leave behind a ghostly legacy. Their last post or final update feels more like a placeholder than an end marker; like a dog-eared page of a book in mid-read, it suggests the promise to return. But often these pages morph into memorial sites where friends and family of the deceased can leave messages, lamenting the shared loss with notes and photos. Or new pages are created for an always-open forum for remembrance for friends, family, and even the public. There are pages for Colton Rusk, for Sean Brazas, for Zainah Creamer, and for Joshua Ashley.

Back at Yuma, Ashley had never seemed what you might call breakable. Standing well over six feet he was, in a word, enormous—his back and shoulders were impossibly wide, earning him nicknames like Lou Ferrigno from the other Marines from II-MEF. The other guys in class had all gravitated to him, laughing at his jokes. He possessed the sure-headedness of a young man accustomed to excelling because he was big and strong. One afternoon, Ashley coaxed Sirius up into the driver's seat of one of ISAK's ubiquitous golf carts and placed the dog's paws on the steering wheel, joking with the other handlers as he'd made it look like Sirius was driving. If at other times Ashley had seemed aloof, even arrogant, in that moment with his dog he'd been gentle, working his large hands and holding Sirius with real delicacy.

On Ashley's page there are photographs of Sirius, of his brothers and his parents; snapshots from proms, where his jet black hair is slick and spiked high with gel, his face rounder, softer, still that of a growing boy. Some of these photos are posted with captions, others come with notes. As one friend wrote, months after he died: "Hey bro, its weird thinking that your [sic] really gone. Its crazy actually. I think about all the good times we had together. . . . My fiance got me this awesome bracelet with your name on it and on the back it has your KIA date and it just gets to me every time I look at it. I miss you man." Elsewhere on Ashley's page someone has posted a photo of a Marine. It doesn't say who the young man is, but that doesn't really matter. On the camouflaged fabric of his helmet the Marine has inscribed a slight alteration of verse 1:9 from the Book of Joshua. In large, black-inked letters it reads: "I will be strong and courageous, I will not be terrified or discouraged, for the Lord my God is with me wherever I go."

But these pages are more than message boards; they are chronicles of loss in wartime. Indeed, these social networking sites play a surprisingly significant role in recording the MWD efforts in these wars.

From time to time as I scroll through my Facebook News Feed, a haunting little box pops up high on the right-hand sidebar. Under the words "People You May Know" I see Ashley's profile picture. He's wearing his helmet sitting on a staircase of bleached earth, Sirius standing on the steps below him, his hand resting on Sirius's big, furry head. "Do you know Joshua?" it asks.

Determining the number of military working dog losses— precisely how many handlers and how many dogs have been killed during combat operations since the first dog teams were sent into Iraq in 2004— proved to be an unexpectedly difficult task. More difficult still is trying to calculate the number of wounded.

A few factors conspire to muddle what, from the outside, should seem easy numbers to tally. The first: there is no *centralized* official record of handlers killed in action. In fact, there never has been.[17] There also is no official record devoted specifically to tracking combat-related injuries or deaths for dogs.

Through a variety of contacts, nonmilitary sanctioned websites, and news articles, I managed to pull together a number I believe is close to what an official number might look like.[18] I started in 2004, the year that dogs first went into combat theater.

Handlers KIA (killed in action) from 2004 to 2013: 30

MWDs KIA from 2004 to present: 20 (2 Missing in Action)

That's not to say that there are not records of military handlers or their dogs, or that these teams are not kept track of while they are on deployment—or that their deaths are not noted. They certainly are.

Across all the different branches there are many different kinds of *required* records kept, and each branch follows its own system. Of the more standard and significant are the dogs' training and medical records, which span their military careers, but this information has many filters and there is no point through which they intersect, save one.

There is a centrally located, official, and, now, thanks to the Freedom of Information Act, publicly accessible record pertaining to military working dogs. This database is maintained by the 341st Training Squadron at Lackland Air Force Base in San Antonio, Texas. (The Air Force, being the executive agent of the Department of Defense's working dog program, tracks all military working dogs from all branches, not just Air Force dogs.) As Master Sergeant (Ret.) Joel Burton, who was formerly responsible for maintaining this annually updated document, puts it, this is the single document that keeps track of all DOD military working dogs "from cradle to grave."

These efforts were initiated on September 27, 2000, as part of a new piece of legislation: the Robby Law. This amendment was designed with a single, specific purpose: "to facilitate the adoption of retired military working dogs by law enforcement agencies, former handlers of these dogs, and other persons capable of caring for these dogs."[19] The law also mandated that the 341st Training Squadron at Lackland Air Force Base in San Antonio, Texas, the head of the Department of Defense's Military Working Dog Program, must provide Congress a full and complete record of every dog whose military service has ended that calendar year, whether by retirement and adoption, euthanasia, or death.

But this mandate wasn't conceived in a time of war and had—and continues to have—nothing to do with the dog teams' experiences in combat. That data is almost exclusively maintained with information pulled from veterinarians' records for each dog. Unfortunately, not all veterinarians follow the same standards or requirements. And there is no *requirement* for the notation of death to include details on how the dog was killed—whether by bullet, IED, heat exhaustion—nor even a requirement to list a dog's death as KIA.[20]

Given that this document and its maintenance was enacted before the United States was engaged in Iraq or Afghanistan, it was not designed to track dogs in combat zones or what happens to them once they're there.

However, in examining each document from year to year, it did not evolve much beyond its original form, instead capturing more pertinent and somewhat detailed information though records were overall inconsistent and incomplete.

Further complicating the collection of these finer details, each military branch—Marine Corps, Air Force, Army, Navy—has different records and different requirements when it comes to keeping track of its dogs. It's a "we take care of our own" mentality. Which means that while each service keeps records of its dog teams—if they've been wounded, if they were killed in action, if they were retired or pulled from service for PTSD or some other reason—this information is not being gathered or reviewed.

It also means that any record specifically devoted to the number of dogs and handlers killed in action is *not* official. Over the years, individuals within the MWD program, some of them program managers or others in administrative roles within the 341st, have attempted to keep tabs on the teams and the losses they suffer. Even then, these records were maintained in haphazard ways, taken on as personal rather than mandated projects.

When Sean Lulofs and Aaslan landed in Iraq in 2004 and started to go out on missions, no one from command knew where they—or the other Air Force and Marine dog teams—were or what had happened to them. All they knew was that the teams had deployed to Iraq and were assigned to bases from there. When he was in Fallujah, Lulofs and Aaslan just went to work every day and did their job. When he finally did reach out to the Air Force Central Command, they were surprised and happy to hear from him. "Holy shit," one guy said to Lulofs. "We were wondering where you guys were and if you were still alive."

That feeling of neglect stayed with Lulofs as he moved away from handling dogs, eventually getting promoted to a job within the Defense Department's MWD program where he was in a position to start, along with a few colleagues, their own handler and dog database.

This inattention to where handlers went, and what fates they met once they reached their deployment destination, persisted after Lulofs's tour ended. The lack of oversight was originally a result from a simple lack of need. Until Adam Cann's death in 2006—the first handler- or MWD-related casualty—there was nothing in place to keep track of handlers killed in action, because no casualties or fatalities had occurred yet.[21]

The deficit of personnel management tracking for dog handlers while they are deployed in a combat zone is an area where, Lulofs believes, the program has failed—miserably. The effort put forth was, "piss poor, at best."

But it's more than just disgust over administrative negligence that spurred Lulofs. For him, keeping some kind of watch over deployed handlers was personal.

Joshua Farnsworth, Lulofs's dog-handler partner and friend in Fallujah, died in July 2007. Farnsworth's obituary is vague, stating only that he "was taken by the angels in his residence."[22] I asked Lulofs what happened. "Well, officially it's written up as an accident," he says. "But I know it wasn't."[23]

After they got back from their tour in Iraq, neither Lulofs nor Farnsworth ever received any medals for their service during deployment—no purple heart, no bronze star, no combat action medals or ribbons.

"I never got him his medals and I promised him I would," Lulofs says. "So I said, 'Somebody's got to keep track of these handlers.' They don't get all the help they need."

Still, the number of handlers and dogs in the MWD program together only represents a minute portion of the military's forces, and no one is, or was, thinking that keeping track of the injured or killed dogs might somehow impact the future.

But this absence of practical record keeping isn't an anomaly in the military. As yet there isn't a standardized medical database that chronicles or catalogs the casualties or fatalities of Iraq and Afghanistan. But during a 2010–2011 deployment in Afghanistan, Colonel Michael D. Wirt, a brigade surgeon with the 101st Airborne Division, created a unique, multilayered database that tracked wounded soldiers with remarkable detail. In this database, Wirt included criteria like "increased or decreased risk factors—whether the victim was wearing larger or smaller body armor, whether a bomb-sniffing dog was present, when a tourniquet was applied" when he listed casualties and deaths during war. He also "mapped where on the human body bullets most often struck."[24] Wirt's work was unique in that the information he added to basic medical record keeping was not only meticulous but also incredibly detailed. His database was intended to build a narrative, and to potentially solve problems.

But for the US military—or even each individual branch—to keep such meticulous track of all their deployed servicemen and women would take an incredible amount of manpower and hours. The MWD program, at minimum, would require an across-the-board change in regulation in the way records are maintained and shared up and down the chain of command, from the veterinarians, to the handlers, to the kennel masters, to the program managers.

By the time he was deputy commander at Blanchfield Army Community Hospital, Wirt told the *New York Times* in 2012, "If you don't take data and analyze it and try to find ways to improve, then what are you doing? . . . A consolidated database with standardized input consisting of mechanism of injury and resulting wounds, classified by battle and nonbattle injuries, would be something you could actually use."[25]

Were the MWD program to maintain something like this, they would be setting a kind of military precedent. But its potential value for soon-to-be deploying handlers, at training facilities like ISAK at the Yuma Proving Ground, could be quite high. Knowing the details of how handlers are getting wounded or killed would be exceptionally useful. Knowing, for example, the type of IED, its size, where it was buried, how deep, how many of them. But the information, if available, is not shared, and the few people who are trying to correct the problem believe it may be impossible to shake up the system enough to inspire real change or true transparency.

Even so, there are worthy lessons to be learned.

part iii

EIGHT

wounds and healing

Thousands of our men will soon be returning to you. They have been gone a long time and they have seen and done and felt things you cannot know. They will be changed.

—Ernie Pyle, *Brave Men*

Usually [dogs] are quick to discover that I cannot see or hear. Truly, as companions, friends, equals in opportunities of self-expression they unfold to me the dignity of creation.

—Helen Keller

They made it into Baghdad on a Monday night. It was already very late by the time Army Captain Cecilia Najera's flight from Tikrit landed. Najera was uneasy about this trip, but when she looked down she was contented. Her partner, a black Labrador retriever named Boe, whom she called her "little shadow," was close beside her.

Lieutenant Colonel Beth Salisbury, commander of the Camp Liberty Stress Clinic, was there to pick them up. Najera and Boe climbed into the vehicle. Salisbury looked and sounded exhausted as she briefed Najera on what they would be walking into that night.

Earlier that day, May 11, 2009, Army Sergeant John M. Russell, a patient, had walked into the clinic and opened fire on fellow servicemen, patients, and staff, killing five people and wounding three others.[1] Russell, who was on his third deployment, had been escorted to the clinic that morning, not by his own choosing but on his commander's insistence. Russell had been exhibiting alarming behavior, openly expressing thoughts of suicide. In fact, he had already been to the clinic on four separate occasions and, only three days earlier, his commander had disabled his weapon by removing the bolt so that it couldn't be fired. But once at the clinic he became belligerent and was told to leave.

Just one hour later, he fought with the soldier placed as his escort and took his weapon, an M16 rifle, and forced the man from the car at gunpoint, intending to return to the Stress Clinic.[2] The soldier had alerted military police but by the time they tried to warn the clinic's staff, it was too late. When the police were on the phone with the clinic, the officers said they had heard shots being fired on the other end of the phone line.[3] The *Washington Post* and the *New York Times* called it the deadliest incident of soldier-on-soldier violence since the invasion of Iraq in 2003.[4]

Najera and Boe weren't in Iraq to find bombs or drugs, or work patrols—this dog team was there as part of a new Army initiative. An occupational therapist, Najera had deployed to Iraq with the 528th Medical Detachment Combat and Operational Stress Control Unit, where she had been previously stationed at Contingency Operating Base Speicher. Boe, her partner, was not a traditional war dog, but a combat-trained therapy dog.

It was just pure coincidence that Najera and Boe arrived in Baghdad on the day of such a tragedy; their plans had been made long ago. Najera and Boe had visited this clinic before, and they knew the people who had been inside during the attack. Which was part of why Najera was uneasy, scared even. She was not only unsure of what she and Boe were about to encounter, but she was at a loss to think of what she could do to be of any real help. The people in this clinic weren't just soldiers, they were therapists and doctors, health-care professionals just like she was. What could she possibly say, she wondered, that would make a difference to any of them?

"I'm not sure that they're going to want to talk to you," Salisbury warned her as they drove, as if reading Najera's mind. The clinic, she said, had been inundated with offers of support, but she doubted any outsider would be able or even welcome to do much for her staff. Not tonight at least, she said. It was too soon.

The military police had sealed off the clinic as a crime scene, so the staff was in the small adjacent building that housed the commander's office. Najera and Boe waited in the hallway with the others who had come to lend their services—chaplains, a social worker, other mental health-care providers. They stood in silence until a sergeant emerged from the room where the clinic staff had gathered together. She addressed the group in the hall. "No one on staff wants to see anyone," she said and told them all to leave. Najera turned to shuffle out with the others, but then she heard the sergeant's voice again. "Ma'am?" The woman was addressing Najera. "You and Boe can come in."

Inside, the clinic staff sat without speaking. Their eyes were red and raw—from crying or exhaustion, Najera couldn't tell. She simply nodded at the group, slipped into a chair, and unclipped Boe's leash, so the dog could have range of the room. Boe wove her way in and around the chairs, sniffing and greeting people as she encountered them. The sergeant who had invited them to stay called Boe over to her and kept the dog next to her, patting her large black head.

Once or twice someone would break the silence. One of the younger staffers, a woman, wanted to talk about what had happened. But after she spoke the group went mute again. It had been a long day for Najera and for Boe, the dog was tired, and they hadn't planned on working straight from the plane so Najera hadn't dressed Boe in her vest—a signal to the dog that she was in work mode. So being tired herself after a long day of traveling, Boe plopped down in the middle of the room with little grace, releasing a heavy, grunting sigh.

A few people chuckled at this, some small smiles showed, even if briefly. And Najera felt reassured. The dog had just done what probably

every person there had wanted to do, and though it was a mild kind of relief, for the smallest of moments the tension broke and the room lightened.

Between 2007 and 2011, there were eight dogs who made up
the very first Combat and Operational Stress Control (COSC) dog therapy teams: Boe and Budge, Zeke and Albert, Butch and Zach, Apollo and
Timmy.[5] They were the first therapy dogs ever trained and deployed to
combat theater in Iraq and Afghanistan.

Hatched in 2007, the idea to deploy COSC dogs evolved after those
working with wounded soldiers at the Walter Reed Army Medical Center
began to notice that the service dogs, assigned to help wounded soldiers get
used to prosthetic limbs, were just as integral to each patient's emotional
recovery as to their physical recovery. Cases of animal-assisted therapy for
people recovering from severe injuries or trauma were well documented.
So why did soldiers have to wait until they were wounded to benefit? Why,
these therapists wondered, couldn't this kind of restorative interaction be
applied preemptively in a combat theater?

The Army partnered with America's VetDogs (a nonprofit started by
the Guide Dog Foundation for the Blind) and developed a program that
would bring skilled therapy dogs into the theater of combat.

The idea was progressive but simple: the dogs would become part of
the combat stress control units, attached to occupational therapists who
would also receive additional training so that they could become therapy-
dog handlers. The COSC units were mobile, meaning that they traveled
from FOBs to PBs, essentially acting as a rotating or even door-to-door
resource, bringing stress and trauma relief to servicemen and women in the
combat zone. The dogs were intended to serve as an adjunct, an icebreaker
so to speak, to the therapy their handlers—and the units they served—were
already offering deployed service members.

In many ways, the COSC dogs required much of the same kind of predeployment preparedness training that being a military working dog neces-
sitates. The dogs had to be exposed to the elements in which they would be
working—the different kinds of terrain, the feel of ear muffs and goggles,

live gunfire, explosions, the sound of large military aircrafts, helicopters—
so that they could become used to them. Unlike MWDs, the COSC dogs
had to be adaptable to multiple handlers and fill different roles. Their demeanor was of the utmost importance: these dogs had to have close to the
perfect temperament to be effective in this demanding job.

In December 2007 the first two COSC dogs deployed to Iraq. They
were a pair of matching black Labs: Special 1st Class Budge and Special 1st
Class Boe.

Boe was a quiet dog, lumbering and sweet, with a molasses-mellow temperament. As an occupational therapist who'd volunteered to be a COSC
dog handler, Najera saw the difference Boe made with her patients almost
instantly. Boe wasn't just popular with the soldiers, but with command as
well. While Najera had anticipated resistance to the idea of therapy in the
theater of war, the stigma of which still looms large, she found that with
Boe, her presence was not just accepted, but welcomed with enthusiasm.

Still, Najera tread lightly, never forcing Boe on anyone. The dog was
gentle enough that Najera could often let her roam off the leash. The dog
had a knack for seeking out reluctant and withdrawn soldiers who might be
too shy or traumatized to ask for help from another soldier.

Boe did not just help soldiers who were deeply affected; she also helped
others with more mundane problems. At one point during their tour, Najera noticed that Boe had gained quite a bit of weight from all the treats she
had been given. Najera realized that a soldier who liked to visit Boe had also
been gaining weight—it was slowing him down and he was having a hard
time finding the energy to motivate himself to exercise. So Najera used Boe
as a way to engage him, never really directly addressing his weight issue. Instead she made it about Boe. Pretty soon, the soldier was taking Boe out on
runs a few times a week—he decided they would lose the weight together.

Boe was effective in even more subtle ways. Najera began to see soldiers put their hands on the dog without any prompting, and then, finally,
begin to open up about their problems. Others simply liked being around
the dog, approaching her because they just wanted to hug her before they
continued about their day.

*Captain Cecilia Najera poses with her COSC dog Boe while they served
together for 15 months in Iraq in 2009.*

When they started their duties in Tikrit, Najera and Boe made regular
visits to the combat support hospital. It was a US military facility but the
staff there treated Iraqi civilians as well—anyone who was injured as a result
of the war, even insurgents. While in the hospital Najera was always careful
not to approach Iraqi patients with Boe, conscious of the cultural differ-
ences between the way Americans and Iraqis regard dogs. In Iraq, dogs are
generally considered unclean and not kept as pets; in urban areas, dogs run
wild in the streets.[6] (The stray dog population reached epic proportions in
2010, and after a spate of attacks on residents of Baghdad, the Iraqi government took action and deployed some 20 teams of veterinarians and police

to shoot or poison the dogs. They killed upward of 58,000 stray dogs in three months.) But Najera and Boe made so many trips to the hospital together that the civilian patients and their visiting families grew familiar with the dog team, sometimes even smiling or laughing when Boe passed by.

There was one young patient Najera would notice, a young Iraqi girl around 12 years old. According to the story Najera was told, the girl's parents were both insurgents who had been killed during a raid by US forces. The girl was badly wounded during the fight, shot after she herself apparently reached for a weapon. The bullet that hit her in the abdomen went into her small intestines, wreaking havoc on her insides and exiting her colon. She had a colostomy bag and was for many months confined to her bed. She was so frail and small that the girl appeared many years younger than she actually was.

Each time Boe passed by, the girl stared out from her bed, watching with large dark eyes. Najera assumed the girl was afraid of the dog. So when one of the nurses approached her and said that she thought the girl would really like it if Boe visited her bedside, Najera was surprised and somewhat reluctant. The nurse insisted. The staff had been giving their patient Play-Doh to occupy the long stretches of confinement to her bed; each time the girl would fashion the clay into small, brightly colored dogs.

Those first visits Najera took it slow, keeping the dog at a distance. The girl would smile. Najera did tricks with Boe, like "sit," "shake," and "lie down," and the girl laughed. It took a few weeks, but finally she reached out a cautious hand and touched the dog to pet her. As she recovered over the six months of her hospital stay, the girl was eventually able to get up from bed. Not long after, she took to walking Boe up and down the hallways. When she was with Boe, the girl seemed genuinely happy.

The night of the shooting at Camp Liberty clinic, there had been a forecast for a huge sandstorm. Najera and Boe had been lucky to catch their flight over to Baghdad. Their stay was extended another week because of some other transportation delays. Initially, Najera was frustrated that she and Boe were unable to find another flight back to Tikrit, but later, she felt grateful. There were five memorial services held that week for the clinic staff, and she and Boe attended each one. That was when the tears came. Those were some very long and challenging days for the COSC dog team—there were no breaks. She and Boe worked straight through the day and into the night. It was the hardest week of their 15-month deployment. Najera felt that she and Boe were meant to be there to help in the aftermath of such a tragic event. That's why she and Boe were in Iraq.

No one is entirely sure why John Russell snapped that day at the Liberty Clinic in Baghdad, or what drove him to kill five people. According to a 325-page report published in October 2009 investigating the incident, he'd been exhibiting erratic behavior for weeks and threating suicide.[7] When this mental break occurred, Russell was just six weeks from finishing what was his third deployment to Iraq. While his rampage was unprecedentedly deadly, he was far from the first soldier to crack under the strain of combat.

Since the Iraq and Afghanistan wars, post-traumatic stress disorder (PTSD) is so prevalent among US servicemen and women that it has earned classification as an outright epidemic, reaching catastrophic numbers in the military. Of the soldiers, Marines, airmen, and sailors coming home from Iraq and Afghanistan, one in five will return with PTSD, adding up to 300,000 so far. (About 380,000 who deploy to these two wars will suffer from a traumatic brain injury.)

Untreated and unaddressed, PTSD frequently leads to volatile behavior and suicide. The recent rate of suicide among active-duty service members, as well as among recent veterans, is rampant. Currently, every 80 minutes a veteran takes his own life. From 2005 to 2010 a service member committed suicide once every 36 hours. The 1 percent of Americans who have served in the US military represents 20 percent of the country's suicides.[8] "Suicide," as journalist Tina Rosenberg reported in September 2012, "is now the leading cause of death in the Army."[9]

The symptoms have been the same war after war: records dating back to the ancient Egyptians tell of warriors and soldiers who were psychologically wounded by the battlefield. The Romans and Greeks also noted similar, damaging phenomena after combat.[10]

In later eras, there was an agreement among the symptoms soldiers felt when they had been damaged by war—anger, anxiety, depression, obsessive thoughts of going home, insomnia, loss of appetite, heart palpitations, and bouts of fever. In the seventeenth century Swiss military doctors called it "nostalgia." The Germans and the French had words for it that meant "homesickness." And the Spanish termed it *estar roto,* meaning "to be broken."[11]

During and after the Civil War, such afflictions took on the name Da Costa Syndrome after a doctor, Jacob Mendes Da Costa, made a clinical study of it with 300 soldiers, publishing his reports in 1871.[12] Afterward, though, it became better known as "soldier's heart." During World War I, physicians fashioned the term "shell shock," originally coined by Captain Charles Myers in 1915 to describe a syndrome in which physical and neurological ailments were thought to be a direct result of the force of a blast, a literal shaking of the brain. Within a year, though, many of these same symptoms—treacherous headaches, ringing in the ears, memory loss, feelings of being disoriented, an inability to sleep—were exhibiting in soldiers who had never suffered a blast. Instead military physicians determined that this was not shell shock but rather a break in nerves, or "neurasthenia."[13] During World War II the syndrome became known as "combat fatigue." In Vietnam the condition was notorious for violent flashbacks and was believed to have been compounded by the poor reception servicemen received upon their return home. To make matters worse, men who reported feelings of depression, paranoia, sleeplessness during wartime were thought to be fainthearted, or cowardly would-be deserters looking for some way out of their soldier duties. This attitude persists today and is still an obstacle to effective treatment.

Though combat stress dogs like Boe are few, canine therapy is a growing trend, one that continues to gain legitimacy in the world of psychotherapy. And dogs have long been regarded as a therapeutic tool for psychologically wounded patients.

Sigmund Freud supposedly brought his dog Jofi, a Chinese chow, into his therapy sessions. The father of psychoanalysis not only felt the dog provided a soothing presence, but also used Jofi to gauge his patient's inner mood. If the dog was relaxed, it meant the patient was at ease. If the dog tried to leave the room during the session or showed any signs of discomfort, it revealed the patient was particularly anxious. Freud loved his dog, but he also believed that the emotions of dogs were exhibited more purely, writing, "Dogs love their friends and bite their enemies, quite unlike people, who are incapable of pure love and always have to mix love and hate in their object relations."[14] Perhaps that is why he relied on Jofi's "judgment" of his patients.

While the idea of using dogs for therapy—actually selecting for breed and temperament and then training them—would take years to take root, it was around Freud's time that militaries started employing dogs to help wounded soldiers, physically and emotionally.

During World War I, military dogs deployed by the French Legion who, for one reason or another, were no longer able to fulfill their combat duties, were retrained to be the companions of blind soldiers. They were taught to anticipate approaching cars, to alert their charge to drops and inclines in the road, and even find the soldier's favorite haunts and guide him safely to the homes of his friends and family.[15] The process for acquiring such a dog was fairly uncomplicated: men who needed a guide dog simply sent letters to the War Dog Service. But as Harold Baynes reported from France, despite the accessibility of the dogs, it wasn't a very popular service. This, he wrote, was largely "because of the feeling that a blind man led by a dog must necessarily appear to be an object of charity." The stigma of helplessness and desperation attached to this kind of handicap must have been so potent that even Baynes (not so sensitively) believed that a soldier making his way through the city with a guide dog would have been indistinguishable from a common beggar.[16]

It seems an obtuse, thoughtless assessment, but it was, disappointingly, representative of the time.

The November 5, 1927 edition of the *Saturday Evening Post* featured a stirring article by a woman named Dorothy Harrison Eustis. Though a native of Philadelphia, Eustis had been living in Switzerland and had just traveled to the city of Potsdam, Germany, where she saw firsthand how the country was rehabilitating its "war blind." What she witnessed had a profound effect on her and would forever change her thinking about the future of any blind person.

> In darkness and uncertainty he must start again, wholly dependent on outside help for every move. His other senses may rally to his aid, but they cannot replace his eyesight. To man's never failing friend has been accorded this special privilege. Gentlemen, I give you the German shepherd dog. . . .
>
> No longer dependent on a member of the family, a friend or a paid attendant, the blind can once more take up their normal lives as nearly as possible where they left them off.[17]

In a small Tennessee town a man by the name of Frank read Eustis's article out loud to his blind son, Morris. The young man had lost his right eye in a riding accident when he was six years old. The left eye was damaged beyond repair ten years later during a high school boxing match. Morris was so inspired by Eustis's experience he sent her a letter four days later, asking her for the address of the school and any other details she would share. She responded and they negotiated a trade—she would bring Morris abroad, where he would receive his education and even be given one of the school's dogs—if, in return, he promised to show off his success and promote the cause once he returned to the States.

Morris agreed and traveled overseas to meet with Eustis. He was paired with a dog named Kiss (whom he quickly renamed Buddy).[18] By the time their training was done, Morris Frank was moving through the sleepy town of Vevey, Switzerland with Buddy with total comfort and ease. When the pair made the trip back home and docked in New York, a crowd of spectators had gathered, including reporters who had come armed with photographers. It was a skeptical if not altogether unkind crowd, and one reporter shouted out, daring Frank to cross West Street to prove to them all what a dog could do for a blind man.

Compared to the roads of Vevey, West Street was a high-speed interstate of danger. Buddy had never ventured anything like this—cabbies jeered out the window, trucks barreled by them, horns honked from all sides. As Frank lifted his foot off the curb he relinquished all control over entirely to his dog, and for three long minutes Frank was completely directionless. To the shock of all watching, they made it across without a hitch. He dropped his arms around Buddy, jubilant and relieved, his heart still thudding. "Good girl, good girl," he commended her.

Eight years later he and Buddy had packed away 50,000 miles behind them preaching the good word of guide dogs. They helped to establish the Seeing Eye School in 1929 for training dogs to lead the blind in Morristown, New Jersey, and by 1936 the school had paired dogs with 250 blind men and women.[19]

When Japan bombed Pearl Harbor, Eustis and Frank, still friends and colleagues, made an immediate decision to rejoin forces. By then Morris Frank was no longer a young man and had another dog, Buddy II. Eustis too had long since retired from their cause, but they reunited to organize and fund this project—veterans of World War II would have guide dogs if they needed them.

The ability of dogs to boost not only a wounded soldier's confidence but also his morale did not go unnoticed. As early as 1919, the US military brought dogs in as a therapy tool for their psychiatric patients at St. Elizabeth's Hospital in Washington, DC.[20] But it was during World War II that dogs made their mark helping veterans recover from war.

The Associated Press filed over the newswire direct from the Anzio beachhead in Italy one such story of a dog named Lulabelle. Lieutenant Colonel William E. King, a chaplain, was making his rounds of a hospital tent visiting the beds of the wounded. On this particular day he'd brought along his dog, who was so small she often made these visits in the chaplain's pocket. One of the nurses stopped the chaplain and pointed out a soldier lying on his back, his gaze fixed on the ceiling. He had lost both hands and was, the nurse said, lucky to be alive. He'd been virtually nonresponsive since they brought him to the hospital. But when he saw

Lulabelle he tried to speak and the chaplain went over to his bed to see what he wanted. The request was a simple one—he asked the chaplain to put the dog on his bed. Lulabelle obligingly scrambled across the man's chest to lick his face.

"I used to have a dog, sir," he explained. "That's the first time a dog has licked my face since I left home." And then he smiled. When the chaplain left the hospital that day he did so without Lulabelle. Instead she stayed on that bed, curled up with the young man, her head resting over his shoulder.[21]

A similar encounter and act of benevolence would bring canines into the halls of the American Air Forces Convalescent Hospital in Pawling, New York. In the summer of 1944, a Red Cross volunteer got the idea that a dog might break the melancholy of one recuperating airman, Lieutenant Colin, who'd shattered his leg. Dogs for Defense, the very same organization responsible for providing the military with its canine fighting force, arranged for Colin to get a dog, a German shepherd puppy named Fritz. The change in Colin was extraordinary: he improved so much that his recovery time exceeded doctors' expectations by six months.[22]

Fritz's presence at Pawling and Colin's undeniable progress kicked off a small movement at the hospital. Soon, other patients were asking for their own dogs.

And, just as they had during World War I, war dogs who had been wounded or for other reasons had finished their tour of service were paired with wounded soldiers to become healing companions. Soon hospitals in Massachusetts and others around New York State were requesting and receiving dogs for their patients. Nearly two years after Lieutenant Colin was paired with Fritz, the hospital in Pawling installed an 80-foot kennel fully outfitted to house the 50 dogs living at the hospital.

As one former pilot, and a Convalescent Hospital patient who benefited from this movement, wrote, "the Red Cross got me Patty, the swellest Irish Setter you ever saw. We're never apart. . . . And I've been feeling better since the day I got her."[23]

Over the next few decades, animal-assisted therapy slowly began attracting attention in the civilian world. Therapist Boris Levinson, owner of a dog named Jingles, once forgot to remove the dog from the room during a therapy session, only to notice that a young patient, a withdrawn boy, became noticeably more relaxed with Jingles in the room. Levinson took note of this canine-inspired improvement and Jingles became a regular fixture in his therapy sessions. In 1962, Levinson published an article on the phenomenon, "The Dog as Co-Therapist."[24]

But while animal-assisted therapy became popular during the 1960s and 1970s, it really wasn't until the 1990s that scientific evidence started to accumulate that suggested more conclusively that dogs have a tremendously positive effect on lowering stress and anxiety. A 1998 study showed that, after a half hour spent with a dog, psychiatric patients exhibited a reduction in their anxiety that was two times the effect of other, more standard stress-alleviating therapeutic activities. In 2003, the woman who conducted this study, Sandra Barker of Virginia Commonwealth University, reported that patients awaiting electroconvulsive therapy were less fearful after spending 15 minutes with a dog.[25] The American Heart Association released a study in 2005 that showed that 12 minutes of time spent with therapy dogs improved "heart and liver function, reduced blood pressure, diminished harmful hormones, and decreased anxiety in heart patients."[26] And finally, in March 2010 Barker published a third study on the "buffering effect" dogs have on human emotions by measuring the cortisol level of their human companions to determine their stress level.[27]

So convincing was this data that in 2009 Senator Al Franken, Democrat from Minnesota, and Senator Johnny Isakson, Republican from Georgia, drafted and passed the Service Dogs for Veterans Act. The bill mandated that no fewer than 200 service dogs would be paired with US veterans, and that these dogs should be divided evenly between those suffering from physical injuries and those suffering "primarily from mental health difficulties." In tandem with this pilot program were plans for a scientific study of the initiative within the Department of Veterans Affairs that would last for no less than three years in order to determine the therapeutic benefits to veterans, from quality of life to savings on health-care costs.[28] And the following year, in 2010, the federal government committed to spending several million dollars to gather scientific evidence on the impact that dogs have on PTSD.[29]

But it wasn't the research that inspired the arrival of the first therapy dog at Walter Reed National Military Medical Center in 2007. It was an accidental observation very much like the one made at Pawling during World War II. At the height of the Iraq War, occupational therapist Harvey Naranjo, a former combat medic, was watching his patients while they were at the stables for equine therapy: riding the horses to help work their core muscles. A few dogs were also ambling around the barn. Naranjo saw his most reticent and withdrawn patient playing with one of the dogs, looking so much happier and more relaxed that his entire demeanor altered. Naranjo commented, offhandedly, to a man standing nearby, that having a dog at Walter Reed would make his job a lot easier. The man turned out to be a retired Army veterinary officer who took Naranjo's idea seriously. Within a short time, they had their first trained service dog on staff—a chocolate Lab named Deuce.[30]

The positive impact that Deuce had on everyone he encountered at Walter Reed was what inspired the Warrior Transition Brigade's Wounded Warrior Service Dog Training Program in 2009. The program was designed to use dogs to prepare recovering patients for the life transition they would make once they left the hospital, whether it was to return to their military service, go back to school, or find employment in the civilian world.

The idea for the program was actually twofold: in addition to spending time with the dogs, the recovering soldiers would be training them to be service dogs for veterans. It worked miraculously well. Patients previously unable to perform everyday tasks were suddenly empowered and able to accomplish them once they were next to a young puppy.

While the program wasn't limited to soldiers struggling with PTSD, they were often the best candidates. The dogs not only provided soldiers who had been withdrawn or depressed with calming and unconditionally loving company, but their presence also gave them the motivation to get out of bed and provided them with a prideful purpose. Despite the fact that these soldiers knew their dog wasn't going to belong to them forever, the effect was profound.

Even the patients' families reported seeing a change. Training a young puppy takes a steady, careful hand and a willingness to emote happiness and praise. The necessary exercise of offering the dog a reward for good work requires a particular tone that combines inhibition with enthusiasm, high pitched and joyful. By interacting with the dogs in this manner, over time, patients relearn a more gentle way to interact with their spouses and children—even if only subconsciously. Their voices were transformed, from the flat, dejected affect so typical of PTSD, into something more upbeat and engaged.

Sara Hook was the chief of the Warrior Transition Brigade's Occupational Therapy Department when the dog program started at Walter Reed. She remembers one soldier in particular who came into the military hospital with a combination of psychological and physical wounds, confined to a wheelchair. Like many newly admitted patients, he was closed off, always with his head down and his eyes low. But when therapy dogs approached him, Hook observed an instant transformation. By the time this patient completed the program some six months later, he was able to stand at a podium and speak from a microphone in front of a crowded room and lead an official military ceremony. Of course he had other traditional rehabilitative therapy while at Walter Reed, but Hook believes this soldier will say that it was the dogs—their unconditional love, that they were always happy to see him no matter how he looked or felt, regardless of his being in a wheelchair—that made the difference.

Hook and her staff at Walter Reed not only saw changes in their patients after the dog program began, but also had case managers report that there was a decrease in prescriptions for medications for pain, anxiety, and depression. Yet, so far the evidence supporting the success of this kind of stepping-stone therapy program at Walter Reed is largely anecdotal. Scientific studies have not yet been conducted to analyze the efficacy of the dog program.

Captain Najera faced a similar problem. Even though Boe's positive impact was clear to the observant eye, Najera had difficulty building a clear case among the military's top brass for continuing the use of therapy dogs.

During her deployment Najera started collecting data for a research paper, one that would examine what evidence, if any, would show that the therapy dogs were making a difference. She compared the dogs with three other therapeutic techniques: guided imagery (envisioning a safe, happy place), deep breathing exercises, and basic education on coping with stress taught in the clinics. But conducting the surveys proved difficult. It was hard to assess the range of the dogs' impact: while Najera and Boe had regular visits with patients, not everyone who might have found relief in Boe's presence could be accounted for. And then, just as they were collecting this data, things for the US military in Iraq began to change. The drawdown of troops started, and servicemen and women were transferred from their bases in Iraq. Najera and the other occupational therapist–dog handlers lost track of the soldiers in their survey pool. One day they were there with Boe and the other dogs then, suddenly, those same people were gone.

Boe was in Iraq for a total of 18 months, serving two deployments back to back. Toward the end of their tour, Najera started to see a change in Boe. She had never been the kind of dog who relished being the center of a large crowd, but she'd always accepted the affection offered to her and indulged the excited fuss the soldiers made with a friendly patience.

But after nearly 15 months of being Boe's handler, Najera noticed that when soldiers approached Boe, she turned away from them. The only time she ever seemed happy was when she was free to just be a dog. She didn't want to engage anymore. It was as if, Najera says, she had absorbed too much sadness.

It would be counterintuitive, even foolhardy, to assume that dogs can experience war but are somehow immune to its hardships, that they do not shoulder its burdens. Dogs experience the same heat, the same chaos, the same injuries, the same violence, and the same trauma. War and combat affect all dogs, just the way they do soldiers. And like people, each dog responds differently. But because working dogs are in such high demand, and their numbers relatively few compared to their handlers, they do not take breaks between deployments as their handlers do. Dogs with good working records who are in good health are, potentially, deployed more times and more often than their handlers, even serving back-to-back tours. This takes a toll. Military working dogs, like soldiers, return from war changed.

In March 2012, at the ISAK course in Yuma, Arizona, a large German shepherd named Jessy stares down the long, sandy stretch of unpaved desert road. She is uneasy. There are bomb-sniffing aids buried about 100 meters from where she is standing, and her Army handler, Sergeant Sabrina Curtis, is trying to coax her forward, commanding the dog to search alone, off leash.

But something holds Jessy back. She moves cautiously, haltingly, casting her head back as if at any moment she expects to turn and find Curtis vanished. Curtis, a diminutive handler with a soft but firm voice, repeats her command to search, this time with more force. Jessy puts her nose to the ground and sets to work, eagerly moving about ten feet ahead. She gives all the cues to indicate she's working on detecting an odor, which is promising. But then she suddenly pulls up away from odor to check again on Curtis, looking torn, almost doleful. After a few more hesitant steps and nervous glances backward, it's clear this dog is more than merely reluctant to search away from her handler.

Jessy's tail is clipped in a short bob, uncommon for her breed. The tail's stubby end looks odd as she walks but it doesn't seem to impede her. When Jessy's previous handler went on leave the dog just broke down, his sudden departure setting off a bout of separation anxiety. During his absence she would spin compulsively in her crate, so frequently that she broke her tail not once, but twice. The veterinarians who treated her removed the length of it rather than have her suffer any further breaks.

They give it a few more tries before Sergeant Charlie Hardesty, who's been observing the pair, walks out to join Jessy, leading the dog to the source of odor to make the find and reward her with the Kong. She still looks back at Curtis, but sits at the source and, when Hardesty praises her, she responds well. The handlers want to keep things positive for Jessy and get her to associate reward and affection with working, rather than with whatever is keeping her from feeling confident and secure on patrol.

To see Jessy's lack of confidence is to know that war wounds—whether skin deep or the kind that are made on the inside—can have an equally damaging and similar effect on a dog.

Canine post-traumatic stress disorder, or CPTSD, is a relatively new term that's only more recently been accepted as a concept, being applied in a serious and consistent way in the military veterinary field. When the number of dogs on the ground in Afghanistan and Iraq reached its height in 2011, it was reported that 5 percent of the 650 dogs deployed were developing CPTSD. The chief of behavioral medicine at Lackland Air Force Base's MWD hospital, Dr. Walter E. Burghardt Jr., estimated that half of those dogs would have to retire from service.[31]

The war dogs that come through the veterinary clinic at Bagram Airfield are right in the midst of the fighting, constantly around the popping of bullets and large explosions. Sometimes they even have to be medevaced for PTSD and treated with drugs, the equivalent of canine Prozac. But it's a tough thing to treat. "You can't tell a dog it's going to be okay, you can't explain to him what's going on," says Captain Katie Barry. Researching the topic is especially challenging, because you can't replicate the trauma of combat at home, nor would you want to, and as a result, research on CPTSD is still scarce and evolving.

Part of the problem might just be that some of the dogs shouldn't be brought into a combat situation to begin with. Not every war dog trainer is like Chris Jakubin, who pushes the dogs at the US Air Force Academy kennels by exposing them to different types of environmental situations—dealing with large crowds, loud noises, even flights of stairs—that they'll encounter in the field. He does it to test their resolve; a dog that might be a daring detection dog inside a quiet building may quickly lose his drive in an unfamiliar setting or a place he finds stressful.

During the ISAK's March 2012 course, the instructors were concerned with 3 of the 17 dogs that attended. These were dogs they felt would need more than three weeks of training before they could be deemed deployment ready. It was possible that these were dogs, like Jessy, whose war dog days were already behind them. It was possible that these were dogs who shouldn't be responsible for the safety of others in a combat zone.

But even capable teams and dogs who show promise and courage in training—giving all the signs that they are ready to tackle a combat deployment—are still just as susceptible to being traumatized once they're downrange.

Which is what happened when US Army handler Staff Sergeant Donald Craig Miller and his Belgian Malinois Ody deployed to Afghanistan in late September 2012, but returned only a few months later in January 2013. What was supposed to be a yearlong deployment ended early. A great detection dog, Ody hit odor and rarely fell victim to distraction during patrols or searches on base back home. When Miller left their home station—Fort Rucker in Alabama—he felt confident in his dog, knowing they would be able to handle the elite missions they were going to be executing.

When they got to Afghanistan, they were attached to a MARSOC unit, bunking in a compound near Camp Leatherneck, the 1,600-acre Marine Corps base that is home to 10,000 troops in Helmand Province. Their initial training together on base went well; Ody was his reliable, happy-dog self, adjusting well to the temperature and their lodgings on base. Miller's pale complexion pinked under the sun and after some time in Afghanistan his strawberry blond hair gave way to a grizzly, paprika-colored beard.

A few weeks into their deployment Miller and Ody went on a mission with the MARSOC team. It was zero dark thirty; they were pressed into the Chinook helicopter with about two dozen other Marines, and he and Ody had the spot closest to the ramp so the dog could stretch out and lie down. The weight of Miller's 90-pound rucksack was weighing down on him, pushing his muscles deeper into discomfort, pinching off his circulation as he crouched on the floor. When the Chinook lowered and they went to make the short drop to the ground, Miller could barely feel his legs.

Into the dark they jumped, running under the loud whir and rush of the blades, kicking up dust and rocks, like a hurricane hitting them hard in the face. As they started to move forward, an air support assault erupted around them. The sound was deafening. As a C-130 shot down from above and the rushing of bodies swarmed around them in the dark, Ody pulled at his leash, practically dragging his handler along the ground, desperate to get away. Miller's dog was freaking out.

Miller tried to calm Ody, offering first a Kong and then the tug toy he always carried with him on missions for Ody. But the dog refused them, and he wouldn't focus on anything, milling aimlessly. He showed no interest in sniffing or investigating anything around him. Ody was in a state of fear and shock.

Miller kept an eye on Ody through his NVGs as they continued with the mission. But even just moving from one point to the next, Ody kept trying to walk underneath his handler, moving against his handler's legs. When Miller took a knee, Ody would push at Miller with his paws, trying to dig underneath him, to get to the only place it seemed he felt safe.

When they got back to Leatherneck, Miller took Ody to the vet right away. He was told to keep him content for the next few days, to just let the dog relax. The dog was locked up the whole night and all the next day—he wouldn't eat, he wouldn't sleep, or even relieve himself. He finally started to relax the following day, spending most of his time in Miller's bed.

But Ody didn't show much sign of improvement beyond that; the trauma from that night hadn't left him. He was jumpy around anyone other than his handler. Miller worried that Ody might bite someone, which, for a dog as easygoing as Ody, meant he was still very afraid.

Despite their poor performance during the mission, the MARSOC team wanted to keep the dog team around. Miller and his team leader decided that Ody should get a three-week retraining session. Their goal was to slowly and gently rebuild the dog's confidence. Each week they introduced a new kind of weaponry at the range—from pistols to rifles, from machine guns to RPGs and mortars—getting louder and louder. On base Ody still proved to be a solid detection dog, doing well on every search drill. So they decided to try a low-intensity mission, a basic foot patrol during the daylight. But as soon as they stepped off the base and outside the wire, Ody tensed up, all his skittishness returning. He knew he was leaving the place where he felt safe.

Miller could have tried another night mission with Ody, but MARSOC uses a lot of mortars and rockets. When he asked himself if it was worth the risk, Miller knew the chance of doing more harm than good loomed too large in the end. Ody's lack of confidence was too big a risk factor, both for him and for the Marines on their missions.

When the pair returned to Fort Rucker, Miller could see the difference in his dog as soon as they drove up to the kennels. He was like a kid on Christmas: Ody knew he was home. Miller is confident, however, that Ody will be a superb garrison dog. He just wasn't meant for war.

NINE

the never
again wars

Many an American boy will survive this war and be restored to his family because some dog gave him warning of an enemy in time to seek cover, or sought him out as he lay helplessly wounded in some jungle thicket. Time and again these dogs have proved their worth in saving human life.

—Clayton C. Going, *Dogs at War*[1]

It was Iraq, 2005. Sergeant Justin Harding and four other Marines sat in a Humvee, blocking a bridge that connected southern Ramadi to the Tameen District and stood over the Tameen Canal, a man-made tributary that ran into the Euphrates. The bridge had once been a railroad thoroughfare, but trains had long since stopped running across these tracks. Instead, pedestrians used it as a walking bridge.

After noticing a suspicious looking speedboat down along the canal, their platoon commander ordered the five Marines to take the Humvee across the train tracks to the other side of the bridge. They rolled along slowly, singing "this shit is bananas, b-a-n-a-n-a-s," a line from a Gwen Stefani song, joking because there was barely any room on either side of their large vehicle and no protective rails, if anything went wrong, to keep their Humvee from dropping 20 feet off the side into the fast-moving waters below.

The Marines had watched civilians walk over the bridge safely all day, so they hadn't even thought to sweep it for explosives. Yet it turned out that there were two IEDs hidden under that bridge. The first blew up right in front of them, the Humvee's grill and hood absorbing the blast. Another second later and it would have exploded right under the vehicle's belly, probably killing everyone inside. The Humvee continued on for another 500 meters before the vehicle overheated. Harding suffered a severe back injury, the pressure from the explosion compressing several discs in his spine. The driver's knees were bruised, and their gunner suffered a bad concussion and had to be medevaced out. As they were waiting for the Quick Reaction Force to come get them, the Medical Humvee was making its way back across the bridge and the other bomb, the one that failed to detonate on their first trip, exploded. The vehicle, nearly destroyed, limped across and everyone inside was put on other trucks.

Harding deployed to Iraq four times; he was there for the initial push of US forces in 2003, deployed two more times in 2004, and returned for a final tour in the US troop surge of 2007. During these four deployments he was hit by more IEDs than he can keep track of. During his second deployment, from 2004 to 2005, he suffered no fewer than three direct hits, a handful in which he was within 50 meters of the blast and another dozen that exploded between 50 and 100 meters away. During one of his Iraq tours in 2004, the Humvee he was in got hit with an RPG. It went through the armor and through their driver, killing him instantly. It took off the leg of their gunner, set another Marine on fire, and knocked out the man sitting behind him. The blast sent shrapnel everywhere, hitting Harding in the face. And then, he says, "we crashed."[2]

Hanging on the wall of Harding's office now is a photograph of ten Marines who were with him in Iraq. Nine of them were killed by IEDs.

These men are the reason why Harding volunteered to be a supervising officer with the Marine Corps Improvised Explosive Detector Dog (IEDD) program, one that pairs single-purpose detection dogs with infantrymen, introduced in 2007 in response to an "urgent-needs request" for bomb-sniffing canines.[3] In 2010, three years after Harding returned from Iraq, he was on his way to Afghanistan, this time as a gunnery sergeant and as the supervisor for a team of 17 IEDD handlers and their 13 detection dogs. Having survived his combat tours, Harding wanted to do something that would help keep young Marines from getting killed by IEDs.

During their seven months in Afghanistan, Harding calculated that his dog teams were responsible for finding approximately 500 IEDs. And while he is infinitely proud of that number, Harding believes that even if only one dog had only found one bomb in the entire seven months that would have been enough. At the very least, he figures, one bomb found would have equaled one Marine's life saved.

At the end of wars, sometimes it's the numbers that make the difference.

In World War II, it is said that war dogs saved 15,000 men. In Vietnam, the dogs were credited with saving the lives of 10,000 men, but many handlers who served there feel that this number is grossly underestimated. Of approximately 87,000 missions, the dogs uncovered 2,000 tunnels and bunkers and enabled 1,000 enemy captures and 4,000 enemy kills.[4]

How big that number will be many years from now, when we are in a position to tally the lives saved by dogs in Iraq and Afghanistan, one cannot say. But Technical Sergeant Justin Kitts was awarded his Bronze Star in 2011 for his detection work with Dyngo during their Afghanistan deployment, and for having secured the lives of 30,000 US, host nation, and coalition forces. And that was just for one dog team on one tour of duty.[5] Equally impossible to tally are the lives that have been recovered, even in some small way, by a dog's cathartic presence, on a battlefield or in a wounded warrior treatment center.

From war to war, these numbers are often forgotten.

It is an unfortunate scenario that's already played out twice in the United States: post–World War II and post-Vietnam. The value of war dogs has been lost as often as it has been found.

These events usually go a little something like this: the United States engages in a conflict. Someone, a person or group, with great resilience and spirit, petitions the military to adopt a canine fighting force, touting their many lifesaving skills. Someone in a position of power gives an order, and a small contingent of dogs is procured, trained, and deployed. Once in-country, the dogs prove to be of great value on the battlefield and save many lives. Next comes an "urgent need" request from the combat arena: "Send more dogs!" And so efforts are pooled, handlers and dogs are trained with fervor and speed. Sometimes concessions are made, sometimes shortcuts are taken, but more dogs are sent to war. The military parades the dogs' successes, the media seizes upon their stories, and headlines capture the hearts of civilians at home.

The wars slow down and eventually end. The tremendous canine force is scaled back, as are the combat-ready aspects of the dog programs, until they are virtually nonexistent.

If the war was unpopular, the lessons are lost all the more quickly. This tendency of the US military to strategize with a selective memory is one with which John Nagl, coauthor of the *Counterinsurgency Field Manual* along with Generals David H. Petraeus and James F. Amos, is well familiar.

The Pentagon is traditionally accused of preparing for the last war. But according to Nagl, who was an operations officer of a tank battalion task force during the Iraq War,[6] that's not exactly what happens. We prepare to refight the last war only if it was the kind of war we had wanted to fight. The wars the US military is interested in fighting again are wars where they've had success, such as the American Civil War and World War II.

The irony of this, Nagl explains to me, is that in recent decades, the American military hasn't spent its time fighting big and successful wars like these. Instead, we have fought small wars, irregular wars—the kind of wars waged with IEDs. Despite this reality, the military still builds the capabilities it needs for those "big" wars, not the capabilities it needs for what Nagl calls the "small nasty wars of peace."[7]

And when the military tries to do that, it makes mistakes, which is when the lessons learned become especially important. In fact, Nagl says, "we have rediscovered many, many lessons that we actually learned and paid for in great cost in Vietnam." One of those lessons, Nagl says, "is the utility of working dogs, who were invaluable in Vietnam. [We] couldn't get enough of them; didn't ever have enough of them." But after Vietnam, he says, the skills of those dogs, as with almost everything about Vietnam, was purged from our memory. "And that's a lesson we had to relearn. We are in danger of forgetting a number of those lessons," Nagl tells me. And that includes the dogs.

In the years following the Vietnam War, the US military began to disassemble its war dog programs little by little, dismantling ten years of combat readiness. In a shroud of shame, the dog programs slipped away—first the tracker dogs, then the scout dog school at Fort Benning. There was no outside organization watching over the military efforts for the dogs deployed to Vietnam as there was in World War II.

The Vietnam chapter, which will remain a perpetual blemish in the United States' war dog history, is perhaps the most troubled and difficult to reconcile. But each war has its own dogs—from the Revolutionary War to Vietnam—and each war has its own saga. How the dogs came in, and how they came out again, is as important, in some ways, as what they did while they were there. Their entry and exit unearths a relevant truth. This discernable pattern of US war dog history is one of building to a great success that is later shelved and forgotten, only to be rebuilt again when the need arises. It's a precedent that creates the kind of disadvantage no one would be able to fully realize until 2004, when it was time to send the dogs back to war, so many years after Vietnam.

Ron Aiello, the Marine handler who served in Vietnam with his scout dog Stormy, remembers how the canine program was dismantled after the war. First they got rid of the Marine Corps scout dogs, the mine dogs, and the booby trap dogs. Then the Army got rid of its tracker dogs. All their combat readiness disappeared. He knew then it was a mistake.

After 9/11 happened and the Iraq war began, Aiello watched the news reports on television, and saw military dogs working checkpoints or sniffing cars as they crossed gates. It infuriated him. He found himself shouting at the television set: "Have them out on patrol! Use them for IEDs!" But he knew the dogs weren't trained for that kind of work because building up those kinds of programs again from scratch would have taken years.

There are many parallels to draw between the wars in Iraq and Afghanistan and that in Vietnam: the wars in Iraq and Afghanistan have not been popular ones, and there is a rush to push our military's attention elsewhere. As the United States closes shop on two wars, the urgent need for dogs is already depleting and will likely continue to lessen over time.

In response, the military working dog program is already downsizing its combat-ready dogs accordingly. All branches of the military are seeing budgetary cuts. The programs that produced the "Dog Surge" of the mid-2000s—the Marine Corps' Improvised Explosive Detector Dogs and the Army's Tactical Explosive Detection Dogs—have already reduced their numbers and will certainly be disbanded. The need for dogs has not been extinguished, but it is no longer urgent now that the United States has withdrawn from Iraq and is preparing to withdraw its troops from Afghanistan. As one of his final acts as program manager at Lackland before retiring, Sean Lulofs was ordered to investigate cutting the program by one-third. In fact, he found a way to cut it in half.

There's no way that what happened in 1975 would happen now. The United States military will never again leave its dogs behind as they did in Vietnam. This is in part because of the government's interest in monitoring the dogs' exit from the military, manifested in the Robby Law, which mandated diligent record-keeping and turned a watchful eye on how the dogs leave service, but also because there is simply too much public visibility for such gross neglect to exist on such a grand scale. But just how far the programs will diminish, and whether or not war dog lessons of the past, which is to say our present, will be remembered, remains to be seen.

Aiello sees the changes happening today—the troop drawdown, the program cuts, and the thinning of dog teams—and he sees the heavy curtain of past mistakes dropping again.

But what is far more likely to make an impact than a tally of numbers at the end of the war are the efforts and living memories of handlers—like

Aiello—who, after their tours of duty ended, became the watchmen of the next generation of dogs, handlers, and war. They are the ones now building memorials and keeping track of the handlers and dogs killed in action. Their memory is institutional and it is long. And just like Aiello and his handler buddies from Vietnam followed in the footsteps of the World War II handlers, so too will the war dog handlers of Iraq and Afghanistan.

When, in 2010, Gunnery Sergeant Justin Harding was with his team of IEDD handlers and dogs in Afghanistan, they made a stop at Camp Dwyer, one of the Marine Corps' largest military bases in the country, so the handlers could bring their dogs to the veterinarians there.[8] While they were waiting on base, their dogs with them, a lance corporal they didn't know approached the handlers. This Marine had been with a unit in Marjah where the fighting had been especially fierce. This young man had returned to Dwyer looking battle shocked and worn, and Harding could tell that he'd seen hell. The grief-stricken Marine had just lost some of his friends, but he wanted to thank the handlers and their dogs. "You guys are the shit," he told them. "You know, you saved our lives and I'm sure not all of you will come back."

Harding's infantry handlers, who hadn't yet been out on patrol, didn't know how to respond. But for Harding, that singular interaction summed up his entire wartime experience: from getting hit with IEDs, to losing so many of his friends, to trying to help protect the younger generation of Marines, to fighting against higher-ups who denied the dogs the legitimacy he believes they deserved.

Harding will never forget watching that young Marine, who was battered and damaged and already showing signs of the scars he'd likely carry for a lifetime, walk up to the handlers with tears in his eyes and reach out to shake their hands. In that moment he was overcome with the certainty that being in Afghanistan with the dogs was the right thing—the best thing he could have done to save lives in this war.

TEN

home again,
home again

My little dog—a heartbeat at my feet.

—Edith Wharton

The good Lord in his ultimate wisdom gave us three things to make life bearable, hope, jokes and dogs, but the greatest of these was dogs.

—Robyn Davidson

Marine Corporal Eric Roethler was back at Camp Lejeune, back in North Carolina, back from Afghanistan.

He'd just gotten called into the head shed where the staff had their offices. They wanted to talk to him about taking on a new dog, the dog he'd take downrange with him when he went back over. When Roethler heard which dog from the kennel they intended to give him, he was thrilled. "Heck yes," he told the staff sergeant. "I would love to take him as my dog." It was a big pat on the back, you could say, being given the responsibility of this dog.

But as soon as Roethler had the leash in his hands he knew he had a challenge in front of him. He was having a hard time clicking with his new dog. Roethler had just spent his deployment with an eight-year-old German shepherd named Kito who'd already been downrange three times.

Their rapport had come naturally, their communication smooth and fluid the whole way through. But this new dog, smart and stubborn, was used to having things go his way. When Roethler would tell the dog to go one way, he would go the other because that's the way he wanted to do it.

From the outside it may have seemed liked the 21-year-old Roethler had something to prove—he was working with another seasoned dog, a dog who had proven himself in training, and a dog who had married up well with his last handler. It's not that Roethler lacked confidence or that he wasn't ready to trust this dog. Maybe part of the issue was that this dog had been so close with his old handler. Or maybe it was because that dog's former handler had been Roethler's corporal in Afghanistan and that corporal hadn't just been any other Marine—it was Joshua Ashley. And this dog, Sirius, had been Ashley's dog.

Roethler had been in Afghanistan with Ashley the summer Ashley was KIA. The night Ashley died, Roethler and another Marine corporal were in the same area of operation, stationed at a MARSOC base in the Helmand Valley. It was the middle of the night and Roethler was gearing up with the Marine corporal for a mission when one of the team chiefs approached them. "Hey, I want to let you guys know that a dog handler got hit," he said. The chief didn't know who it was or if that man was alive or dead; he just wanted to let the handlers know that one of their own was down.

Roethler and his friend didn't believe it could be any of their guys. The hit had happened in Zombalay, and none of their guys were supposed to be on missions there. But when the chief came back and told them the handler's initials they started to piece it together. It had to be Ashley.

Roethler still went out on the mission that night and did his job no better or worse than he would've any other night. But there wasn't a moment that Ashley wasn't in the back of his mind.

Before Ashley was killed, Roethler had been able to watch him work Sirius in Afghanistan while they were training with the MARSOC guys. He'd seen what a solid detection dog Sirius was. He could tell what a good team they were.

But now it was September 2012. Ashley had been killed in action in July. It was time for Sirius to have a new handler. And after about a month of working with Sirius at the Lejeune kennels, things had improved between Roethler and the dog.

In January 2013 they traveled together to Yuma Proving Ground for their predeployment training. Some of the same instructors who had coached Ashley through the March class the year before were still there— Sergeant Charlie Hardesty and Staff Sergeant Lee McCoy. It threw them a little to see Sirius come through again, but it was also like they got to have a little piece of Ashley back.

One afternoon, Roethler and Sirius were running drills in McCoy's lane, searching the compound's exterior. This drill was one of McCoy's specialties; there was nothing for the dog to find here, just a visual plant for the handler. There was no associative odor, so if they were going to find the bomb, it wouldn't be Sirius's nose but his handler's eyes that should catch it. Roethler had his weapon raised and was using the scope on his rifle to scan the area. Sirius was out in front, sniffing and searching the ground. And then, through the lens he spied something glittering in the gravel. And no sooner did he raise his head to take another look and call back his dog than Sirius sat right in the middle of the road, turned his head back, and stared straight at Roethler. The dog turned back again to look in the direction of that shiny material and then looked back again at his handler. Somehow he'd picked up on that IED plant and was letting his handler know there was something up ahead and he didn't like it.

McCoy let out a low whistle and turned to Roethler. "That's a solid dog right there," he told him. After that day, Roethler felt the difference between him and Sirius. That was the day their bond took root.

Now when they're not working Sirius is as gentle as big teddy bear; he only wants to get petted and lay around. But when they're working he's still the same hardheaded dog. His stubborn streak is still strong. Just like Ashley was. They were exactly the same way, obstinate and hardheaded, wanting to do everything their own way. But Roethler says, "That is why they were such a good team." And every time that streak shows in Sirius, Roethler

*Marine Corporal Eric Roethler and MWD Sirius wait to board an aircraft
aboard a multipurpose amphibious assault ship in March 2014.*
Photo by Specialist 1st Class RJ Stratchko

shakes his head, chuckles, and thinks about Ashley. "My first thought," he
says, "is, 'dammit Josh, you left me with a hardheaded dog.'"

Roethler and Sirius are set to head to Afghanistan sometime in 2014.
But they're ready, he says, 100 percent. He doesn't worry that what happened to Ashley will happen to him. "You can't live your life in fear," he
says. "You think of the good, forget the bad." Roethler is almost defiantly
proud that he took over Ashley's dog. And he has put all the faith he has in

Sirius, a commitment that he feels the dog has earned. "First thing is trust your dog. You trust your dog, you follow him where he goes. If you don't trust your dog you need to rethink your situation. You should have total faith to trust and walk behind him."

There are some other guys from II-MEF out there in Afghanistan, Beauchamp and Garcia, who were at YPG with Ashley in March 2012. They're both partnered up with new dogs but they're out there together, stationed at Camp Leatherneck. Peeler did a tour in Afghanistan with Lex, his tracker dog, and came back. Now he's an instructor at YPG. Kitts and Mendoza, the instructors running lanes at YPG, left the program when the Air Force pulled their branch out of ISAK in 2012 and started its own predeployment course. The two of them had both gotten assignments at the United States Air Force Academy and had moved out to Colorado. Mendoza had actually joined Chris Jakubin's team at the Academy's kennels. Kitts took a job working with cadets and wasn't working with dogs anymore, at least not as an Air Force handler. Dyngo had already gone and come back from Afghanistan. It was his last deployment. He was back at his old home station in Arizona. He's getting to be an old dog, ready to retire.

The way things are looking, Roethler and Sirius might very well be one of the last Marine dog teams to deploy in this war. Then maybe they'll all be ready to come home again. Some of the animals will work as military police dogs and others will retire from service and just be dogs. Some will even go home with their handlers.

It was just about six o'clock when Matt Hatala met his mother in the Target parking lot so they could swap cars—he traded her the keys to his diesel truck, a 2006 Chevy, and she handed over the ones that went with the borrowed Pontiac Vibe. When Hatala had realized how much gas it was going to take to drive his truck down to South Carolina, it was his mother who'd called up a car salesman she knew at a local car dealership. The people there had been remarkably supportive of their veterans in Waverly, Iowa, and when he heard what her son was doing and why he needed a vehicle, he'd arranged to get Hatala a car, and for free. Hatala threw his clothes into the hatchback and hugged his mother good-bye. Thirty minutes later he was on his way, with nothing but the June night and open road in front of him. He pushed his foot down and drove about as fast as the little Pontiac Vibe would go.

His first stop was Peoria, Illinois, to pick up Keegan Albright; he'd also been a dog handler in Afghanistan. They drove through the night until they reached Indianapolis, where they met up with Shea Boland, the Marine who'd been Hatala's point man during all his patrols in Afghanistan. Pumped up on energy drinks and the buzz of reunion, the guys spent the whole time talking, napping, and driving. The car was filled with metal and country music, laughing and bullshitting. They hadn't been together since Afghanistan; they'd all gotten caught up in their own lives, but for Hatala, inside the small space of that car, it felt like no time had passed at all. He was back with his brothers and they'd be with him all the way to kennels in South Carolina. They were going to get Chaney.

After Hatala got back from his tour in Afghanistan, he'd left the Marines. And even though he was home and employed, he was struggling. His job wasn't what he wanted it to be, things weren't going the way he planned. But then a couple of weeks ago, he got a call letting him know that his request to adopt the bomb-sniffing dog he'd had with him in Afghanistan had been approved. The news that he could pick up his dog filled him up with a kind of lightness he hadn't felt in a long time.

When they finally arrived at the kennels, Hatala just wanted to get his dog. After he filled out all the final paperwork and they waited for someone to bring Chaney out of his kennel, Hatala's excitement started to twist into a jittery ache. He hadn't laid eyes on Chaney since September 2011; a gap of nearly two years had gotten between them. In their lull Chaney had been paired up with other handlers and redeployed to Afghanistan. The small worry that his old partner might not remember him started expanding. And then he saw the dog, ambling along with another handler coming toward them. The dog's eyes seemed to take them in but he didn't get excited at the sight of his old friends. It was like Chaney couldn't tell who Hatala

was. Though Hatala could hardly blame him—he'd grown a beard, he'd
gained a little weight, and he wasn't wearing his cammies. But then his old
partner had changed too. Chaney wasn't quite the hulking mass of black
dog that Hatala had pictured in his mind—he'd lost a bit of weight, and
though still a large dog, he didn't seem quite so big anymore. His paws were
white and his beard had grayed.

Hatala gave a good loud call of "Chaney!" in the dog's direction. The
reaction was immediate. Chaney went nuts, pulling and straining to get
to him. Relief flooded him; his dog knew him. In all their time together
Chaney had proven himself a mellow and well-mannered dog. The only
thing that ever really riled him up was a cat. So when Hatala saw Chaney
respond to the sound of his voice, he knew his dog not only remembered
him—he was incredibly happy to see him.

They handed Hatala Chaney's leash and that was it. He had his dog
back. The guys climbed into the car, their mission accomplished. Boland
rode in the back with Chaney; they had to fold down the right side of the
backseat to fit in his crate, broken down into halves so it resembled a big
white bathtub, almost overtaking the car. Chaney lounged comfortably;
when he moved around, his giant head grazed the roof of the car. The four
Marines drove back the way they came, all of them finally together in a
holy communion of brotherhood. It was bliss for Hatala. The only thing he
wished was that their trip had lasted longer than four days.

When they first got back home to Iowa, Chaney followed his old handler everywhere he went—into one room and then the next—always by
his side, just like he did when they were in Afghanistan. Every time Hatala
went to the front door Chaney was at his feet, face upward, eyes seeking as
if he was asking: "Where we going? Are we working?" But there were no
patrols to make in Iowa, no drills to run. There were also different rules. In
Afghanistan, Chaney had gotten used to sleeping wherever he wanted, and
usually that meant Hatala's cot and not alone on the square doggie bed on
the floor. It took a few weeks for Chaney to settle into being a house dog,
but he adjusted. He stopped following Hatala to the door; he got used to
being left in the house.

When the excitement of bringing Chaney home to Iowa faded into something more like normal, Hatala realized just how profound an effect having Chaney back was having on him. He'd been sleeping better since Chaney moved in, he was less stressed—he was somehow more comfortable in his own home.

There was a while, at first, when having Chaney back felt surreal, like it hadn't really happened, as if the whole thing had just been a dream. But when he wakes up each morning, Chaney is still there.

The Rusk family home has always been populated with dogs. From every Christmas going back to when the first of their three sons was born, all the photos of their boys during the holidays have a dog or two crowded into the frame somewhere. Colton was the middle child, a dark-haired little boy with a determined sense of independence. He never needed to be told to do his homework; he always took care of himself. He wanted to be a veterinarian when he grew up. That is, until he decided he wanted to be a Marine. And Colton always did what he set out to do.

Colton Rusk was born on September 23, 1990, and 20 years later, exactly to the day, he left for Afghanistan with Eli, his bomb-sniffing dog.

When Rusk would call home, he had a way of talking to his mother, Kathy—he knew just what to say to set her at ease. He was more forthcoming with details when he spoke to his father, Darrell, but he was protective of his mother. After all, he had a big, red-hearted tattoo with the word *Mom* scrawled across the top of his right arm. From the way he sounded, Kathy could almost imagine that her son was somewhere else entirely, somewhere safe and happy, as if he were only away at summer camp instead of in a combat outpost in Afghanistan. And he always talked about Eli.

The last time he called home, the phone rang early Sunday morning in Texas. Rusk told his mom that the Marines of the 3rd Battalion, 5th Marine Regiment were moving to a safer location and that she shouldn't worry. He'd written a letter, he told her, and it was already on its way. He told her to keep an eye out for it. After not hearing from her son for months, to have the sound of his voice come through so buoyant, so happy, talking about how Eli was sleeping in his sleeping bag or taking up all the space on his cot, it all but pushed away her worry. And that night Kathy went to sleep and actually got some rest.

That following Monday, December 6, 2010, Kathy and Darrell got the notification that Rusk had been killed. Kathy's memory of that day is hazy, but she remembers hearing Darrell ask about Eli—had Eli made it? Where was the dog now?

And Kathy thought of that letter Rusk sent and realized it was still on its way. It arrived the day before they buried him. At the top of the paper was a discernable smudge. Next to it Rusk had written: "Eli kisses."

Rusk's story and the news that Eli had shielded his body after he was shot, had garnered a lot of attention. It does not happen often, but the Marine Corps offered the dog to the family.

Kathy never dreamed that they'd get Eli. And when the Marine Corps first contacted them about adopting the dog, Kathy and Darrell balked. They wanted him, yes, but how could they take him away from the other young men in Rusk's unit? But they were assured that the dog couldn't stay with Rusk's unit, he would have to come back to the States, and start all over again with a new handler before he could redeploy to Afghanistan. If he redeployed at all.

On February 3, 2011, the Rusks drove to Lackland Air Force Base to pick Eli up. Kathy was worried. It'd been months since they'd seen him, and she doubted that he would remember them. While they signed the adoption papers, questions ran through her mind: What if Eli was traumatized or didn't want to go with them? The small room they were waiting in felt even smaller in spite of the fact there were only a few people in there with them. When a Marine finally came in with Eli, from the moment he entered the room she was filled with a contented kind of certainty—the dog was meant to be with them, he was back with his family. She watched the way he strained at the leash to get closer to them, like he knew exactly who they were and he'd been waiting all this time to see them again.

After they drove the two hours back from Lackland, they brought Eli into the house and let him off the leash so he could explore his new home.

He made a beeline straight for Rusk's room and went right on his bed as if he knew exactly where he was going.

Every night Eli sleeps with Brady, the Rusks' youngest son. Brady was only 12 when Colton died, but even though he's a teenager, Eli still sleeps in his bed—not curled at the end of the bed, but under the covers, wrapped in Brady's arms. He may shift around at night if he gets too hot, but he never moves until Brady falls asleep.

The Rusk family home in Orange Grove, Texas, has become something of a sanctuary for the Marines in Colton's unit. Every one of the young men in Rusk and Eli's unit has an open invitation to come and stay. A handful of Marines have already made this pilgrimage to call on the family of their fallen brother—to pay their respects, to visit and to see Eli.

Kathy intuits that they wish to be alone with the dog, to visit with Eli in private. She senses they worry about her, her husband, and their other sons, as if they think somehow the family stopped living too when Colton died. "We tell them we want what is best for them, we want them to live their life to the fullest," she says. "We know Colton's life is over, but he would want them to live their life."

The Marines take solace in these visits and in the Rusk house. Some have stayed days; one even lived with them for a couple of months after he got out of the service. They act as big brothers to Brady. A few of them have taken to calling Kathy "mom." That was hard for her.

Three years later there are still days when Kathy can't bring herself to get out of bed, and it's Eli who comes and finds her, who licks the tears off her face. The dog that lives in her house needs taking care of and it's that need that pulls her up. Eli has his bad days too, when the ghosts of his past come to haunt him—to this day he doesn't like the sound of gunfire, and when there are fireworks going off she sees the change in him. She sees in his face that he's afraid. And then it's her turn to comfort him.

Every now and again Kathy comes across something that belonged to Colton, something that still carries his smell—an old shirt or his watch, the one he was wearing in Afghanistan that she keeps safely tucked away in a small pouch in a small cabinet. The Marines in Rusk's unit brought back all the toys and gear that Colton used with Eli, like his Kong, and gave it to the family. But those things are special and the Rusks only bring them out on rare occasions. One day she caught Eli sniffing the cabinet, just sniffing and sniffing, and she couldn't think what he was after—until she remembered the watch was in this cabinet. He was sniffing out Rusk's scent. Now when she finds Colton's things she shares them with Eli; she drops down her hand to offer whatever she's holding to the dog. They inhale and remember the young man they loved together.

While ruminating on the loss of one of his longest-living pets—a crew that included a variety of well-loved animals—writer James Fallows remarked that "we take animals into our lives knowing that, in the normal course of events, we will see them leave. . . . Nothing lasts forever, and small animals are here for only a brief while."[1] And yet, despite knowing that we engage in this short-lived sojourn destined to mourn, we invite these creatures into our lives, again and again, knowing that however long their lives span, it will have been worth it in the end.

In the spring of 2014 Eli will be seven years old. His joints ache a little. He's slowed down some. Kathy is more careful now not to let him wear himself out chasing tennis balls in the sun.

Before they went to pick Eli up and bring him home, Kathy wrote to the Marine Corps and asked that they please not neuter him because she wanted to breed him. They didn't want to make money off the puppies, she explained in her letter, they wanted to give Eli's puppies to the Marines in Rusk's unit. And so when they brought Eli home, they did so with his fatherhood abilities still intact. The first litter of puppies has already been born—Eli mated with a chocolate Lab, but all 11 of the puppies are black like him. Kathy had intended that they would go to anyone from Colton's Marine battalion who wanted one, but so many of them were still in service. One puppy went to Colton's older brother Cody, who named the little dog Tough; another went to Colton's cousins, who named the puppy Fern, after *Where the Red Fern Grows*, Colton's favorite movie. Still another puppy went to the casualty officer who helped the Rusk family through the worst of their grief following the notification of their son's death. The next of Eli's offspring will be going to the boys of the 3rd Battalion, 5th Marine Regiment.

Kathy Rusk knows that Eli isn't going to live forever. She knows the dog will die, but she won't dwell on the thought, choosing instead to think of other things.

When his dog Aaslan retired, Sean Lulofs hadn't been able to adopt him. His wife had just had a baby and Aaslan didn't have the right temperament for children. He kept tabs on the dog for a while; he knew about the family that had taken him in and where the dog was living. But around the time Aaslan would've been 14 years old, Lulofs stopped reaching out to hear news of his dog. It wasn't because he stopped caring, but he couldn't face the possibility that the dog might've died. So he just left it alone, preferring to keep the fantasy that he was alive and well.

Ron Aiello never found out what happened to Stormy, but when he went to that reunion for the World War II handlers, he met another Vietnam handler who'd worked with Stormy after he left. He showed Aiello a photo of them together, taken in 1970. As far as Aiello knew, this was the last time there was any real record of her. Of all the fates that could have befallen his dog, Aiello prefers to believe that Stormy was killed in action rather than being handed over to the South Vietnamese Army where she would've likely been euthanized. To think of that (or worse, to think she might've been killed and then eaten) fills him with anger.

After his tour ended, Aiello was certain he would never be able to have another dog again. It wouldn't be possible, he thought, that he could love another dog as much as Stormy, and it wouldn't be fair to another dog to always be comparing the next animal to her. But when his younger son pleaded for a dog, he made him a deal. He told his son that if he could keep a hamster alive for one full year, they would get a dog. Aiello thought it was a bet he couldn't lose. His son's first hamster hadn't lasted more than a few weeks. But the next hamster made it one year. A promise was a promise. So Aiello took his son to the pound and they adopted a shepherd-Lab mix called Sampson. Aiello grew to love this dog. It wasn't as hard as he thought it would be.

That hamster died exactly one week later, perhaps knowing he had served his purpose—or, Aiello reasoned, the new big dog in the house had frightened the little thing to death. Either way, a dog had found its way into Aiello's home and into his heart again. Somehow, there had been room. There is always room.

what we talk about when we talk about war dogs

The only thing of which I am sure is that the dogs will be around if we are. They are too valuable in all regards to give up. They are too much a part of who we are.

—Mark Derr, *A Dog's History of America*[1]

After one especially fierce battle, Napoleon Bonaparte had a singular, soul-enlightening encounter with a dog. Surveying the aftermath of the bloody fight he had waged with Italy, Napoleon walked among the fallen men, their bodies still scattered on the ground. A dog appeared before him, and it soon became clear that he had been keeping watch over his master's corpse. The animal was distressed and ran back and forth between the dead soldier and Napoleon, licking the man's lifeless hand in an attempt to signal the general, and, in a sense, implore him for aid, which of course Napoleon had no earthly ability to offer. Many years later, while in exile, Napoleon would write of the deep impact this dog had made on him:

Perhaps it was the spirit of the time and the place that affected me. But I assure you no occurrence of any of my other battlefields impressed me so keenly. I halted on my tour to gaze on the spectacle, and to reflect on its meaning.

This soldier, I realized, must have had friends at home and in his regiment; yet he lay there deserted by all except his dog. . . . I had looked on, unmoved, at battles which decided the future of nations. Tearless, I had given orders which brought death to thousands.

Yet, here I was stirred, profoundly stirred, stirred to tears. And by what? By the grief of one dog. I am certain that at that instant I felt more ready than at any other time to show mercy toward a suppliant foe-man. I could understand just then the tinge of mercy which led Achilles to yield the corpse of his enemy, Hector, to the weeping Priam.[2]

When we talk about war dogs, we are not simply talking about war, and we are not merely talking about dogs. These dogs are a connective thread, a great conveyer bringing events of consequence and people, who would otherwise exist at a great distance from one another, much closer together. By proxy, these dogs can become the thread of war's experience, a link between us or a mirror by which we are more easily able to see things as they really are.

One dog trainer I spoke with while writing this book was employed by a private canine contractor; he'd been hired to prepare Marine dog handlers for their deployments in Afghanistan. This man had already had a long career working dogs for sporting competitions; it's a kind of training that demands very precise execution from the dogs at each particular task. He enjoyed the work, yes, but for a long time, he'd been caught up not with the dogs as much as with winning ribbons. He had never thought of his dogs as just a means to an end, exactly, but when he started training dogs to find explosives, he was startled by what he saw. He began to see the animals he'd worked with his whole life with a newfound appreciation. He'd always known that dogs could save lives, he told me. But, he said, his voice quiet, "until I actually put my hands on them, I really never understood it."

Author Mark Derr doesn't write about dogs to understand them, he told me; he writes about dogs to explore the many ways they help us understand ourselves. He believes dogs are a great gift. He perceives them to be our connection to the natural world, bringing about a more significant sense of meaningfulness to our existence than perhaps we deserve.

And when it comes to understanding and talking about war, Derr muses that dogs offer us a way to discuss the more complicated aspects of war that we otherwise might not—the ugly, darker parts of war—in a way that I believe is quite profound. "It's just that using the dogs to discuss these things is somehow cleaner, as it were, somehow simpler," he reasoned. But, he added, "there's nothing wrong with that, because the only way they get discussed is by distilling them down to their raw essence."[3]

To know war dogs is not to know war, but they can help us understand it better. Knowing the bond between a handler and his dog, we are able to see the people at the other end of the leash more clearly. To know a military handler and his dog's lot in war is to better understand our military and our country's lot in war. And just as war dogs save lives, they enrich them.

Because I've known war dogs, I will never look at dogs the same way again. Because I've known their keepers, I will never look at the military, or the people in its community, the same way, either. And because I knew Lance Corporal Joshua Ashley—despite the fact that I only knew him a little, and gleaned much of what I know about him from those who taught him, loved him, and mourned him—I will never think of war the same way. It's not that I now think of these things—conceptually or otherwise—as necessarily better or worse than I did before I started writing this book; they are just far more layered, complex, and complicated, and infinitely more interesting.

When we talk about war by talking about war dogs, I believe Derr is right—dogs make war more palatable, but also more tender, and more human. Dogs have a way of bringing us back to our senses. They cut a path to our emotions, and more often than not that emotion is love, whatever form it takes.

acknowledgments

When I was a kid I had a habit of "rescuing" animals (though some might have called it kidnapping). There were the neighborhood dogs—the Chinese chow across the street who always needed a cold drink or the beagle from down the block who used to follow me to the bus stop—and the litter of kittens living in the woods at my summer camp. My mother endured this, and whatever strange dog or wounded bird I had brought into the yard, with good-tempered exasperation while my sister, in a show of sibling solidarity, championed my efforts. But if my affinity for animals comes from anywhere it is from my father, a Connecticut farm boy who taught me how to befriend a dog, how to hold a cat, and how to love animals and treat them with dignity and respect.

He also told me (often) to count my blessings, so here they are: my mother, Sheila; my father, Meyer; and my sister, Gail.

When it comes to this book, however, offering thanks must begin with Tom Ricks. For while I found the photo that set me on the war dog path, the journey that followed would not have been without Tom's encouragement. He recognized a good idea and then gave me full reign over it, and for this, I'm forever in his debt. If it was Tom who opened the reporting door, then it was Chris Jakubin who shepherded me through once I was on the other side. As my war dog mentor, he not only gave me his time but also his trust, going above and beyond to make sure I was connected with the best in the business, linking his reputation to mine.

After more than four years reporting on war dogs, I feel privileged to be a part of the military working dog community and all the communities—private, professional, and familial—that surround it by extension. I will always admire their fierce commitment to the dogs—it is selfless and without end. I owe thanks to so many people, among them: Bill Childress, Mike Dowling, Master Sergeant Kristopher Reed Knight, Captain John Brandon Bowe, Antonio Rodriguez, Sean Shiplett, Joel Burton, Sean Lulofs, Ron Aiello, and Richard Deggans; Bill Krol and Lisa Yambrick of American Vet Dogs; and the handlers who run the Military Working Dogs Facebook page. And for the men and women, some of them handlers, who for various reasons couldn't take credit by name for the help they gave me but offered it anyway, I'm grateful. In many ways I feel as though they gave me pieces of themselves around which I simply put words.

I do not know where this book would be without the creative and wonderful team at Palgrave Macmillan, though I do know how lucky I am to have had the erudite and discerning Elisabeth Dyssegaard as my editor. She appreciated what I appreciated about these dogs and their handlers, and with kindness and knowing saw how to best bring their stories full circle. Special thanks to Donna Cherry for organizing the many facets of this book's production, and to Bill Warhop, who copyedited the manuscript and whose line-by-line comments gave me much-needed encouragement in the last and most grueling phase of editing this book. I also wish to thank Lauren Dwyer-Janiec and Christine Catarino for their amazing work getting *War Dogs* out into the world.

Whatever challenges this book brought with it, I never took them on alone, for I had the counsel of Esmond Harmsworth, my brilliant and uncompromisingly lovely agent. I will always be thankful—and better off—for the guidance and support he offered.

Thanks to Ali Rhodes, Jared Mondshein, and Rick Carp, who all contributed their time and talent—fact-checking, transcribing, hunting down the most reluctant of contacts and most obscure details of military history—helping to guard against error, ultimately ensuring this book was better and smarter.

I am—and will always be—eternally grateful for the friendship of David Rothkopf. He was always there to remind me that the sky was not falling after all. I don't know where I would be without his humor and un-flagging support. The crew at *Foreign Policy* magazine, a brilliant and wickedly funny band of creatives who are still relentlessly encouraging of my war dog endeavors, will always have my admiration and adoration—chief among them my friend Ben Pauker and my colleague Ty McCormick.

Thanks must be paid to Karin Tanabe, Jeremy Berlin, and Jennie Rothenberg-Gritz, who are not only among my dearest friends but are exceptional writers. Each of them provided insight, reassurance, and edits when I truly needed them most.

Book writing was, at least as I experienced it, a sometimes terribly solitary exercise. But because of these friends, I was never lonely: Rachel Wozniak, Chris Wozniak, Michal Mizrahi, Jessica Pavone, Claire Bohnengel, Brandon Van Grack, Sarah Longwell, Erica Sandler, Molly Smith, Kyle Kempf, Nick Vilelle, Mitchel Levitas, James Fallows, Deborah Fallows, and, of course, Mike Fallows, and most especially my Great Uncle Benny, who was the very best kind of friend.

notes

introduction: dogs in the time of war

1. "Dogs of War in Conflict," *New York Times*, February 21, 1915.

chapter 1: when dogs become soldiers

1. Jeffrey Gettleman, "Enraged Mob in Falluja Kills 4 American Contractors," *New York Times*, March 31, 2004, http://www.nytimes.com/2004/03/31/international/worldspecial/31CND-IRAQ.html?pagewanted=all.
2. Marine Sergeant Clinton Firstbrook, "Newfound Respect: A Combat Correspondent's Tale of the Battle for Fallujah," *Marines Magazine*, July 2004, http://web.archive.org/web/20060301190608/http://www.usmc.mil/magazine/304/Feature1stPerson.pdf; Robert D. Kaplan, "Five Days in Fallujah," *The Atlantic*, July 1, 2004, http://www.theatlantic.com/magazine/archive/2004/07/five-days-in-fallujah/303450/.
3. President Bush Addresses the Nation, White House Press Release, March 19, 2003, http://georgewbush-whitehouse.archives.gov/news/releases/2003/03/20030319-17.html.
4. "Improvised Explosive Devices (IEDs)—Iraq," GlobalSecurity.org, http://www.globalsecurity.org/military/intro/ied-iraq.htm.
5. From interviews with Colonel Mike Hanson (retired) on January 24, 2013, and Major Jim Griffin (also retired) on January 30, 2013, who were given orders to look into this. Their Marine battalion was part of the first invasion into Iraq in 2003.
6. When Lulofs and Aaslan left Iraq, the bounty on their heads had been upped two-fold to $20,000.
7. Tony Perry, "Snipers Stalk Marine Supply Route," *Los Angeles Times*, December 28, 2006.
8. Though a final tally of how many dogs actually served in Vietnam isn't known—official records of their enlistment weren't kept until 1968—it's estimated that somewhere between 4,000 and 4,900 dogs were used; the confirmed number based on official records is 3,747. This number is taken from the United States War Dogs Association website, which credits Dr. Howard Hayes, veterinarian (retired) of the National Institutes of Health, who, as of March 1994, reviewed these records and counted the dogs by brand number, the tattoo the dogs get in the inside of their right ear. "U.S. War Dog History," The United States War Dog Association, http://www.uswardogs.org/id10.html.

chapter 2: the house of misfit dogs

1. E. H. Richardson, *British War Dogs: Their Training and Psychology* (London: Skeffington & Son, LTD, 1920), 55.

2. Ibid., 65.

3. Ibid., 66.

4. Almost all domestic adult dogs have 42 teeth: 4 canine, 10 molars, 12 incisors, and 16 premolars.

5. "Bite Force," Season 1, Episode 2, *Dangerous Encounters*, National Geographic Channel, May 27, 2005, http://events.nationalgeographic.com/events/speakers-bureau /speaker/brady-barr/.

6. Ibid.

7. Dr. Stanley Coren, "Dog Bite Force: Myths, Misinterpretations and Realities," online article from his blog "Canine Corner," *Psychology Today*, May 17, 2010, http:// www.psychologytoday.com/blog/canine-corner/201005/dog-bite-force-myths -misinterpretations-and-realities.

chapter 3: the trouble with loving a war dog

1. Alexandra Horowitz, *Inside of a Dog* (New York: Scribner, 2009), 57.

2. Ibid., 58.

3. Ibid., 57.

4. Marc Bekoff, *The Emotional Lives of Animals* (Novato, CA: New World Library, 2007), 125.

5. Ibid., xviii.

6. Phone interview with Marc Bekoff, September 10, 2012.

7. John Black, "Darwin in the World of Emotions," *Journal of the Royal Society of Medicine* 95, no. 6 (June 2002), http://jrsm.rsmjournals.com/content/95/6/311.long.

8. John P. Wiley Jr., "Expressions: The Visible Link," *Smithsonian*, June 1998, http:// www.smithsonianmag.com/science-nature/expressions-the-visible-link-1538449 51/?no-ist.

9. Charles Darwin, *The Expression of the Emotions in Man and Animals* (London: John Murray, 1872), 57, 60.

10. The bulk of this information was relayed to me via email by Dr. Jaak Panksepp, the Baily Endowed Chair of Animal Well-Being Science and Professor, Veterinary and Comparative Anatomy, Pharmacy, Physiology (VCAPP), at Washington State University, on September 22, 2012.

11. J. Brauer, J. Kaminski, J. Riedel, J. Call, M. Tomasello, "Making Inferences about the Location of Hidden Food: Social Dog, Causal Ape," *Journal of Comparative Psychology* 120 (2006): 38–47; Monique A. R. Udell and C. D. L. Wynne, "A Review of Domestic Dogs' (Canis Familiaris) Human-Like Behaviors: Or Why Behavior Analysts Should Stop Worrying and Love Their Dogs," *Journal of the Experimental Analysis of Behavior* 89, no. 2 (March 2008): 247–261, http://www.ncbi.nlm.nih .gov/pmc/articles/PMC2251326/?report=classic.

12. "Dogs Decoded," *Nova*, PBS documentary, original airdate November 9, 2010, http://www.pbs.org/wgbh/nova/nature/dogs-decoded.html.

13. Anaïs Racca, Kun Guo, Kerstin Meints, and Daniel S. Mills, "Reading Faces: Differential Lateral Gaze Bias in Processing Canine and Human Facial Expressions in Dogs and 4-Year-Old Children," *PLoS ONE*, April 27, 2012, http://www.plosone.org/article/info%3Adoi%2F10.1371%2Fjournal.pone.0 036076.

14. J. K. Vormbrock and J. M. Grossberg, "Cardiovascular Effects of Human-Pet Dog Interactions," *Journal of Behavioral Medicine* 5 (October 11, 1988): 509–17, http:// www.ncbi.nlm.nih.gov/pubmed/3236382.

15. Ashley Balcerzak, "How Your Dog Helps Your Health," *Men's Health*, November 7, 2013, http://www.menshealth.com/health/how-dogs-make-you-healthy.

16. "Oxytocin is a nine-amino-acid peptide synthesized in hypothalamic cells, which project either to the neurohypophysis or to sites within the central nervous system." Thomas R. Insel, "Oxytocin—A Neuropeptide for Affiliation: Evidence from Behavioral, Receptor Autoradiographic, and Comparative Studies," *Psychoneuroendocrinology* 17, no. 1 (March 1992): 3–35, http://www.sciencedirect.com/science/article/pii/030645309290073G.

17. Dr. Z, "How Owning a Dog Extends Your Life," Stresshacker.com, November 17, 2010, http://www.stresshacker.com/2010/11/how-owning-a-dog-extends-your-life/; "People & Animals—For Life,"12th International IAHAIO Conference, July 1–4, 2010, Stockholm, Sweden, http://www.iahaio.org/files/conference2010stockholm.pdf.

18. Phone interview with Marc Bekoff, September 10, 2012.

19. E. H. Richardson, *British War Dogs: Their Training and Psychology* (London: Skeffington & Son, LTD., 1920), 151.

20. Known as the father of ethology, the study of animal behavior, especially in nature, Lorenz's most notable contribution is thought to be his work identifying the pattern of imprinting in the Greylag goose. Born and raised in Austria, much of his work came during Hitler's rise to power. That he was a willing and ardent member of the Nazi Party and contributed to the science of eugenics, however, is, in the discussion on dogs, perhaps best overlooked but not forgotten. He would later recant this affiliation and expressed regret, as he wrote, for having "couched my writing in the worst of Nazi-terminology." "Konrad Lorenz—Biographical," Nobelprize.org, http://www.nobelprize.org/nobel_prizes/medicine/laureates/1973/lorenz-bio.html. The source cited on the page is from *Les Prix Nobel en 1973*, Editor Wilhelm Odelberg, Nobel Foundation, Stockholm, 1974.

21. Konrad Lorenz, *Man Meets Dog* (London: Methuen & Co. LTD., 1954), 139.

chapter 4: beware the loving (war) dog

1. This stirring quote is taken from an impassioned speech made in a court of law and known as "Eulogy of the Dog," by Mr. George C. Vest. Vest would serve in the United States Senate from 1879 to 1903, but in the fall of 1870 he was a trial lawyer and he made this speech while defending his client, whose dog, "Old Drum" had been shot and killed by a neighbor (or someone who worked for him). With this closing argument Vest is said to have brought the jury to tears. His client was awarded damages. Even after all his years in the Senate, this speech is his legacy. 101 Cong. Rec., S4,823–24 (daily ed., September 23, 1870), http://www.senate.gov/artandhistory/history/common/generic/Speeches_Vest_Dog.htm, speech text: http://www.senate.gov/artandhistory/history/resources/pdf/VestDog.pdf.

2. Maria Cristina Valsecchi, "Pompeiians Flash-Heated to Death—'No Time to Suffocate,'" *National Geographic News*, November 2, 2010, http://news.nationalgeographic.com/news/2010/11/101102/pompeii-mount-vesuvius-science-died-instantly-heat-bodies/.

3. "Pliny Letter 6.20," online translation provided by University of Texas at Austin Classics Department, https://www.utexas.edu/courses/classicalarch/readings/Pliny6-20.html.

4. Albert Payson Terhune, *A Book of Famous Dogs* (New York: Triangle Books, 1941), 6. Terhune writes that the Museum of Pompeii keeps "two distorted figures, side by

side, amid the horde of other gruesome casts"—a child and a dog. Found on the inside of the dog's collar is the following Latin inscription: "Thrice has this dog saved his little master from death: once from fire, once from flood, once from thieves." How they gathered this information, or if Terhune traveled to the museum to read the dog's collar for himself, is a mystery I was not able to solve.

5. Mark Derr, *How the Dog Became the Dog* (New York: Overlook Press, 2011), 33.

6. Ibid., 40–41.

7. Sam Anderson, "Entering Darkness," *The New York Times Magazine*, June 10, 2011, http://www.nytimes.com/2011/06/12/magazine/entering-darkness.html?pagewanted=all; Michael Balter, "Chauvet Cave Does Not Stand Alone," *Origins of History* blog, *Science*, February 19, 2009, http://blogs.sciencemag.org/origins/2009/02/chauvet-cave-does-not-stand-al.html.

8. Derr, *How the Dog Became the Dog*, 25–28.

9. Jan Bondeson, *Amazing Dogs* (Ithaca: Cornell University Press, 2011), 11.

10. Ibid., 11; Agnes Strickland and Bernard Barton, "True Stories And Historical Anecdotes of Dogs," *Fisher's Juvenile Scrap Book* (London, Paris & New York: Fisher, Son, & Co., 1839), 60, http://books.google.com/books?id=UG4EAAAAQAAJ&printsec=frontcover&source=gbs_ge_summary_r&cad=0#v=onepage&q=sabinus%20&f=false.

11. Terhune, *A Book of Famous Dogs*, 84.

12. Mari Yamaguchi, Associated Press, "Mystery Solved in Death of Legendary Japanese Dog," *Washington Post*, March 2, 2011, http://www.washingtonpost.com/wp-dyn/content/article/2011/03/02/AR2011030201491.html.

13. Terhune, *A Book of Famous Dogs*, 78–100.

14. "After Brazil Flooding, Loyalty to the Dead," CNN.com, January 17, 2011, http://news.blogs.cnn.com/2011/01/17/in-brazil-flooding-loyalty-to-the-dea/.

15. "Chinese Dog Refuses to Leave Dead Owner's Graveside," BBC.com, November 21, 2011, http://www.bbc.co.uk/news/world-asia-china-15825892.

16. Rebecca Frankel, "Rebecca's War Dog of the Week: Time to Lift the 'Don't Pet, Don't Feed' Ban," foreignpolicy.com, October 15, 2010, http://ricks.foreignpolicy.com/posts/2010/10/15/rebeccas_war_dog_of_the_week_time_to_lift_the_don_t_pet_dont_feed_ban; "Rufus, Target and Sasha Save U.S. Soldiers," Oprah.com, October 4, 2010, http://www.oprah.com/oprahshow/Rufus-and-Target-Save-US-Soldiers.

17. "General Order 1B (Go-1B)," Memo from Central Command, March 13, 2006. http://img.slate.com/media/42/061101_Exp_GO-1B.pdf, linked in Adam Weinstein, "Iraq's Slumdog Massacre: One Million Dogs Face Death," *Mother Jones*, June 18, 2010, http://www.motherjones.com/politics/2010/06/iraq-kbr-one-million-dogs-death.

18. Doc's owner, David Inham, brought Doc along to an Iowan Army Reunion, where the pair gave the local paper an interview, and a man by the name of Frank Stamper sold the dog's photo on a piece of stock card for 25 cents apiece. John P. Zeller, "Iowa View: Patriotic Pooch Has Place of Honor in Civil War Lore," DesMoinesRegister.com, May 12, 2012, http://archive.indystar.com/article/D2/2012 0512/OPINION/120512009/Iowa-View-Patriotic-pooch-has-place-honor-Civil-War-lore.

19. "Rags, Dog Veteran of War, Is Dead at 20; Terrier That Lost an Eye in Service is Honored," *New York Times*, March 22, 1936, http://query.nytimes.com/mem/archive/pdf?res=FA0914FA345C167B93C0AB1788D85F428385F9.

20. Mark Derr, *A Dog's History of America* (New York: North Point Press, 2004), 257–58.

21. "Dogs and Horses Often War Heroes," *New York Times*, October 17, 1917, http://query.nytimes.com/mem/archive-free/pdf?res=F20F14FB385F1B7A93C3AB178BD95F438185F9.

22. Captain William W. Putney D.V.M., USMC (RET.), *Always Faithful* (New York: Free Press, 2001). No page number is available; it is included in the book's glossy insert, a scan of a clipping from the author's "hometown paper, the *Farmville Herald.*" No date is given.

23. Michael G. Lemish, *War Dogs: A History of Loyalty and Heroism* (Washington, DC: Brassey's Inc., 1996), 176–78.

24. "War Dogs Remembered," The United States War Dog Association, http://uswardogsmemorial.org/id16.html.

25. Rebecca Frankel, "Rebecca's War Dog of the Week: Eli, Brother and Protector, Goes Home," ForeignPolicy.com, February 4, 2011, http://ricks.foreignpolicy.com/posts/2011/02/04/rebeccas_war_dog_of_the_week_eli_brother_and_protector_goes_home.

26. Ibid.

27. E. H. Richardson, *British War Dogs: Their Training and Psychology* (London: Skeffington & Son, Ltd.,1920), 150.

28. Ibid., 151.

29. This description of Bronco's injuries comes from the vet who treated him at Bagram Airfield and operated on him twice, Captain Katie Barry, Facebook message, dated January 9, 2013.

30. Phone interview with Kevin Behan on August 30, 2012.

31. Ibid.

32. Obituary, "Ernie Pyle Is Killed on Ie Island; Foe Fired When All Seemed Safe," *New York Times*, April 19, 1945.

33. Ernie Pyle, *Brave Men* (New York: Henry Holt, 1943), 197.

34. Sebastian Junger, *War* (New York: Twelve, 2010), 239–240.

35. Phone interview with John Mariana, January 5, 2013.

chapter 5: a dog of many talents

1. There are quite a few alternatives for the word *nose*, some more fitting in the context of dogs than others for obvious reasons. Thesaurus.com offers: "adenoids, beak, bill, horn, muzzle, nares, nostrils, olfactory nerves, proboscis, schnoz, smeller, sneezer, sniffer, snoot, snout, snuffer, whiffer . . ." http://thesaurus.com/browse/sniffer.

2. Mark Derr, *Dog's Best Friend* (New York: Henry Holt, 1997), 95.

3. Ibid.

4. Julio E. Correa, "The Dog's Sense of Smell," *Alabama Cooperative Extension System*, Alabama A&M University, June 2011, http://www.aces.edu/pubs/docs/U/UNP-0066/UNP-0066.pdf.

5. *The Parent Trap*, dir. David Swift, Walt Disney Productions, 1961.

6. Section 5-2, "Explosives Used for Training," Army Manual, Department of the Army, September 30, 1993, http://armypubs.army.mil/epubs/pdf/p190_12.pdf.

7. Ibid.

8. Email exchange with Sean Lulofs, Lackland Air Force Base MWD program manager, on February 2, 2012.

9. Bloodhounds have even more sensory receptors/olfactory cells in their nose than most breeds of dogs. "Underdogs: The Bloodhound's Amazing Sense of Smell," *Nature*, PBS series, original airdate January 29, 2006, http://www.pbs.org/wnet

/nature/episodes/underdogs/underdogs-the-bloodhounds-amazing-sense-of-smell /350/.

10. Stanley Coren and Sarah Hodgson, *Understanding Your Dog For Dummies* (Hoboken: Wiley Publishing, Inc., 2007), 103; see also http://www.dummies.com/how -to/content/understanding-a-dogs-sense-of-smell.html.

11. Alexandra Horowitz, *Inside of a Dog: What Dogs See, Smell, and Know* (New York: Scribner, 2009), 124.

12. Andrea Seabrook, "Why Do Animals' Eyes Glow In The Dark?" NPR.org, October 31, 2008, http://www.npr.org/templates/story/story.php?storyId=96414364.

13. "How Well Do Dogs See At Night?" *Science Daily*, November 9, 2007.

14. Horowitz, *Inside of a Dog*, 125.

15. Irit Gazit and Joseph Terkel, "Domination of Olfaction over Vision in Explosives Detection by Dogs," *Applied Animal Behaviour Science* 82, no. 1 (June 3, 2003): 65–73.

16. The Israel Defense Forces (IDF) has an extremely powerful dog program. In many ways they have set the recent standard of war dog training. In the mid-2000s the US Marines sent a small contingency of dog handlers to train with IDF handlers. One of the more revolutionary training methods those handlers brought back and made standard was the "off-leash capability."

17. Lieutenant Colonel E. H. Richardson, *British War Dogs* (London: Skeffington & Sons, Ltd., 1920), 79.

18. Michael G. Lemish, *War Dogs* (Washington, DC: Brassey's Inc., 1996), 207.

19. Stanley Coren, *How Dogs Think* (New York: Free Press, 2004), 37.

20. Maxwell Riddle, *Dogs Through History* (Fairfax: Denlinger's Publisher, 1987), 174.

21. Ibid., 174–75.

22. Fairfax Downey, *History of Dogs for Defense* (New York: Dogs for Defense, Inc., 1955), 1.

23. Ibid., 2.

24. Caroline Tiger, *General Howe's Dog* (New York: Chamberlin Bros., 2005), 95.

25. Dogs weren't captured in early photography because they weren't able to sit still for the time it took for the camera to flash and capture the subject. (Which explains why in so many Civil War–era battlefield photos the dogs appear so blurry.) It's believed that the first photo of a living dog wasn't taken until 1840, and that photo was of Elizabeth Barrett Browning's dog, Flush; the image was captured by photographer Nicholas Henneman. Grace Glueck, "A Multitude of Dogs, From Cuddly to Cranky," *New York Times*, February 1, 2002, http://www.nytimes.com/2002/02/01 /arts/photography-review-a-multitude-of-dogs-from-cuddly-to-cranky.html.

26. Lemish, *War Dogs*, 18.

27. Somewhere close to 7,500 were killed in battle (though some believe that number to be too low given the relatively low loss overall and the extreme danger of their tasks).

28. "Dogs of Battle and Dogs of Mercy," *Vanity Fair*, September 1916, http://www .oldmagazinearticles.com/WW1_dogs_pdf.

29. Downey, *History of Dogs for Defense*, 16.

30. Ibid.

31. Ibid., 65.

32. Ibid., 21–22.

33. Clayton G. Going, *Dogs at War* (New York: The Macmillan Company, 1945), 9.

34. According to the US War Dogs Association

35. Lemish, *War Dogs*, 81. Author cited from a report on the dogs' progress in New Guinea issued on December 6, 1943, written by 2nd Lieutenant Robert Johnson, the unit's senior officer.

36. "Mentioned in Dispatches," *New York Times*, January 23, 1944.

37. Fairfax Downey, *Dogs of Destiny* (New York: Charles Scribner's Sons, 1949), 171.

38. Mark Derr, *A Dog's History of America* (New York: North Point Press, 2004), 293.

39. Downey, *History of Dogs for Defense*, 110.

40. Lemish, *War Dogs*, 269.

41. Ibid., 287.

42. Ibid., 185.

43. Ibid., 197.

44. "Medical Innovator: Finding New and Effective Ways to Treat Wounded Troops: Q&A with Lieutenant General Eric B. Schoomaker Surgeon General US Army," *MMT* 15, no. 3 (May 3, 2011).

45. Ibid.

46. Michelle Tan, "DoD Says Amputations Reached Wartime High," *Army Times*, March 14, 2012, http://www.armytimes.com/news/2012/03/army-amputations-reach-war-time-high-031212w/.

47. Andrew W. Lehren, "Calculating the Human Cost of the War in Afghanistan," *New York Times*, August 21, 2012, http://atwar.blogs.nytimes.com/2012/08/21/calculating-the-human-cost-of-the-war-in-afghanistan/.

48. Department of Defense, "Operation Iraqi Freedom (OIF) U.S. Casualty Status," Fatalities as of April 8, 2014, 10 a.m. EDT, and "Operation Enduring Freedom (OEF) U.S. Casualty Status," fatalities as of April 8, 2014, 10 a.m. EDT, http://www.defense.gov/NEWS/casualty.pdf.

49. James Dao and Andrew W. Lehren, "In Toll of 2,000, New Portrait of Afghan War," *New York Times*, August 21, 2012, http://www.nytimes.com/2012/08/22/us/war-in-afghanistan-claims-2000th-american-life.html?_r=0.

50. Peter W. Singer, "Robots at War: The New Battlefield," *The Wilson Quarterly*, Winter 2009, http://www.wilsonquarterly.com/essays/robots-war-new-battlefield.

51. Joseph Giordono, "New Army Program Aims to Put Soldiers on Higher Alert for IEDs," *Stars and Stripes*, May 25, 2005.

52. James Dao, "Afghan War's Buried Bombs Put Risk in Every Step," *New York Times*, July 14, 2009.

53. Formerly the Joint IED Defeat Task Force founded in 2004: http://www.globalsecurity.org/military/agency/dod/jieddo.htm.

54. Spencer Ackerman, "$19 Billion Later, Pentagon's Best Bomb-Detector Is a Dog," *Danger Room* blog, *Wired*, October 21, 2010, http://www.wired.com/dangerroom/2010/10/19-billion-later-pentagon-best-bomb-detector-is-a-dog/.

55. Ibid.

56. Statement By Lieutenant General Michael D. Barbero, Director Joint Improvised Explosive Device Defeat Organization, United States Department of Defense, before the United States House of Representatives Committee on Appropriations Subcommittee on Defense, September 20, 2012, https://www.jieddo.mil/content/docs/20120920_JIEDDO_Statement_for_the_Record.pdf.

57. Otto Kreisher, "IEDs Replace Artillery As Battlefield's Biggest Killer, JIEDDO General Says," *Breaking Defense*, October 17, 2012, http://defense.aol.com/2012/10/17/ieds-replace-artillery-as-battlefields-biggest-killer-jieddo-g/.

58. Associated Press, "Bomb Explodes in Parked Plane," *Evening Independent* (St. Petersburg, FL), March 8, 1972; Richard Witkin, "Bomb Found on Jet Here After $2-Million Demand," *New York Times*, March 8, 1972; Richard Witkin, "T.W.A. Jet Damaged in Las Vegas Blast," *New York Times*, March 9, 1972; "Nixon Orders Tighter Air Security," *Daytona Beach Morning Journal*, March 10, 1972; "President Orders Tighter Security by U.S. Airlines," special edition, *New York Times*, March 10, 1972; Robert Lindsey, "Air Security Tightened to Meet Order by Nixon," special

edition, *New York Times*, March 11, 1972; *ABC News*, aired March 8, 1972; "1972: TWA Jet Explodes at Las Vegas Airport," *On This Day*, BBC, http://news.bbc.co.uk /onthisday/hi/dates/stories/march/8/newsid_4268000/4268151.stm.

59. "Bomb on TWA Plane," *ABC News*, aired March 8, 1972, http://abcnews.go.com /Archives/video/march-1972-bomb-twa-plane-13078635.

60. Ken Dilanian, "Good Dog? Homeland Security May Want You," *Los Angeles Times*, July 17, 2010, http://articles.latimes.com/2010/jul/17/nation/la-na-dhs -dogs-20100717. The *Los Angeles Times* article doesn't mention it, but at the time they were reviewed in 2006–2007 they were under a different—and much longer—name: "On October 1, 2009, the U.S. Border Patrol (USBP) Canine Training Program and the Office of Field Operations (OFO) Canine Training Program were merged to create the Customs and Border Protection Canine Training Program," http://www.cbp.gov/border-security/along-us-borders/canine-program.

61. "TSA Oversight Part 2: Airport Perimeter Security," Serial No. 112–75, July 13, 2011, http://oversight.house.gov/wp-content/uploads/2012/04/7-13-11-Subcomm ittee-on-National-Security-Homeland-Defense-and-Foreign-Operations-Hearing -Transcript.pdf.

62. Melissa Mertl, "Dogs Can Smell Land Mines, But Humans Cannot. Sensitive New Chemical Sniffers Could Fix That," *Discover Magazine*, September 1, 2001, http:// discovermagazine.com/2001/sep/feattech#.UyzFiV5RHyw.

63. Henry Fountain, "Devices Go Nose to Nose With Bomb-Sniffer Dogs," *New York Times*, October 15, 2012, http://www.nytimes.com/2012/10/16/science/explosives -detectors-aim-to-go-nose-to-nose-with-sniffer-dogs.html.

64. Phone interview with Staff Sergeant Taylor Rogal, October 10, 2012.

chapter 6: the road to war leads through Yuma

1. "In detection work, a false response is when the dogs exhibits their defined final response in an area where the target odor is not present." Sometimes the cause of a false response is easy to assess and wouldn't be counted against the dog during cer- tification or training. During my time at the Yuma course I watched dogs alert on spots where there were no buried aids. Often times there would be lingering odor from training exercise from days before. Other times though a dog will alert because he knows if he does, he'll get his toy. A handler has to know his dog's tells well enough to be able to determine the difference. Steven D. Nicely, "Record Keeping," K9 Consultants of America, http://www.k9consultantsofamerica.com/training_info rmation/RECORD%20KEEPING.htm.

2. Michael G. Lemish, *War Dogs* (Washington, DC: Brassey's Inc., 1996), 208.

3. Ibid., 208–211. The British used Labrador retrievers for their trackers; their tem- peraments were more easygoing, and the British found the breed better suited for the work.

4. Phone interview with Charlie Hardesty, June 2012.

5. Phone interview with Gunny Knight, April 17, 2012.

6. Interview with US Army Sergeant George Jay and Army Specialist William Vidal (from Bagram Airbase), June 20, 2012.

7. John F. Burns, "On Way to Baghdad Airport, Death Stalks Main Road," *New York Times*, May 9, 2005, http://www.nytimes.com/2005/05/29/international/middle east/29road.html?pagewanted=all.

8. Sebastian Junger, *War* (New York: Twelve, 2010) 144.

9. Robert Rosenblum, *The Dog in Art: From Rococo to Post Modernism* (New York: Harry N. Abrams, Inc., 1988), 9.

chapter 7: the fallen

1. I first came across this quotation in June 2012. It was listed as canine handler Sean Brazas's favorite quotation on his personal Facebook profile—he was killed in action in Afghanistan in May 2012.

2. A handler at Camp Lejeune, who wished to remain unnamed, confirmed the events as Josh's father described them to me, relaying the details as they were circulating at Camp Lejeune, II-MEF home station.

3. When the military pronounces someone killed "during combat operations," it makes for an entirely vague and unsatisfying qualifying of the account of someone's death. It's the description that came with the military death notices for Coffey, Brazas, and Ashley.

4. Mike Joseph, "37th TRG Honors Belgian Malinois: MWD Gets Heroism Medal for Action under Fire," *Air Education and Training Command* (News), September 27, 2012, http://www.aetc.af.mil/news/story.asp?id=123319933.

5. Chuck Roberts, "Working Dog Reunites with Handler During Bedside Hospital Visit," US Army News, September 24, 2012, http://www.army.mil/article/87806 /Working_dog_reunites_with_handler_during_bedside_hospital_visit/.

6. Andrew deGrandpre, "3 MARSOC Marines, Dog Die in Afghan Blaze," *Marine Corps Times*, August 3, 2011.

7. "Sgt. Christopher Wrinkle Died Trying To Save Dog," YouTube post of WGAL Channel 8, Local News Report, August 8, 2011, http://www.youtube.com/ watch?v=ga-qJLi8pmc.

8. Thomas Lynch, *The Undertaking* (New York: Penguin Books, 1997), 21.

9. Email correspondence from Captain Katie Barry sent in early October 2012 from her new station in Germany.

10. Jeff Donn, "Soldiers Find Loyal Companions in War Dogs," Associated Press, NBC, August 12, 2007, http://www.nbcnews.com/id/20151076/ns/health-pet_health/t /soldiers-find-loyal-comrades-war-dogs/#.U3GQHC9RHyx. Some records incorrectly state that Bruno was killed in this attack. Master Sergeant (Ret.) Joel Burton confirmed that this was not the case. He wrote to me on September 27, 2012, that three dogs were wounded in this attack—Flapoor, Bruno, and Kevin all survived. The 341st Training Squadron at Lackland Air Force Base is responsible for keeping the records as mandated in The Robby Law. Burton, who was stationed at Lackland for eight years, was responsible for maintaining this document that tracks MWDs (from all branches) as he puts it, "from cradle to grave."

11. Corporal Micah Snead, "Military Working Dog, Marine Stick Together Through Battle, Injuries," Leatherneck.com, February 7, 2006, http://www.leatherneck.com/ forums/archive/index.php/t-26186.html.

12. Interview with Charlie Hardesty, March 2012.

13. "Five Camp Lejeune Marines Killed in Iraq," Associated Press, http://www.milit arytimes.com/valor/soldier/1459367. No publication date is listed, but given that it was a wire story, it was likely January 2006.

14. Mike Dowling, "SGT Adam Leigh Cann—Semper Fi War Dog," post from his now defunct blog *K-9 Pride*, April 22, 2008, http://k9pride.wordpress.com/2008/04/22 /sgt-adam-leigh-cann-semper-fi-war-dog/.

15. Mike Pitts, "First Marine Scout Dog Killed in Action," photographer and publication unknown, 1966, at US War Dog Memorial Site, http://uswardogsmemorial .org/id16.html.

16. "Video: LCpl Ferrell and Zora," American Forces Network Afghanistan, DVIDS video, 7:54, taken June 25, 2012, http://www.dvidshub.net/video/148955/lcpl -ferrell-and-zora#.URcd6eh9_K4.

17. Master Sergeant (Ret.) Joel Burton confirmed that this was an accurate statement.
18. I verified this number against two different sites, my own blog posts, and checked it with two different sources who had worked within the 341st at Lackland Air Force Base. This number does not include Special Operations or Special Forces dogs. I believe that if it did the number would increase significantly.
19. The Robby Law, Bill H.R. 5314, http://save-a-vet.org/d7/sites/default/files/docs /GOV-RobbysLaw-HRBILL.pdf.
20. From my study of these reports dating from CY00–CY11, with few exceptions, when the status of death was qualified as KIA, it was not followed with a notation on the cause of death—bullet, IED, etc.
21. Interview with Master Sergeant (Ret.) Joel Burton, January 2013.
22. Obituary for Joshua Brandon Farnsworth, MailTribune.com, July 8, 2007, www .mailtribune.com/apps/pbcs.dll/article?AID=/20070708/NEWS04/307089996&c id=sitesearch.
23. Phone interviews with Sean Lulofs, September 20, 2012, and October 1, 2012.
24. C. J. Chivers, "Cataloging Wounds of War to Help Heal Them," *New York Times*, May 17, 2012.
25. Ibid.

chapter 8: wounds and healing

1. "U.S. Soldier Charged with Murder in Iraq Shooting Deaths," CNN.com, May 12, 2009, http://edition.cnn.com/2009/WORLD/meast/05/12/iraq.soldiers.killed/.
2. Rod Nordland, "Report Finds Lapses in Handling of G.I. Accused of Murders in Iraq," *New York Times*, October 20, 2009.
3. Luis Martinez and Martha Raddatz, "Camp Liberty Shooting: Alleged Shooter's Dad Says Soldier 'Just Broke,'" ABC.com, May 12, 2009, http://abcnews.go.com /Politics/story?id=7565251.
4. James Dao and Paul von Zielbauer, "Among 5 Killed, a Mender of Heartache and a Struggling Private," *New York Times*, May 17, 2009; Ernesto Londoño, "U.S. Soldier in Iraq Kills 5 Comrades at Stress Clinic," *Washington Post*, May 12, 2009.
5. William Krol, "Training the Combat and Operational Stress Control Dog: An Innovative Modality for Behavioral Health," *United States Army Medical Department Journal: Canine Assisted Therapy in Military Medicine* (April–June 2012): 46.
6. Bushra Juhi, "58,000 Dogs Killed in Baghdad in Campaign to Curb Attacks by Strays," *The Washington Post*, July 11, 2010, http://www.washingtonpost.com/wp -dyn/content/article/2010/07/10/AR2010071002235.html.
7. Nordland, "Report Finds Lapses in Handling of G.I. Accused of Murders in Iraq."
8. Margaret C. Harrell and Nancy Berglass, "Losing the Battle: The Challenge of Military Suicide," Policy Brief by Center for New American Security, October 2011. The policy brief's authors got these numbers from the Department of Defense and the Department of Veterans Affairs. It was of particular interest that the authors made a special note in the report that they intentionally "refrain from using the phrase 'commit suicide . . .' because the word 'commit' portrays suicide as a sin or crime . . . [and] contributes to a stigma that prevents individuals from getting help."
9. Tina Rosenberg, "For Veterans, a Surge of New Treatments for Trauma," *New York Times*, September 26, 2012.
10. Steve Bentley, "A Short History of PTSD: From Thermopylae to Hue Soldiers Have Always Had A Disturbing Reaction To War," *VVA Veteran* (March–April 2005; originally published January 1991).
11. Ibid.

12. In 1871, after conducting his clinical study of 300 Civil War veterans, Dr. Jacob Mendes Da Costa wrote a paper outlining that such symptoms were the manifested stress a soldier weathered in the battlefield.

13. Caroline Alexander, "The Shock of War," *Smithsonian Magazine*, September 2010.

14. "Beside Freud's Couch, a Chow Named Jofi," *Wall Street Journal*, December 21, 2010, http://online.wsj.com/news/articles/SB1000142405274870388690457603163012408736.

15. Ernest Harold Baynes, *Animal Heroes of the Great War* (New York: The Macmillan Company, 1925), 198.

16. Ibid.

17. Dorothy Harrison Eustis, "The Seeing Eye," *Saturday Evening Post*, November 5, 1927. To no great surprise the Germans, who proved ahead of the canine curve in most instances, were the first to use guide dogs, training them with innovation and then assigning them to soldiers who had been blinded in battle by mustard gas.

18. Most unbelievably, on his voyage over, because he was sightless, the 20-year-old man was deemed not another passenger but a "parcel." The crew on the ship went so far as to restrict his activity while he was aboard the vessel until the trip was over. "Through Buddy's Eyes," *Vanderbilt Magazine*, Fall 2010, http://www.vanderbilt.edu/magazines/vanderbilt-magazine/2010/12/through-buddys-eyes/.

19. "Guide Dog, at 10, Still Aiding Blind," *New York Times*, October 16, 1936.

20. Perry R. Chumley, "Medical Perspectives of the Human-Animal Bond Within the Department of Defense," *The United States Army Medical Department Journal* (April–June 2012): 18–20.

21. Clayton G. Going, *Dogs at War* (New York: The Macmillan Company, 1945), 164–65.

22. Fairfax Downey, *Dogs for Defense: American Dogs in the Second World War 1941–1945* (New York: Dog for Defense, Inc., 1955), 114–115.

23. Ibid.,117.

24. B. M. Levinson, "The Dog as Co-Therapist," *Mental Hygiene* 46 (1962): 59–65.

25. Mark Thompson, "Bringing Dogs to Heal," *Time*, December 5, 2010.

26. Major Arthur F. Yeager and Captain Jennifer Irwin, "Rehabilitative Canine Interactions at the Walter Reed National Military Medical Center," *The United States Army Medical Department Journal* (April–June 2012): 57–60.

27. Thompson, "Bringing Dogs to Heal."

28. "Franken-Isakson Service Dogs For Veterans Act Passes Senate: Legislation To Help Wounded Veterans Included In Defense Authorization Bill," press release, July 24, 2009, http://www.franken.senate.gov/?p=press_release&id=592.

29. Janie Lorber, "For the Battle-Scarred, Comfort at Leash's End," *New York Times*, April 3, 2010, http://www.nytimes.com/2010/04/04/us/04dogs.html.

30. Phone interview with Harvey Naranjo, January 27, 2013.

31. James Dao, "After Duty, Dogs Suffer Like Soldiers," *New York Times*, December 1, 2011.

chapter 9: the never again wars

1. Clayton G. Going, *Dogs at War* (New York: The Macmillan Company, 1944), 3–4. This is a selection shared by Going but is excerpted from *The National Humane Review of the American Humane Association;* no author is noted.

2. Phone interview with Justin Harding, January 30, 2013.

3. Dan Lamothe, "Dogs Become Essential in Fight against IEDs," *Marine Corps Times*, March 25, 2010.

4. Michael G. Lemish, *War Dogs: A History of Loyalty and Heroism* (Washington, DC: Brassley's, 1996), 240. Lemish has compiled this number from after-action reports, which he notes were "spotty at best" and not filed by Marines.

5. Airman 1st Class David Owsianka, "SFS Handler, MWD Receive Bronze Star," 56th Fighter Wing Public Affairs, August 12, 2011, http://www.luke.af.mil/news /story.asp?id=123267984.

6. Peter Maass, "Professor Nagl's War," *New York Times* Magazine, January 11, 2004, http://www.nytimes.com/2004/01/11/magazine/professor-nagl-s-war.html.

7. From an in-person interview with John Nagl, June 12, 2012.

8. Dan Lamothe, "Afghanistan Drawdown Keeps Logistics Crews Busy," *Marine Corp Times*, June 11, 2012, http://www.marinecorpstimes.com/news/2012/06 /marine-logistics-afghanistan-equipment-leaving-061012/.

chapter 10: home again, home again

1. James Fallows, "Mike the Cat," *Atlantic*, December 11, 2013, http://www.the atlantic.com/personal/archive/2013/12/mike-the-cat/282238/.

epilogue: what we talk about when we talk about war dogs

1. Mark Derr, *A Dog's History of America* (New York: North Point Press, 2004), xvi.

2. Albert Payson Terhune, *The Book of Famous Dogs* (New York: Triangle Books, 1937), 240–241.

3. Phone interview with Mark Derr, June 21, 2012.

index